W9-CEB-012

ESSENTIALS OF GENERAL SPEECH

McGRAW-HILL SERIES IN SPEECH
CLARENCE T. SIMON,
Consulting Editor

ARMSTRONG AND BRANDES
The Oral Interpretation of Literature
BAIRD · American Public Addresses
BAIRD · Argumentation, Discussion, and Debate
BAIRD AND KNOWER · Essentials of General Speech
BAIRD AND KNOWER · General Speech
BLACK AND MOORE · Speech: Code, Meaning, and Communication
CARRELL AND TIFFANY · Phonetics
HAHN, LOMAS, HARGIS, AND VANDRAEGEN · Basic Voice Training for Speech
HENNING · Improving Oral Communication
KAPLAN · Anatomy and Physiology of Speech
KRUGER · Modern Debate
OGILVIE · Speech in the Elementary School
POWERS · Fundamentals of Speech

ESSENTIALS OF GENERAL SPEECH

A. Craig Baird
Department of Speech and
Dramatic Art
State University of Iowa

Franklin H. Knower
Department of Speech
The Ohio State University

Third Edition

McGRAW-HILL BOOK COMPANY
New York St. Louis San Francisco
Toronto London Sydney

ESSENTIALS OF GENERAL SPEECH

Library of Congress Catalog Card Number 68-12262
03250

2 3 4 5 6 7 8 9 0 MAMM 7 5 4 3 2 1 0 6 9 8

PREFACE

Essentials of General Speech, third edition, is a streamlined introductory text for students in a service course in speech. It has been designed for the short-term or limited credit hour course where the required textbook reading must be kept to a minimum. The material has been so developed that it may be used in either the course with major emphasis on the communication processes of speech or the introductory course in basic speech activities.

This text and the more detailed *General Speech* are alike in the attempt to combine in a single book the core philosophy of classical rhetoric and the major contributions of the behavioral sciences to communication. We believe that the theory and history of rhetoric has a significant contribution to make to the modern study of communication. We also believe that the behavioral sciences are as important today to the progress of our knowledge about communication as rhetoric has been in the past. We do not deem it practical to concern the introductory and service course student with the documentation of the many sources which support and elaborate the facts and principles herein reviewed. We believe that the general principles of education for better communication should be made the focus of attention in this book.

This edition, like earlier ones, recognizes speech as a form of social behavior. It includes but goes beyond the study of speech as process and expression only. It is aimed at the student seeking excellence of social impact or effect through communication. It recognizes the need for the speaker to read and adjust to the responses of his listeners with care and precision. Speech is recognized as a learned activity. The student's improvement in communication is as much a matter of the communication principles he comes to understand, and the feelings, attitudes, and motivations he develops, as it is a matter of his practice. We therefore lay much stress upon those procedures in teaching which provide an educational balance in cognitive, affective, and motor goals.

Much of this edition has been updated in its treatment of communication, in its use of examples cited, and in its citation of the literature of the field. The sequence of chapters has been rearranged to progress from the study of speech as communication process to the study of speech as communication activity. A wide variety of projects has been provided to give the instructor substantial latitude in his selection of the types of assignment he prefers to make.

The McGraw-Hill Book Company has prepared a series of teaching films to accompany the text. Those who have used the films have found them a stimulus to the student. Also available is a separate *Teacher's Manual* developed expressly for this edition of *Essentials of General Speech*. The manual provides course outlines, and discussion and examination questions, as well as suggestions for the use of the teaching films.

A. Craig Baird
Franklin H. Knower

CONTENTS

ESSENTIALS OF GENERAL SPEECH

GENERAL PROCESSES OF SPEECH

1 INTRODUCTION

COMMUNICATION IN TODAY'S WORLD

Our first objective in this book will be to take a good look at our communication behavior. You no doubt have given some consideration to the subject or you wouldn't have started to read this book. Perhaps you have read enough from various sources to be confused by the conflicting explanations which abound. In your experiences you have encountered barriers to communication which have made little sense. Or you have tried to get your message through to someone, and have felt a disappointing failure. Perhaps you have aspired to the achievement of some personal goal in your association with your peers but have backed away from action with the feeling that you lacked confidence in your own ability to be of service. In some disagreement with another perhaps someone has said: "It's just a communication problem." Do you know what problems are communication problems and what problems are not?

There are other reasons for the study of communication. The very amount of communication around us is a challenge to participate. If we do not do so, our goods, our social values, and our very way of life may fail for want of adequate explanation and defense. The population explosion and an expanding world of knowledge have given rise to an information explosion in which there is a tremendous struggle for men's minds. This competition operates not only on national and international levels, but in the everyday person-to-person behavior of our social, business, and professional lives as well.

Aristotle's justification of good speech in politics is still one of our guides in any course that views speech as a social force. Aristotle concluded that first, we must speak up if truth and justice are to prevail over error. Second, our political tenets must be so stated that the rank and file will understand and respond accordingly. Third, both sides of a problem need to be presented so that the better choice may be made clear and thus adopted. Finally, every citizen should be able to expose the barrage of bad propaganda and to help set the logical or factual record straight.[1]

New technologies are ever expanding the range and speed of our travel. Yesteryear there was safety in distance. Competing ideologies were not as powerfully equipped to search out and speedily destroy the opposition as they are today. Everywhere observers agree that our world is a changing world. Most of us recognize that the kind of communicating we do may have some values in directing these changes for the better. This can happen only if our communication is the very best. There is more to know about today. College-educated men and women of this generation are generally accepting their responsibilities to keep abreast of their developments; to absorb more information at a faster pace than has been necessary before; to learn to use this information to explain, to predict, to make decisions, to inform, and to persuade for personal as well as for common good. To accomplish such objectives we need to know more than most of us do about the nature and potential of effective communication.

COMMUNICATION AND PEOPLE

Too much of the communication of too many people fails. It fails because a failure of one or more parts has its influence on producing a failure of the whole. Communication above the most simple stages is a very complex affair. Perhaps the greatest barrier to better communication is the delusion that it is simple and easy. Sometimes in our admiration for our communication technology, we ignore the need for developing ourselves as human beings, as participants, and as benefactors. Our machines will be no better than the people who make and control them. It follows therefore that our first step is the

[1] Paraphrased from Aristotle's *Rhetoric*, book 1, chap. 1 (1355a).

better understanding of our subject. If you have taken up this book with the hope that there are simple, infallible formulas for the development of communication, you will be disappointed. There are no easy roads to excellence in communication. The understanding of this process involves a cognitive process: a set of ideas, a way of thinking, a philosophy. In contrast with the simple conditional reflex expression habits of infants, the serious speaking of superior adults deals with ideas about communication as well as ideas we communicate about. Communication achievements are also influenced by affective or feeling processes. The good speaker has developed feelings, attitudes, sets, and value systems which motivate and direct his communication behavior. The actual speaking behavior is also a motor or muscular process. Motor skills often develop slowly. Their growth, however, is also influenced by what one knows and how one feels about it. The whole man speaks, and in superior speaking he speaks as a whole man. We can think of his cognitive, affective, and motor systems as subsystems of his total integrated communication production system. We place greater emphasis here in the cognitive study of communication. Since the motor system comes into play regularly in everyday talk all one's life, there is much opportunity for its practices. The opportunity for the development of understanding and of useful attitudes is usually not so readily available.

WAYS TO STUDY COMMUNICATION

There are many ways of studying communication today. First let us look at standard procedures. Some scholars are primarily concerned with the study of communication as such processes as thinking, language, articulation. This process approach may be designated as a basic principle approach. We seek to understand the principles of speech we employ in the use of speech processes. We shall deal with several of these processes in various chapters of the book. Thought, adjustment, language, voice, and action are some of them to which we shall devote more time later. We may study speech as activity, as in reporting, interviewing, discussion, debate, etc. The prototype of all communication activity is person-to-person talk. Communication activity involves concepts of purpose and situation. It is also concerned with the patterns of procedure which, for example, differentiate an interview from a debate, a pep talk from a persuasive discourse. We shall be very much concerned with content, for indeed, the message—what we communicate about—is the essence and the body of communication. We shall also be concerned with impact or effect. The major test of our achievement is the test of our effects upon others. Does the speech give our listener some useful information, develop or modify an attitude, motivate action towards some useful goal, or help our listener in problem-solving discussion? In all these cases we are concerned with the development of an excellent, ethically sound, and socially responsible communication. As Carroll Arnold has said, "Every event of speech is to some degree a fundamental and socially significant event for the speaker, the spoken to, and perhaps for those who come after."[2] Although all levels of communication are important, we shall not be much concerned with pathological or remedial communication for it is a distinguished area of specialized study in the field.

SPEECH AND COMMUNICATION DEFINED

We see from this introduction that speech is more than language. The concept of speech as indicated by the sentence "He speaks German" is obsolete in this context. The study of speech is not merely the study of voice or articulation. It is not social adjustment alone; it is not merely the way one thinks. All these are part of a broader field of study which includes also such subjects as confrontation or face-to-face speaking, and social sensitivity or people reading. It is feedback, it is listening, it is visual cues as symbolic stimulation. *Speech is ongoing multisymbolic behavior in social situations carried on to achieve communication. We define communication as a social achievement in symbolic behavior.* Communication is something that happens, an event of the moment when one person uses symbolic stimulation to create in another some response. It's an understanding, a feeling, or an overt act which is consistent with the intent of the communicator, and which would not have occurred at the time if there had been no communication. It is an achievement when it works because the message received is not always the message sent. Successful communication behavior for complex messages is a skill of the highest order. A mutual interest in communication provides a favorable social environment for its success.

A communication problem is any social situation which can be corrected or improved by the use of symbolic behavior. A communication failure occurs when there is a misunderstanding of the nature and functions of communication, or an inability of participants to

[2] Carroll Arnold, "Speech: A Liberal Study," before the Pennsylvania Speech Association, Philadelphia, Oct. 7, 1959.

use it efficiently to accomplish appropriate communication purposes.

Speech is socially direct and instantaneous. It is an event in time. We can prepare for it, we can reminisce about it afterward, but once we have spoken out, we cannot change what we have said. We can try to correct an error, but we cannot change the fact that an error was made. Perhaps this is what Bacon had in mind when he said that "conference maketh a ready man." At a time when speed is so much a part of our lives, small wonder that speech as a means of communication plays such an important part in them.

Speech employs symbolic behavior as a stimulus for the meanings we seek to communicate. It is multisymbolic because it employs language, tones, and behavior simultaneously to represent what we mean. We must recognize that meaning arousal in the human mind may occur as a result of stimuli other than symbols. In fact we may refer to such meaning arousal as "learning the hard way." If it were necessary to get all our meaningful experiences from objects and events, including people, directly rather than through our vicarious associations with symbols, there would be little we could call civilization. We have learned to use symbols as a way of accomplishing our social relationships short of the exercise of force. The use of force upon another to achieve an end is the barbaric, the primitive, and the uncultured way. De Laguna has said that "speech is the great medium through which human cooperation is brought about." [3] The fact that the senses with which we perceive the speech of another are our distance rather than our contact sensors lends emphasis to the communication of meaning as a process economical in our use of energies as well as cultured in our respect for the personal integrity of our fellowmen.

To declare that speech is economical in the use of energies does not imply that it is easy. Skillful speech requires that the speaker be a person of a huge repertory of communication resources, that he be sensitive to a whole range of variables to be taken into account, and that he so command the use of his resources in adapting his message to his listeners that he maximizes the possibility that the messages received will approximate the messages he sends. This is no mean achievement. Since such behavior is all learned behavior it follows that a capacity to learn is important for communication. Such learning in some may occur by chance. It is more commonly a product of high aspiration and diligent efforts to achieve excellence in communication.

[3] Grace A. de Laguna, *Speech: Its Function and Development*, Yale University Press, New Haven, Conn., 1927, p. 19.

A COMMUNICATION MODEL FOR SPEECH

A systematic understanding of communication demands more than a definition. Ultimately one's knowledge is formulated as a systematic explanation—a theory of communication. This book sets forth such a theory in considerable detail.[4] A useful step between the definition and the theory is the communication model. We have found the following model meaningful as a graphic presentation of the main points of this theory:

A GRAPHIC SPEECH MODEL

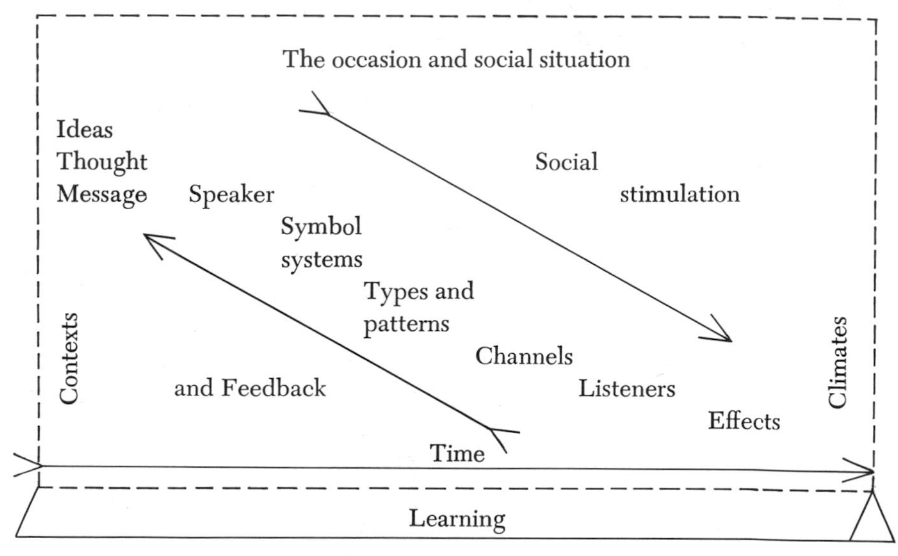

CRITERIA FOR EVALUATION

Most of the major points in this model have been dealt with briefly earlier in this chapter. These points will be further developed in chapters later in the book; the beginner's problems in speech im-

[4] See also Wendell Johnson, "The Spoken Word and the Great Unsaid," *Quarterly Journal of Speech,* 37:419–429, December, 1951; Franklin H. Knower, "Communication: A Model for Communicology," *Ohio State Journal,* 3:181–187, 1963; Gerald R. Miller, *Speech Communication,* Bobbs-Merrill Company, Inc., New York, 1966, chap. 3, "Process and Speech Communication"; Keith Brooks (ed.), *The Communicative Arts and Sciences of Speech,* Charles E. Merrill Books, Inc., Columbus, Ohio, 1967, pp. 98–148.

provement are the subject of Chapter 2. We do want here to consider further the matter of the criteria on which your communication exercises can be evaluated. In the following page we present a speech performance scale. You should study this scale and the discussion of each major process or criterion which follows.

SEVEN PROCESSES IN SPEECH IMPROVEMENT

This view of speech as an act involving speaker, speech, communicative act, audience, and speaking situation suggests a number of processes basic to speech improvement. From the speaker's point of view, they are:

1. Speech attitudes and adjustment
2. Voice
3. Articulation
4. Physical activity
5. Language
6. Ideas
7. Organization

Speech improvement may be facilitated by your cooperation in these basic processes. You need to analyze and apply each of them not as an end in itself but as it is related to audience demands, needs, and characteristics. Moreover, you must measure your improvement in speech not only as discrete and separable items of the process but also as a unit—as an interdependent network. These activities make up the so-called fundamental speech processes to distinguish them from speech activities with their various applications in teaching, business, and public service, and scores of other speaking situations. These processes are foundational to all communicative applications, including oral reading. Some teachers restrict their attention to the procedures of voice, articulation, and physical activity. The authors of this text and many others include also among these adjustment, ideas, organization, and language, in each case as expressing itself in an audience situation.

The following brief explanations of these seven processes are a description of the goals you may well set for yourself as a speaker. Few will reach a high level of achievement in all of them. With reasonable concentration and application, however, your performance will be adequate in speech generally and in most of these fundamentals, and perhaps even exceptional in some of them.

SPEECH PERFORMANCE SCALE

Name	Date	Instructor
Subject		

CRITERIA	RATING 1–9 *	COMMENTS
1. General Effectiveness:		
2. Speech Attitudes and Adjustments: Indifferent — Loses thought Fidgety — Evasive Tense — Inappropriate		
3. Voice: Weak — Loud Fast — Slow Poor pitch — Poor quality Monotonous — Poor rhythm Excess vocalization		
4. Articulation: Substitutions — Foreign dialect Additions — Regional dialect Slighting — Mispronunciation		
5. Physical activity: Indirect — Unresponsive Random — Inappropriate		
6. Language: Ambiguous — Wordy Inaccurate — Needs force Needs vividness — Needs variety		
7. Ideas: Poor purpose — Not clear Poor central idea — Dull Weak support — Needs originality Undeveloped — Insignificant Inaccurate		
8. Organization: Introduction — Sequence Division — Conclusion Transitions		
Total		

* Rate the speaker on a scale of 1 to 9 for each of the numbered items, with 1 the low point and 9 the high point of skill. Add ratings to get the total score.

1 The effective speaker adjusts to his audience

The basic principle of all speech preparation and presentation is that speech is social; that communication is effective only when it adapts itself to the comprehension, interests, and attitudes of those who listen and observe; and that audience response is the test of a satisfactory speech. Such adaptation does not mean that you surrender your ideas, purposes, and personality as you attempt to identify with your group. Such surrender to the crowd is sophistry or demagoguery. Your speaker-audience integration, however, does mean that you enter fully into the personalities and concerns of those you address. Psychologically you put yourself in their place, and thus keep constant contact with them and in turn secure circular response.

Adaptation to the audience is a form of intellectual integrity. It shows that you respect the comprehension of those by whom your ideas are to be assimilated. This adaptive spirit means also your goodwill toward those whose beliefs, attitudes, and experiences you would affect. Furthermore you look to the best interests of your immediate and larger audience and thus you are governed by more than your own self-centered motives. Audience adaptation, then, determines the character of the speaker's psychological appeals, his thinking, organization, language, voice, bodily action, and all other elements of a given speech.[5]

The effective speaker adjustments include attention to a well-developed personality. What you are as a person has great significance for the impression you make as a speaker. Good coordination of your physical, intellectual, and emotional characteristics is a great asset in winning acceptance for your ideas and attitudes. A well-developed personality will enable you to make full use of your intellectual ability, achieve audience adaptation, and remain aware of your ethical responsibility.

Emotional maturity. One of the most significant aspects of emotional maturity is freedom from undue aggressiveness and undue compliance. The tendency to dismiss or ignore opposition, to dominate others, to be smug, or exhibitionistic is as much to be resisted as the tendency to fear holding a dissenting opinion or to withdraw into a shell and let others make your decisions and do your talking for you.

[5] See Chaps. 7 and 10.

Intellectual ability. Speakers are often confused and flustered because they have not carefully thought through their material. Knowledge is power only when you know how to select, organize, and communicate your ideas. As a speaker, you must thoroughly understand your material and keep uppermost in your mind the central idea of your speech. The rational ramifications and the factual underpinning of this idea can then submit to logical order in your mind.

Ethical responsibility. One aspect of the functioning of the personality in the speaking situation is the demonstrated fact that you are an ethically responsible person, aware that you may do much harm or much good through your remarks. You cannot adopt the philosophy that "talk never hurt anyone"; rather, you must accept the responsibility of discriminating between fact and fiction, between truth and error. As a speaker, you have a secret alliance with moral principles—a commitment which will be reflected in your handling of ideas and your attitude toward the audience.

As Gerald Miller states it, "But every communicative act, of necessity, involves a value dimension; it stems from certain ethical and/or aesthetic premises. Not only do we seek to understand how speech communication motivates men, we also reflect upon the question of whether it is *good* for them to behave as they do." [6]

Although these seven criteria constitute an adequate guide to the understanding of speech performance and provide a definite pattern for improvement in specific aspects of speaking, the ultimate evaluation of speaking effectiveness may be something more or less than the sum of these seven processes. It is determined not simply by judging the ideas, organization, language, voice, articulation, physical activity, and speaking personality as separable aspects of the speech, but by taking full account of the interaction effects of these skills. The total pattern of what happens as you become audible to a group is the standard for measuring your effectiveness as a speaker.

2 The effective speaker uses voice control

Vocal pitch, intensity or loudness, rate of speech, and voice quality determine the nature of the speaker's voice. The proper regulation of these elements enhances its pleasantness.

Pitch. The speaker's natural pitch level on the musical scale and his pitch should not jar listeners. His voice should come neither from

[6] Miller, *op. cit.*, p. 8.

too near the top nor from too near the bottom of the scale. And he should avoid continually rising inflection and singsong delivery.

Loudness. The speaker should adjust his voice to the size of the room or auditorium, or to the microphone or open-air situation. If he is relaxed, he will probably be free from breathiness, loudness, and monotony of delivery. His volume should be produced without undue strain on the vocal mechanism; clear articulation rather than loudness will help the audience to easy comprehension.

Rate. Speeches should be neither so fast as to baffle comprehension nor so slow as to bore. Avoid "and-uh's" and pauses that make listeners squirm or look to the ceiling. Talk at the speed that is normal for you. It will be found that a conversational address to the audience will help maintain a steady pace.

Voice quality. The teeth, mouth, tongue, and hard and soft palates are so constructed as to provide voice resonance. If the voice-producing organs are functioning normally, the speaker will not be troubled by nasality, harshness, guttural heaviness, shrillness, stridency, or a metallic or muffled quality. A balance between tension and relaxation will make the voice pleasing to the ear.[7]

3 The effective speaker is efficient in articulation and pronunciation

A normal, unaffected method of articulating syllables will produce vowels that are pure and unmistakable and consonants that are fully yet not heavily sounded. It is unwise to make a fetish of perfection in the shaping of sounds, yet one should avoid being what Edward Bok once called a "lip-lazy American." Substitutions such as *agin* for *again;* additions such as *acrost* for *across;* omissions such as *reconize* for *recognize;* and conspicuous slighting of some sounds should be avoided. It is wise to adhere to the generally accepted standard for the sounds and accents of words.[8]

4 The effective speaker uses appropriate bodily activity in speaking

In communication, visual effects are almost as important as auditory reactions. Most people are eye-minded; hence posture, gesture,

[7] See Chaps. 10 and 11.
[8] See pp. 147 ff.

and other bodily movements become key agents of oral expression. Focus your physical energies so as to maintain contact with your audience. Physical activity that is constructively purposeful rather than forced or random will help to interpret your ideas to your audience and will demonstrate that you are physically spontaneous and alert.

5 The effective speaker uses language well

In working to formulate, present, and clarify ideas and their factual bases, strive for accuracy in the use of words and their combinations; for clearness, so that the meaning will be understood by the listeners; and for attention-getting and interest-sustaining effects.

The language of the effective speaker must not be ambiguous; rather, it must be concrete and specific. The grammar is standard. Avoid triteness and undue use of technical and abstract words; employ colorful, even figurative language. Do not be verbose; your words have weight and economy in number. Make use of interest-getting devices such as periodic sentences, questions, parallel constructions, and emotionally charged language. Thus the style of the effective speaker is always idiomatic and oral, clear, interesting, mature, and personal. Avoid the style of a person delivering an oral essay.

6 The effective speaker communicates ideas

Ideas are probably the most important process of the speech act. Basically we view the speaker as a thinker—as a person dealing with facts and expressing judgments concerning those facts. The comprehension, insight, and convictions of the speaker are thus of great importance if he is to speak to a specific purpose.

Satisfactory expression of ideas may be judged by the purpose in speaking. Select and develop ideas with a view to their impact upon or relationship to your particular audience and your purpose with regard to them. Organize your speech around a central idea, clearly conceived and well worded. Your thought should reflect a sound and informed analysis of the subject and able management of your "forms of support"—the facts, analogies, comparisons, illustrations, and statistics that bolster your ideas.

7 The effective speaker organizes his ideas systematically

Your talk should be characterized by unity, coherence (order), and proportion (emphasis, force). Even though the talk may be impromptu, it should reflect planning. The effective speaker resists the temptation to indulge in wide and purposeless excursions from the theme. Arrange your ideas in an appropriate order, with the relation of subordinate topics to the central theme apparent. Begin purposefully, move through the main body of your talk, and conclude decisively. Use summaries, transitions, and introductory statements to link the parts of the pattern together in order to make clear its progression. The result is much more than a mechanical unfolding of an outline; it is a well-organized demonstration of clear thinking.

PROJECTS AND PROBLEMS

Project 1

Try engaging a friend in discussion about some of the ideas suggested in this chapter and in the references cited. Present them together with some ideas of your own or that you have read elsewhere. Report your experience to the class when called upon. Make an appointment for a conference with your instructor about your experience together with your evaluation of the responses of your listeners, or write out a brief report for him on this experience.

Project 2 An introductory test of general speech achievement

Purposes of this assignment: (1) To provide a basis for a preliminary analysis of your speech characteristics and achievements; (2) to provide a basis for self-analysis of your needs in speech education.
Subjects for this speech:

1. Some problems I have observed in communication
2. What coming to college means to me
3. The effective speaking techniques of a teacher (or preacher, salesman, radio or TV commentator) I know
4. Why I have selected my chosen vocation
5. A valuable principle of a human relationship worth remembering

Procedure: Your instructor will record his judgment of your speech on a rating scale but will not criticize you in class. After you sit down, make notes on what you feel were the strong points of your speech and on the things that gave you the most difficulty in presenting it. Consult the section on seven processes in speech improvement in this chapter for suggestions on the preparation of your speech.

Project 3 An introductory test of oral-reading achievement

Purposes of this assignment: (1) To facilitate the evaluation of your speech needs by your instructor; (2) to help you develop insight into your speech achievement.
Subjects for this project: Select a short piece (300 to 500 words) of argumentative or expository prose which expresses an idea you find interesting.
Procedure: Read it over until you can present it without hesitating or stumbling. Concentrate on communication of the meaning when you read the selection to the audience. Your instructor will evaluate your speech skill in reading. You also should attempt to make an objective self-evaluation of your skill in using speech processes.

Project 4 An analysis of the speech in oral reading of others

Purposes of this assignment: To develop analytical and critical habits of evaluating speech and oral-reading performances.
Procedure: Use the seven processes in speech improvement discussed in Chapter 1 for a systematic analysis of speech and oral-reading performances of at least three of your classmates. Make notes and write a page or two of critical analysis of each performance. Your instructor will judge your paper on the quality of the critical evaluations you have made.

For the instructor: Show the film *Is There Communication When You Speak?* prepared by the McGraw-Hill Book Company to accompany this text. Note in the *Teacher's Manual* the suggestions for showing this film.

REFERENCES

Baird, A. Craig: *Rhetoric: A Philosophical Inquiry*, The Ronald Press Company, New York, 1965, chap. 1.

Berlo, David K.: *The Process of Communication*, Holt, Rinehart and Winston, Inc., New York, 1960.

Brooks, Keith (ed.): *The Communicative Arts and Sciences of Speech*, Charles E. Merrill Books, Inc., Columbus, Ohio, 1967.

Bryant, Donald (ed.): *The Rhetorical Idiom*, Cornell University Press, Ithaca, N.Y., 1958, pp. 71–95.

Miller, Gerald R.: *Speech Communication*, Bobbs-Merrill Company, Inc., Indianapolis, 1966.

Nilsen, Thomas R.: *Ethics of Speech Communication*, Bobbs-Merrill Company, Inc., Indianapolis, 1966.

Reid, Ronald F.: *Introduction to the Field of Speech,* Scott, Foresman and Company, Chicago, 1965.

Ross, Raymond S.: *Speech Communication,* Prentice-Hall, Inc., Englewood Cliffs, N.J., 1965.

Schramm, Wilbur: *The Science of Human Communication,* Basic Books, Inc., Publishers, New York, 1963.

Weaver, Carl H., and Warren L. Strausbaugh: *Fundamentals of Speech Communication,* American Book Company, New York, 1964.

Wilson, John F., and Carroll C. Arnold: *Public Speaking as a Liberal Art,* Allyn and Bacon, Inc., Boston, 1964.

YOU THE SPEAKER

2 BEGINNERS' PROBLEMS IN SPEECH IMPROVEMENT

How good are you as a speaker? Review again the processes of speech discussed in the previous chapter to guide you as you examine your own case. Did your early life at home and school encourage you to read much, to write and speak often? Or was the influence of your family and your surroundings hardly favorable to such communicative habits? Did your high school studies in science, history, English, and other requirements and electives include for you little or nothing in speech? Or did you have a speech course but one which you largely neglected because your teacher was uninspiring, or because athletics, music, or special affairs took your time? Perhaps you were active in debating, extempore speaking, oral interpretation, or school plays. Or perhaps some speech difficulty of yours increased your timidity and led to your avoidance of formal speaking occasions. Or perhaps you were so engrossed in your prospective engineering, nursing, or other profession that speech and similar subjects meant little to you.

Whatever your experience, your purpose now is to make the most of the classroom speech opportunities. If your earlier methods and speech practices have been bad, you can certainly move on to better things. If you have been more or less successful in class and extra-class speaking, you can no doubt increase many of your skills. The principles and specific suggestions that follow attempt to help you toward systematic improvement in your speaking abilities.

These principles of learning are not unlike the principles of improvement in most fields of study. Educational psychologists [1] tell us that those who learn best are those who recognize their needs and values in every learning assignment. You may need orientation to this kind of learning experience. You should know what is important and what is of less importance. If you find yourself frustrated by attempts to learn, you should seek a better understanding of the whole process.

Perhaps you know some things expounded in the text or by the instructor. Don't let yourself conclude that there is nothing more for you to learn. If you find yourself thinking in this manner, raise your sights. Set your goals for what others may consider impossible. Most students are satisfied with far less than their potential. It is also important to be realistic. Don't try to do too much at one time. One great scholar admonished his pupils to do a little bit for genius every day. Relate the assignment to your life, your experience, your aspirations. In this way it takes on an added meaning.

You may consider yourself fortunate; you may have resources; or you may have won honors. You have it made. Don't kid yourself. It's what you are, not just what you have, that determines your future.

Practice, rehearse, simulate, play roles, try different ways of accomplishing your ends, vary your directions, seek suggestions.[2] Beware of excuse, delays, simple formulas, wasting your time, hoping to find the easiest way of learning. Keep at it. When you get tired trying one way, don't give up. Try a new way. If you can do these things, you may be pleasantly surprised at what there is to learn and what you can do about it.

I PRINCIPLES FOR YOUR IMPROVEMENT AS A SPEAKER

The eleven questions following introduce principles basic to speech improvement. Use these as a guide in analyzing your problems, needs, and goals in your own speech-improvement program.

[1] Lee J. Cronbach, *Educational Psychology*, Harcourt, Brace & World, Inc., New York, 1963.

[2] Gardner Lindzey, *Handbook of Social Psychology*, Addison-Wesley Publishing Company, Inc., Cambridge, Mass., 1954, chap. 6.

1 What is your attitude toward speech and speechmaking?

What are the incentives that may have stimulated you in this field? Your review of your vocational and occupational interests in relation to speech will no doubt find you more appreciative of communication in your special field. At least you will be more inclined to respect the facts that confirm the communicative uses of speech. And you will be more sympathetic to its significance in your career.

2 What of your desire to communicate?

Almost everyone, sooner or later, whether he realizes it now or not, needs to exchange talk with others. If you analyze your specific situations in recent days, you will readily note how constantly you have been impelled to speak up and how equally talkative have been those with you.

For example: Perhaps you may have recently been summoned to court for allegedly fast driving in a 35-mile-per-hour zone. According to you, you were unfairly penalized. Perhaps as a business or local agricultural agency employee you would like to exchange ideas about installment buying, union dues, or soil banks. Perhaps you are much concerned about the smog or air pollution you recently experienced in Chicago or New York. Perhaps you would like to seek information and counseling concerning a job with the CIA, or some antipoverty program. Perhaps you have discussed with fellow students whether you should join a campus protest march. Or you, with thousands of other Americans of your age, have argued about the Peace Corps, the shortage of school and college teachers, the pros and cons of the draft. These oral experiences in which you and fellow talkers have joined all reveal genuine interests that call for your added information, your attitudes, and your energetic but controlled utterances.

3 What of your ability to improve in speech?

According to Eugene White, Harry Truman stated that he always experienced some nervousness before a speech and that in his early career this condition caused him concern. As he acquired experience he learned to control tension. "My first speech was a complete failure," he admitted. "It took a lot of appearances before I felt at home on the platform and could put my ideas across the way I wanted."[3] Truman's experience is a common one.

Each year speech instructors deal with scores and scores of beginners. Some of these beginners are excellent at the start; others are immature or are otherwise handicapped. By the end of the course they have definitely improved. In hundreds of cases these young men and women, continuing their speech development, demonstrate mature ability in speaking in business, law, teaching, and other areas of community life. Skill comes as a result of understanding, direction, and practice. Learning to speak is a matter of acquiring systematic knowledge and positive attitudes about communication as well as improvement in its practice.

4 Have your background and personality affected favorably or otherwise your speaking habits?

What personality factors account for your being better or worse than others in speaking situations? What past experiences and training explain your personality? Your intellectual, social, moral, and other attitudes undoubtedly affect your speaking ability and method. They color the subjects you choose, the illustrations you insert, your way of approaching and developing subjects, and your way through conversational exchange.

There are many questionable notions about speech and its improvement in our culture. These have been studied as false images among students. These notions can be corrected. If you should find yourself accepting such rationalizations for inaction you should learn to distinguish the truth from the half-truths in such ideas as "Anyone who knows his subject can adequately explain it"; "If you have adequate command of English, you will be a good speaker"; "Glib talkers are often shallow thinkers"; etc.[4]

To get a better picture of yourself, it will help to organize information about your background. Include material on your family and home influences, your past and present reading habits, your extracurricular activities other than speech—for example, journalism, music, athletics—your hobbies, your habits and experiences as a listener-observer (do you, for example, often watch television?), your attitudes toward political parties and issues, your religious interests and activities, your attitudes toward speaking and your ex-

[3] Eugene E. White, *Practical Public Speaking*, The Macmillan Company, New York, 1964, p. 10.

[4] Franklin H. Knower, "The College Student Image of Speech, Communication, and Speech Education," *The Speech Teacher*, 15:108–112, 1966.

periences with it. Self-examination will not only provide you with the subjects for speeches but will indicate to what areas you will want to give special attention in speech training.[5]

5 What are your chief speech needs?

What are your abilities with regard to language, ideas, voice, and the other elements of speech? Objective analysis will help you discover the answers. Review the speech fundamentals outlined in the preceding chapter and get evaluations of your speech from others. Your speech instructor will no doubt guide you in obtaining this information.

For purposes of evaluation, rating charts similar to the one on page 10 are often used. Note that this scale is based largely upon the processes in speech improvement listed in Chapter 1,[6] and to be discussed in detail in later chapters. Have someone rate your speech performance from a normal speaking situation, for example, a short extempore speech, or perhaps oral reading from material that you have previously examined. The judgment of an expert is better than that of a layman; but if a specialist is not available, the combined judgments of a number of fellow students will ordinarily produce a reliable evaluation. Student critics may not always pinpoint your specific abilities and shortcomings, but, on the average, their judgments are a fairly good index of your general effectiveness. The scale items checked and the accompanying comment should give you a considerable understanding of yourself and many clues for your improvement. Although rating charts do not provide final answers, if you view them in relation to the supplementary comments and in relation to your background, the results may be very helpful.

6 What are your purposes in speaking?

What is the purpose of speech? Its aim, we are told, is to affect the behavior of listeners, or to get a favorable reaction from them. Your goal, then, is not primarily to coin catchy phrases or to perfect your tone, but rather to shape your words and voice qualities toward

[5] See project 1 at the end of this chapter.

[6] These items have been validated as significant variables in speech performance. See Howard Gilkinson and Franklin H. Knower, *Psychological Studies of Individual Differences among Students of Speech*, University of Minnesota, Minneapolis, 1939. Recent analysis of speech variables tends to support these variables.

a worthwhile end. That end is to influence others—to inform them, persuade them, impress them, or inspire them. And, we should add, this influence is always to contribute toward a better immediate and wider community.

7 How well do you understand the general principles of communication?

Prospective speakers need to do more than practice this art. You also need to have some intellectual comprehension of the bases of the art. Knowledge concerning the basic speech processes is important for several reasons. First, although practice is important, an intelligent rather than a trial-and-error method of learning speech is preferable. At the college level, moreover, you are concerned with insight into facts and principles as well as with the acquisition of skills. Knowledge, in this sense, is not merely something added to skill; it is insight that makes it possible for you to develop your personality as well as your speaking. Skill without such knowledge is hardly worth your while academically.[7,8]

Second, intelligent understanding of principles will enable you to adjust more effectively to a variety of situations than you could if your education were either strictly trial and error or a matter of developing blind and limited mechanical habits in a specific situation.

Third, many objectives of speech education require more time for attainment than is available in any specific course. If you have a reasonable understanding of the facts and principles involved, you will continue to work at these objectives long after the specific course is completed. Knowledge of the history of public address, for example, will afford you insight into the basic principles of speech. You may learn much from the record of William Jennings Bryan, who studied speech at Illinois College; of Albert J. Beveridge at Asbury College (Depauw University) in Indiana; of Daniel Webster at Dartmouth; of John C. Calhoun at Yale; and of Franklin D. Roosevelt at Groton Academy and Harvard.[9]

[7] See Benjamin S. Bloom (ed.), *Taxonomy of Educational Objectives,* Handbook I: *Cognitive Domain,* Longmans, Green & Company, New York, 1956.

[8] Richard C. Anderson and David P. Ausubel, *Readings in the Psychology of Cognition,* Holt, Rinehart and Winston, Inc., New York, 1965.

[9] Laura Crowell, L. LeRoy Cowperthwaite, and Earnest Brandenburg, "Franklin D. Roosevelt: A Study in Leadership through Persuasion," in Loren Reid (ed.), *American Public Address,* University of Missouri Press, Columbia, 1961, pp. 209–244; Loren D. Reid, "Gladstone's Training as a Speaker," *Quarterly Journal of Speech,* 40:373–380, 1954.

8 What are the speaker's responsibilities?

Speaking carries with it responsibilities. Your right to speak is morally based on your desire to benefit those who listen and the rest of the human family. Your responsibility as a speaker is to tell the truth as you understand it and to avoid distortions of fact and logic.

Each member of the medical profession takes the Hippocratic oath, one section of which affirms that the prime end of the profession is "the service it can render to humanity; regard or reward or financial gain should be a subordinate consideration." Your unofficial speech code should be not unlike that of the medical profession.

9 Why is it important to aim at a broad education?

Effectiveness in speaking calls for a broad education. The effective speaker should have some background in history, economics, natural resources, literature, and philosophy. Narrow specialization in one field may have detrimental effects upon young students as well as upon mature persons. The broadcaster who has only a knowledge of gadgets and the art of talking over the air is in a shallow groove. Similarly, speech correctionists, oral readers, or dramatic arts majors, who acquire knowledge of their own brands of speech and sidestep the humanities and the behavioral sciences, are often limited to the lower levels of service. In most cases, early and complete specialization limits the perspectives for possible expansion.

General education aims to relate one field to another—for example, economics to literature, history, and philosophy—and so gives you a richer variety of details on which to draw for talks. It will help you relate yourself and your specialty to make what you have to say more intelligible to other educated persons. Furthermore, your liberal arts training will help you in the immediate preparation of specific speeches, since you may tap your storehouse of accumulated learning. Both theoretically and practically your speech training calls for knowledge of speech, but this knowledge must be buttressed by ample learning in other areas of thought.

10 What shall be the purposes and methods of your practice?

Certainly any speech program requires practice as well as knowledge. Practice means preparation for and participation in speech-learning activities, including oral performance in your room or before extra-classroom groups, as well as in the classroom itself. The effectiveness of these practice sessions, however, depends upon the methods by which you conduct them. The following suggestions may help you to practice effectively.

Practice with the intent to learn. Commit yourself to what you are trying to do. Your vicarious learning now may keep you from having to learn the hard way.

Practice for achievement of definite objectives. Know what you are trying to do and stick to your program. As your skill in a given direction improves, continue to revise your objectives.

Practice on projects related to your own level of achievement. If you tackle projects that are too easy, you will soon lose interest. On the other hand, if you attempt projects that are too difficult, you may bog down. For example, do not attempt a thirty-minute talk on "A program to prevent the worldwide extension of the nuclear bombs," on the basis of twenty-four hours preparation.

Practice participation in a variety of realistic speaking activities. When you speak, set out to accomplish a specific purpose. Whenever possible, accept opportunities for nonclassroom speaking experiences. Talk before a campus or community club; interview someone for a well-defined purpose; talk for three minutes over a radio station; participate in a panel with three classmates on some campus or community project or engage in an informal discussion in which you both listen and speak. The greater the number of major types of activities in which you participate, the easier it will be for you to adapt to variations in these types of situations.

Practice under conditions comparable to those under which you expect to speak. Rehearse speeches aloud rather than silently. If you are to make your speech on your feet, stand when you rehearse it. If possible, get somebody to listen to you. Private and mail-order lessons in speech obviously provide no opportunity for practice before a real audience. Unless you have had experience before listeners, their presence later may disorganize you. Avoid practice by reading from a manuscript if you expect to extemporize in the real performance. Practice in a room comparable to the one in which you will later perform; and get speaking experience without a speaker's stand or table. Practice interrupting your train of thought, then picking it up and proceeding.

Practice with efficient control of time, energy, and speaking environment. Budget your time. If you are to prepare a speech, get your subject early. Apportion your time for selection of the subject, for securing and organizing materials, for written composition (if you are to write your speech), and for rehearsing the speech itself.

Practice more than the minimum indicated. You may occasionally get by with meager preparation, but it is unwise to curtail your practice in speech. You have something more to depend upon than the good fortune of the moment.

11 How will you evaluate your achievement?

Your study of speech should begin with an analysis of your abilities and needs, and this process of evaluation should be repeated at intervals throughout your training and at the end. You will want to know what you have accomplished; written examinations (on the principles of speech) and oral testing (by speech performances) should give you accurate information. The evidence of your progress, which these evaluations will provide, should spur you on to further development.

II SPECIFIC SUGGESTIONS FOR YOU THE SPEAKER

Most beginners in speech ask: Shall I plunge ahead with my talks and oral readings and later catch up with the principles expounded in the textbook? Or shall I read and assimilate the fundamentals and techniques before attempting practice? Or shall I work on both principles and practice at the same time? The writers of this book emphatically prefer the third of these possibilities. We believe that from the beginning you should combine principles and practice in speech activity. We learn not only by assimilating information but also by doing.

Here are the steps you should take in preparing and making a speech:

1. Follow systematic methods for preparing and delivering each speech and the related speaking assignments. Your problem here is that of systematic study habits. Most speeches fall short because of the last-minute preparation.

2. Prepare carefully the substance or ideas of your speech. Whether it is brief or long, you will bore into its content and have something worthwhile to say.

a. Select for your subject a topic of some interest to your listeners; one about which you know something and in which you are really interested; and one that can be handled in the short time at your disposal. See Chapter 6 for detailed suggestions concerning the subject.

b. Adapt to the audience situation. Analyze the interests, knowledge, and attitudes of those who are to attend to you. Adjust your preparation and procedures to your listeners at every step. This means reading their reactions as you speak and adapting your remarks to them as you go along. See Chapter 4 on audience adaptation.

c. Listen as well as talk. See Chapter 5 on you as the listener.

d. Select and frame the purpose of your speech. See details in Chapter 6.

e. Word carefully the central ideas of your speech.

f. Gather materials. Take stock of your knowledge and substantiate your information from sources that will strengthen your speech. See Chapter 6; also note sources of materials in the Appendix.

3. Organize the main ideas and subordinate points.

a. Work out an appropriate beginning and end. Link the parts together with proper summaries and transitions.

b. Make an outline, but don't reduce your speech to a mechanical document. See Chapter 7 on organization and outlining.

4. Compose your speech. Write it in full if you wish, but do not memorize it or plan to read it. Your compositional style should be extemporaneous, one that reflects your ideas and one that relates to the audience situation. Oral composition before the public event may be preferable to studied, written composition. See Chapter 9 on language.

5. Practice systematically your proposed talk.

6. Deliver your speech as effectively as possible. Your delivery will no doubt be more satisfactory to you and to your audience if you have carefully followed the steps outlined above. See Chapters 10 to 12 on voice, articulation, and bodily action.

7. Welcome criticism and profit by it. Seek out reactions from your instructor and fellow students. Try to discover your strong and weak points.

In following these steps, you will prepare systematically by beginning your preparation, including practices, at least two weeks before your scheduled talk.

The stages of your preparation may not always unfold in the exact order indicated here. But the general pattern of surveying your subject and organizing and rehearsing the speech will obviously call for some such sequence. Follow the steps indicated above as long as they help you. Then vary the procedure to meet your needs.

PROJECTS AND PROBLEMS

Project 1 A self-analysis interview

Purposes of this assignment: (1) To develop objective habits of self-analysis in speaking; (2) to formulate appropriate goals for speech improvement; (3) to carry out an effective personal interview with your instructor; (4) to have your speech evaluated in an interview situation. The content in the self-analysis interview is the analysis of your speech achievement and what you can do to improve yourself.

Procedure in preparing the interview: Make an appointment with your instructor and carry it out according to schedule. On the basis of the outline for speech criticism presented in this chapter, prepare a systematic and objective résumé of your speech achievement. Describe the goals for improvement or the standards toward which you expect to work in the course. Prepare to control the interview with the instructor by organizing your presentation, asking questions where necessary, and terminating the interview on time. Use your basic speech skills to the best of your ability in the interview.

Project 2 A brief talk four or five minutes

Prepare a brief talk according to the procedure in project 1 at the end of Chapter 1.

Subjects for this talk:

1. Revolt on the campus of today
2. How I passed the college entrance examinations
3. My impressions of *Who's Afraid of Virginia Woolf?*
4. Tennis for college women
5. My bowling championship
6. Why I believe in extracurricular music (or athletics, or theater, or debating)
7. A superior woman speaker
8. My summer in the Rockies (or elsewhere)
9. My career as a baby-sitter
10. My high school overemphasized extracurricular activities
11. Should my state have a higher or lower sales tax?
12. The football players on this campus should be subsidized

13. Who is my neighbor?
14. The new mathematics

For the instructor: Assign for review the topics in the *Teacher's Manual* under Improving your Speech Habits.

REFERENCES

Anderson, Richard C., and David P. Ausubel: *Readings in the Psychology of Cognition,* Holt, Rinehart and Winston, Inc., New York, 1965.

Becker, Samuel E., Carl A. Dallinger, Harry N. Crosby, and David Gold: *Communication Skills: An Experiment in Instructional Methods,* The University of Iowa, Iowa City, 1958.

Bloom, Benjamin S. (ed.): *Taxonomy of Educational Objectives,* Handbook I: *Cognitive Domain,* Longmans, Green & Co., New York, 1956.

Cronbach, Lee J.: *Educational Psychology,* Harcourt, Brace, & World, Inc., New York, 1963.

Douglas, Jack: "The Measurement of Speech—the Classroom," *The Speech Teacher,* 7:309–319, 1958.

Knower, Franklin H.: "What Is a Speech Test?", *Quarterly Journal of Speech,* 30:485–493, 1944.

———: "The College Student Image of Speech, Communication, and Speech Education," *The Speech Teacher,* 15:108–112, 1966.

Lindzey, Gardner: *Handbook of Social Psychology,* Addison-Wesley Publishing Company, Inc., Cambridge, Mass., 1954.

Mednick, Sarnoff A.: *Learning,* Prentice-Hall, Inc., Englewood Cliffs, N.J., 1964.

Mowrer, O. Hobart: *Learning Theory and the Symbolic Process,* John Wiley & Sons, Inc., New York, 1960.

Watson, Goodwin B.: *What Psychology Can We Trust?* Teachers College Press, Columbia University, New York, 1961.

White, Eugene E.: *Practical Public Speaking,* The Macmillan Company, New York, 1964.

3 DEVELOPING CONFIDENCE

YOUR FEAR OF AUDIENCES

Your oral communication obviously requires that you relate yourself actively to the one or more listeners who compose your audience. You may be a listener part of the time. But sooner or later you are to stand—or sometimes sit—as speaker, with your ideas, language, voice, and the physical accompaniments of your personality on display. You hope that you will be clear-minded and relatively at ease with those who respond to you and to whom you respond. Often, however, in this process a kind of disturbing emotionalism pervades you, a genuine fear of your auditor-hearers. You know that they wish you well. But your nervousness and self-consciousness limit, or you think they limit, your speaking effectiveness. This relatively disorganized relationship of the communicator and his audience produces what is called *stage fright*, an extreme metaphor often applied even though the speaker may not be on a "stage" nor have full-fledged "fright."

Stage fright is an acute anxiety condition in which fear symptoms appear and higher mental processes are reduced in efficiency. It is accompanied by lack of confidence. It should not be confused with a normal sense of responsibility in speaking and a keen desire to do a credible communication job. There is little evidence that stage fright is psychologically different from fear reactions to other situations, although its immediate stimulus is a social situation rather than a physical danger to one's person. Its lack of confidence is a conflict-creating condition causing unpleasant dissonant states.

The emotional response of the organism is an allover response; hence it has cognitive, affective, and motor manifestations.[1,2] Since most individuals possess different degrees of intensity of response and of control of these psychological systems, it follows that the manifestations of stage fright are not always uniform in feeling, thinking, and muscular systems.

Since the total psychological systems in the long run will seek consonance and abhor dissonance there exists a tendency to achieve integration and consistency. The speaker is often aware of a more intense feeling of stage fright than he demonstrates muscularly to others. We do not interpret this fact as indicating different kinds of stage fright. These variations merely suggest different kinds of response. In fact the dissonance of these response systems is an aggravating and confusing feature of the condition in the organism.

Stage fright is also a relative term. It affects different persons in various degrees of intensity. It is more common, however, than most people realize.[3] Among college students 60 to 75 percent will admit that it bothers them and 30 to 35 percent think it their most serious speech problem. Even if you are one of the fortunate few who have not experienced fright, don't assume that you will never experience it. We cannot predict when it will occur. Persons free from it at one time will suddenly find themselves experiencing it. It is distressing and confusing to those who do not understand the psychology of emotion. Since understanding this psychological state is one of the techniques for controlling it, we shall devote much of this chapter to explanations.

We have learned from work with the speech attitudes scale that speech is a unitary system. Although we cannot predict levels of confidence from one specific situation to another, when we have measured a fairly large sample of an individual's reactions, we can

[1] Theodore Clevenger, "A Synthesis of Experimental Research in Stage Fright," *Quarterly Journal of Speech,* 45:134–145, 1959.

[2] Howard Gilkinson and Franklin H. Knower, *Psychological Studies of Individual Differences among Students of Speech,* University of Minnesota, Minneapolis, 1939.

[3] *Ibid.*

predict how confident he will be in another fairly large sample of speech behavior.[4]

What are the symptoms and causes of stage fright?

The causes of stage fright are usually complex and varied. To say categorically that stage fright is the result of inadequate preparation or sensitivity or conditioning or conflicts is an unwarranted oversimplification of the facts. But it is, in part, a learned type of behavior.

Man's basic emotional responses appear to be adapted to physical dangers, since these have been the most obvious dangers he has had to meet.[5] But the speaking situation is usually not one the speaker consciously perceives as a response to immediate physical danger. This may explain why the sufferer from stage fright is embarrassed by it. The absence of physical danger, however, does not mean that there is no danger. We realize unconsciously even more than consciously that our welfare depends upon social approval. What others say about us can hurt us. We therefore covet and court their goodwill, and if we lack assurance in anticipation or feedback of this goodwill, we are alarmed at the consequences. The person with stage fright has panicked. The cortical processes for the time are largely bypassed. He makes a signal response to his emotional behavior.

Failure to understand the nature of emotional response arises when it seems unwarranted, and causes a person to be mystified and worried about it. He begins to doubt his adequacy and his confusion generates confusion. This frequently occurs even to one who speaks reasonably well but who is unfamiliar with speech standards and therefore unable to judge his achievements with objectivity.[6] If a speaker thinks his audience has reacted with disapproval, his self-criticism is sufficient stimulus to release the emotional response. A correlation of degrees of stage fright with general ability across the entire range of intelligence in the population would no doubt find stage fright negatively correlated with intelligence. Not only would those of higher intelligence have higher levels of aspiration, sensitivity to failure, and consequent tension,

[4] Franklin H. Knower, "A Study of Speech Attitudes and Adjustments," *Speech Monographs*, 5:130–203, 1938.

[5] Paul Thomas Young, *Motivation and Emotion*, John Wiley & Sons, Inc., New York, 1961, pp. 17–20.

[6] Raymond B. Cattell, *The Scientific Analysis of Personality*, Pelican Books, New York, 1965, p. 12.

but also those with lower levels of ability will be less motivated and less critical of themselves regardless of their behavior. Familiarity with these characteristics of the stage-fright reaction should bring home to you the need for an understanding of the nature of emotion. When the responses are understood the cortex tends to inhibit precipitating causes.

Symptoms. Where and how do we get information concerning this problem of fear in speech situations? Part of it obviously comes from the speaker's own testimony concerning his weakness and other organic conditions; part of it from our observations of speakers; part of it results from experimental measurements of organic activities, such as pulse and blood pressure. We study stage-fright symptoms not merely to control them but to provide that understanding through which we learn to inhibit the emotional response which produces them.

Withdrawal. Most of the symptoms of stage fright are subject to reasonably precise explanations. Withdrawal behavior, such as looking at the floor or ceiling, out the window, or over the heads of the audience, and leaning backward with the weight principally on one heel, represents incipient retreat or flight from the unpleasant stimulus. Indirect eye contact results from the speaker's feeling that he needs all his powers of concentration to recollect and utter what he has to say. If he looks at the audience, he anticipates that their reactions will distract him. The desire to run away and to apologize for one's behavior are other characteristics of the withdrawal reaction. Students have been known to withdraw from school rather than take a required speech course.

Physiological reactions. Pounding of the heart, increase of the pulse rate, gasping for breath, dry mouth, perspiration, blushing, and blanching are the results of changes in physiological processes associated with fear reactions. These reactions have survival value only when they release sufficient energy in the organism for struggle or flight. To provide such energy, glycogen (a form of food reserve) is released into the bloodstream from the liver by reflex action.[7] This energy is then made available through metabolism. Metabolic action is dependent upon oxygen supplied to the blood by the lungs. We gasp for breath when we are afraid, not because we have any less air in the lungs than under normal conditions, but because we

[7] Young, *op. cit.*, p. 369.

need more. For the body to make use of the energy from glycogen and fresh oxygen, blood must be pumped by the heart into the muscles of the legs, arms and hands, face, and so forth, and waste materials must be carried away. An emotion-arousing stimulus speeds up heart action in order that blood may circulate more rapidly. Tension in the muscles of blood-vessel walls is relaxed. Warm blood rushes to the surface of the body to rid itself of waste matter through perspiration. Blushing or blanching depends upon whether the blood is allowed to circulate rapidly close to the surface of the body or whether an excessive amount of blood is drawn from the surface of the body to fulfill physiological functions primarily in the trunk. The sinking feeling which is sometimes felt in the pit of the stomach is probably associated with an animation-arousing stimulus which inhibits digestive processes of visceral organs. The mouth becomes dry also as a result of disruption of the digestive processes.

Tension and muscular conflict. When the organism is energized in conflict and then fails to use up this energy in the biological responses of struggle or flight, it tends to use up the energy in tension (the straining of antagonistic muscle groups against each other), in trembling (the intermittent relaxation and tension of the muscles of antagonistic groups), and in fidgeting and random behavior (the attempt of the organism to return to normalcy from an unpleasant state of tension). Trembling occurs in those regions most easily responsive to the conflicts of antagonistic muscle pairs—the vocal folds, the finer muscles of the face, the arms and hands, and the knees. The feeling of awkwardness results from the fact that the abnormally tense muscles do not respond as readily and flexibly as they do in their normal state.

Conflict of intellectual and emotional behavior. Man's intellectual behavior is largely learned. The use of languages and other complex psychological and social skills are possible for us because we learn them. To use these skills, memory must function well. What we remember we have learned. One common aspect of the training of children is teaching the inhibition of emotional responses. As one matures intellectually the capacity to inhibit emotional responses may be developed as a form of intellectual behavior. Its achievement is probably dependent upon both the intensity of the emotional reaction and the strength of cortical or intellectual resistance to the emotion. The two types of behavior in a sense compete for control of the organism. If intellectual reactions are to function at their best, it would seem necessary to inhibit intense emotional reactions. When we find it impossible to inhibit intense emotional reactions, many of our other capacities for intellectual behavior are also seriously interfered with or bypassed. Thus the inability to think on one's feet, forgetting what one had to say, slips of the tongue, the mind experiencing a block or temporarily going blank, and the inability to control muscular action are traceable directly to the fact that for the time being emotional reactions have taken control. To illustrate by analogy, we may say that when the charges of emotional reaction become too great, the cortex blows a fuse and the lights of the intellect go out, or at least become badly short-circuited. This situation leads to what we may call the law of stage-fright control: *Anything that increases the efficiency of intellectual control or reduces the intensity of emotional responses helps develop confidence in the speech situation.* We shall discuss the methods by which this law may be applied in a later, more detailed exposition of procedures in reducing the severity of stage fright.

Voice reactions. Nervous reactions in speaking affect voice control in many ways. The stress of emotional reactions acts to produce high pitch. Monotony and harshness of voice arise from the difficulty of controlling muscles under tension. Weakness or inaudibility of voice in the person who can scarcely speak above a whisper when nervous may have a similar physiological foundation in the adjustment of the vocal folds to the altered breath stream during an emotional state. Together with the increase in rapidity of rate of speech, weakness of vocal tones may be explained as a characteristic of the withdrawal behavior of the nervous speaker. He tries to make himself inconspicuous and to get it over with in a hurry. An inflectional monotone and characteristic flat or harsh resonance of the voice under fear reactions also serve to signify an anxiety-ridden speaker's attitudes and emotional condition to his hearers.

Psychological reactions. A final factor descriptive of stage fright may be referred to as the psychological reactions of the speaker to his condition; although all symptoms are in a way psychological. The speaker may feel weak, confused, mystified, disgusted, apologetic, sheepish, and altogether unhappy. Some persons are disturbed by these symptoms and others by entirely different ones. In some cases the individual has the characteristic physical symptoms, but does not seem to be disturbed by his perception of them. Such cases no doubt result from a combination of intense emotional response together with strong cortical inhibitions, or from a previous condition of intense stage-fright reactions now partially overcome.

Reeducational technique may develop control over basic emotional response patterns, eliminate causes, and prevent the development of this type of reaction. We shall consider first those methods which contribute most directly to reduction of the intensity of the fear response.

LEARNING TO DEVELOP CONFIDENCE

Developing confidence involves two major factors: reducing the intensity of emotional reaction and increasing the efficiency of intellectual activity. Following are some specific methods that can help you reach these two goals.

Reducing the intensity of emotional reaction

Study the psychology of emotion. It is a well-known fact that we are afraid of what we do not understand. When we acquire insight into the nature of our emotional responses and learn that what was considered a mystifying, embarrassing peculiarity is a commonplace experience subject to natural law and reasonably precise explanations, the panicky feeling which aggravates fear gives way to hope and determination to develop new habits of response. William James long ago pointed out that when we become curious about emotional responses and "abstract the mind stuff" from the emotions, i.e., think about them as they are experienced in order to analyze and report on their nature, the full force of the emotional reaction is greatly reduced.

Think and talk about your emotions as objective facts. Confession is good for the soul. When we are troubled about almost any kind of emotional response, it is helpful to find someone to listen to our story. Acute emotional distress is much relieved by the feeling that someone is interested in hearing a personal account of the experience. Sharing the feeling with others not only releases emotional tension but also raises the emotional response to a conscious level where one may function more intellectually. The admonition to talk about our emotions does not mean that we must intrude them upon others at every opportunity.

Resolve personal conflicts. Inferiority complexes appear as frequently in persons who merely imagine or accept irresponsible suggestions of inferiority as they do in persons who may really be inferior. Red hair, freckles, fatness, bowlegs, a facial scar or birthmark, shortness in boys and tallness in girls, living in the country or on the wrong side of the tracks, belonging to a minority racial group, failure in competitions or examinations, and hundreds of other minor characteristics and experiences are often magnified by active imaginations or unrealistic self-accusations into blemishes or weaknesses out of all proportion to the facts.

Conflicts sometimes develop as a result of competition among desires and ambitions. Examples of such conflicts are found between the accepted need for expression of self-confidence and abhorrence of egotism, the recognized value of doing one's best and the dislike of pretension, the value of rendering useful service and the objection to butting in, the interest in talking about ourselves and the fear of being considered a braggart, the desire to maintain reputable moral standards and fear of being considered a prig, and the recognized need for persistence in attaining social objectives and an aversion to becoming a bore. Such conflicts usually remain on the unconscious level until one recognizes or has pointed out for him the need for solving them. When the necessity for formulating clear-cut decisions on such motives is recognized, a speaker or writer, at least with wise counseling, ordinarily can formulate an intelligent plan for action which will in time largely relieve him of emotional reactions toward these personal conflicts. Consult your teacher about conflicts you experience.

Fight unpleasant, frustrating emotions with pleasant, stimulating responses. We have already mentioned the value of the development of habits of intellectual objectivity toward one's emotions. Such habits may be considered one's means of applying the principle of fighting unpleasant emotions with pleasant responses. The value of this technique is that most persons are incapable of experiencing two opposite types of emotional reactions or conditions at the same time. It also involves a role-playing technique widely recognized as a method of developing personality and social adjustment. If the speaker becomes strongly interested in what he is to accomplish by his speaking, if he can exercise a sense of humor or stir himself by righteous indignation over a cause he expounds, if he feels a keen sense of pride in the accomplishments of wholesome rivalry, if he acts as if he were confident even when he is not,[8] if he enjoys the pleasant emotion of participation in group activities where success is enjoyed with others or where it accompanies work

[8] Robert West, *Purposive Speaking*, The Macmillan Company, New York, 1924.

well done, the disorganizing and unpleasant effects of fear may be effectively inhibited.

Develop habits of voluntary relaxation and control of activity. When someone has been keyed up and must relax in order to attain vitally needed rest, the natural method of achieving this objective is simple —yawn, stretch, let the muscles become tense, take a deep breath of air, let the air out slowly, and then let the muscle tensions collapse. A considerable degree of general relaxation may be attained by taking several deep breaths of air in fairly rapid succession. Habits of localized control over relaxation may be attained by first vigorously tensing the particular muscles involved and then collapsing the tension quickly. Grasping the speaker's stand is a device often used to induce tension as a step in achieving relaxation. Some speakers report that they can speak more easily when seated than when they stand up. This device works because it facilitates relaxation.

Do not submit unnecessarily to severe mental and physical strain. Control your environment. The speaker who realizes that he can expect to do his best only when he is rested and well will see to it that he takes the necessary care of his health. For a great many people, speaking is hard work. It may burn up a considerable amount of energy. What one can take as all in a day's work under optimal conditions may be just too much for the maintenance of poise and self-control when one is spent by fatigue or affected by loss of energy in ill health.

Increasing the efficiency of intellectual activity

Know what can be reasonably expected of a speaker. We have seen that speech is a complex process made up of many different elements contributing to the total effect. The speaker who is conscientious about his work wants to handle all these elements as well as possible. Some listeners are influenced primarily by one element, some by another. It is the speaker's duty to know fairly well when he has satisfied all reasonable requirements. He is probably overly optimistic if he hopes to please everyone. He may realize that he is not doing his best upon a particular occasion. That, too, is something he should understand as a normal variation in human achievement. If he knows what is a reasonable expectation of his audience, and if he has attained sufficient objectivity in speech analysis to know that he has no justifiable cause for embarrassment, then he can dismiss his worry and concentrate on the job at hand.

Use devices in speaking which facilitate memory for speech materials. We have already referred to the fact that organized material is more easily remembered than unorganized material. A story is commonly remembered more easily than the ordering of points in an analysis of an abstract or technical proposition because the sequence of events in the story has a more obviously inherent order or organization. In planning to discuss subjects of an abstract type it is desirable to try to find the best possible arrangement of points for retention. Materials which are prepared, or on which one's memory is refreshed just before the speech is made, are more recent and therefore are recalled more readily than ideas prepared some time in advance. Prepare the beginning of the speech with special care. These techniques will be recognized as application of the laws of learning which have been discussed in Chapter 2.

Use directed movement to keep the mind active. Among directed movements commonly used by speakers to collect and organize their thinking are deliberate pauses, moving from one side of the table or stand to another, picking up and putting down an object, taking a drink of water, rewording a previously stated idea, and making a general comment about the subject. Occasional movements of this type are not misinterpreted. If the speaker forms the habit of exercising them too frequently, his speaking loses effectiveness. The use of autosuggestion, in which the speaker assumes confidence, may be classified as a form of directed movement to facilitate thinking.[9]

Develop an effective philosophy for speaking. It has been pointed out by James that "confidence equals success over ambition." [10] In a situation where one's ambition is indicated by the symbol 2 and his success by the symbol 1, it follows that his confidence is indicated by the fraction ½. It should be apparent that the strength of confidence can be changed by modifying either of the values of the fraction. If one hopes for more than he has the right to expect, he will probably be disappointed and unduly worried. Few speeches are sufficiently important to be chiseled in marble, cast in bronze, or even set in type. When the beginning speaker learns that his best

[9] *Ibid.*

[10] William James, *Psychology: Briefer Course,* Henry Holt & Company, Inc., New York, 1900.

efforts, even though they fall short of perfection, are probably fair expressions of himself and that there is no justification for deceiving others in speech, he is on the road to the development of goals within the realm of possibility. The numerator in the fraction can be modified if he sees to it that his best efforts do not fall below a minimum standard of achievement. Although we interpret the success of speech on the basis of results attained, we must remember that success is what we make it. As beginners we cannot afford to make success so difficult that all satisfaction of achievement is lost.

PROJECTS AND PROBLEMS

Project 1 An interview with an off-campus community leader

Interview an off-campus community leader. Find out what he has observed about achieving self-confidence and control in speaking. One member of the class should consult a psychology professor or counselor. Report to the class on your findings.

Project 2 A personal-experience narrative

Purposes of this assignment: (1) To increase self-objectivity, directness, relaxation, and enthusiasm; (2) to improve the ability to extemporize in a conversational manner; (3) to develop skill in effective projection to the audience.

Subjects for this speech:

1. The message received was not the message sent
2. An experience which gave me a thrill
3. A good intention which went wrong by accident
4. A practical joke which was enjoyed by all
5. A most embarrassing experience
6. An experience with hobbies
7. My first job
8. Experience with my teachers
9. A travel experience
10. "It's an ill wind that blows no good"

Project 3 A speech with visual aids or demonstrative action

Purposes of this assignment: (1) To help overcome the feeling of awkwardness and tension in the speech situation; (2) to develop some facility in using the symbolism of bodily action in speech.

Subjects for this speech:

1. The city of tomorrow
2. Fencing
3. The grip and swing of a golf club
4. A musical instrument
5. The cancer cell
6. Cartooning or sketching
7. Pantomime of a character
8. Diagram of the organization of a company
9. First-aid practice
10. Handling a flying rod
11. Adjusting the sights on a rifle
12. A "bit" of information

Project 4 A speech of strong conviction

Purposes of this assignment: (1) To develop skill in the effective defense of a conviction; (2) to facilitate the development of confidence in speaking; (3) to improve effectiveness in fluency, projection, directness, and expressive action; (4) to increase awareness of the responses of your listeners.

Subjects for this speech:

1. A firm conviction which I believe my audience should share
2. A cause which I believe to be misunderstood
3. A principle for which I feel a deep and moving loyalty

Consider such specific subjects as:

The hypocrite
The war profiteer
The coward
The yes-man
The schemer
The double-crosser
Getting out of Vietnam
Low moral standards on my campus
College queen contests
Critics of the younger generation
Women drivers
Why I believe in America
Some common annoyances
Pioneering in medicine
Classroom cheating
Defacing library periodicals
Abolishing grades
Martin Luther King

For the instructor: Show the film *Getting Yourself Across* prepared by McGraw-Hill Book Company to accompany this text. Note suggestions in the *Teacher's Manual* for use of the film.

REFERENCES

Arnold, Magda B.: *Emotion and Personality,* Columbia University Press, New York, 1960, vol. 2.

Bruton, Eugene: "Colorimetric Measurements of Anxiety," *Speech Monographs,* 26:282–287, 1959.

Cattell, Raymond B.: *The Scientific Analysis of Personality,* Pelican Books, Inc., Baltimore, 1965.

Clevenger, Theodore: "A Synthesis of Experimental Research in Stage Fright," *Quarterly Journal of Speech,* 45:134–145, 1959.

Gilkinson, Howard, and Franklin H. Knower: *Psychological Studies of Individual Differences among Students of Speech,* University of Minnesota, Minneapolis, 1939.

Gruner, Charles R.: "A Further Note on Stage-fright," *Speech Teacher,* 13:223–224, 1964.

Hebb, D. O.: *Organization of Behavior,* John Wiley & Sons, Inc., New York, 1949.

James, William: *Psychology: Briefer Course,* Henry Holt & Company, Inc., New York, 1900.

Janis, Irving: *Psychological Stress,* John Wiley & Sons, Inc., New York, 1958.

Knower, Franklin H.: "A Study of Speech Attitudes and Adjustments," *Speech Monographs,* 5:130–203, 1938.

Leefer, Robert W.: *Some Needed Developments in the Motivational Theory of Emotions,* University of Nebraska Press, Lincoln, 1965, pp. 25–125.

Lerea, Louis: "The Verbal Behavior of Stage Fright," *Speech Monographs,* 23:229–233, 1956.

West, Robert: *Purposive Speaking,* The Macmillan Company, New York, 1924.

Young, Paul Thomas: *Motivation and Emotion,* John Wiley & Sons, Inc., New York, 1961.

YOUR AUDIENCE

4 ADAPTING TO THE AUDIENCE AND THE OCCASION

In the adaptation of the speaker to his listeners we come face to face with the problems of speech as a form of social behavior. What we have to say about the audience in this chapter will apply to most listeners whether they are in a formal audience or in an informal communication situation. Effective communication is not a kind of target practice in the dark. You want to succeed in accomplishing your purpose with your message. To do this you must adapt that message to those who receive it. You will expect to draw upon all your communication resources to accomplish your purpose, but you cannot expect to represent your message or express yourself in the same way to all listeners. The success of your speech is largely in their response. The more you can know about the way they respond to speaking, the greater the probability that you can get from them the response you would like.

We use the word *audience* to represent one or more persons receiving a spoken communication. The speaker is in direct confrontation with the listener as in person-to-person discourse or seemingly in direct communication as in watching a film or television tape. In most direct communication there is also a visual code which parallels the vocal and linguistic codes. Because auditors typically confront the speaker, the communication situation is a social situation. The word audience is inappropriate for a readership. An audience is not just an aggregate of people. They are people with a curiosity, a wish, or an assignment to listen to a message. Members of an audience may have or acquire some of the characteristics of groups, but their joint presence in listening to a message doesn't make them a group, nor is a group necessarily an audience. When there is social facilitation of audience response the audience tends to function as a group.

Most cultures, just as ours, have norms for audience behavior, although norms will vary in different situations. In general we expect persons in an audience to give the speaker a chance to speak, to attend to his message whether they like it or not, and to avoid distractions which will interfere with the listening of others. The speaker is expected to respect the commitments of his listeners. He will avoid keeping them after the allotted closing time, or making unwarranted requests of them. An old tradition calls for thanks by the speaker to his audience, but when still used is often a hollow and perfunctory courtesy. Except for cases in which a special courtesy has been shown, thanks are no longer considered necessary.

It is the speaker's duty to protect the interests of his audience and the speech situation. Although heat, light, and ventilation are now ordinarily provided automatically, if automatic controls are not in operation, the good speaker will make adequate arrangements for the physical comfort of his listeners. He will also protect them from persons who take advantage of their gathering for selfish reasons. This is one reason why the participation of members of an audience in a forum is limited to the asking of questions. Although we devote this chapter to audience analysis and adaptation, you should keep your audience in mind in the use of every process of speech.

ANALYZING THE AUDIENCE AND THE SITUATION

If you are to use the tools of communication most efficiently you must select and use them in many adaptive ways. First you must know about the nature and functions of communication in general social behavior. You take such information into account in determining what you will say and how you will say it. Then you need to know about the nature of your specific listener or audience. You will ask what are their expectations of you? You ask: "How can I make what I want to say more meaningful for this particular occasion?" Finally you will continue to study your audience as you speak. You will note their behavior to initial remarks, and then you will make continuous adjustments in what you say and how you say it with the intention of getting the greatest possible favorable response to your purpose from your listeners. This latter type of adaptation is now generally called feedback, although it has long been considered a type of monitoring. You may make a post-speech analysis to study the effects of your communication. This can be helpful in future adaptations to this audience.

The recognition of the response of your listeners is their feedback to you. Your adjustment to that response is the consummation of feedback in the total process of communication in social behavior. If feedback ends with your perception of listener response, it has little purpose or value. If it reinforces your previous behavior you will continue speaking in the same manner. If it suggests that your communication is not achieving your purpose, you will carry out planned alternative behavior which may be more successful. This doesn't mean you capitulate when the going is tough. It does mean that you have given your effort. No man can do more.

GENERAL ANALYSIS OF AUDIENCE

Although no two people or audiences can be expected to react exactly alike, they are all human beings. Audiences will differ in size, interests, knowledge, attitudes, and habits of behavior. Yet, since people who are similar in one or more ways tend to congregate, you can expect many similarities among members of an audience. They all want something for which they have chosen to be listeners. Their interests are intrinsic. If they are a captive audience, as many student audiences are, they have this condition in common. Their interests are extrinsic and may need to be developed and polarized. All will want to be respected. In general they will want you to succeed. Many will be interested in you as a person. Identify yourself to them as a person worthy of their expectations by means of anecdotes, references to your common experiences, by use of common knowledge, and by putting substance into your remarks. Your ability to establish credibility will greatly influence their acceptance of your message.

Find out the proposed procedure for the occasion. Will the talk be one of a number of classroom talks? Will you be a member of a panel? You must learn the order of speaking, the length of the speeches, and the size of the audience.

Know the kind of persons you are addressing. If it is a mass meeting of college students, the audience will be in one respect homogeneous. But the extent of homogeneity or heterogeneity can be measured only in connection with your purpose in speaking. A current-events club, for example, is more homogeneous in its interests than members of an alumni association. Appeal to as many elements of your audience as you can within the scope of your speech. The more heterogeneous your audience the more dependence you must place on the development of the more universal aspects of your topic.

Analyze the general economic, social, political, and religious views of the audience, their specific interests, their characteristic attitudes, and the likelihood of their being well informed on your subject. You will need to learn whether they are generally alert to new information; whether they will be favorable to your point of view, or neutral, or indifferent; whether they have a stake in the outcome of the discussion. Age, sex, national origins, and occupations will give you valuable clues as to what interests them, and as to what they know or believe.

You need to know something of the situation in which your talking will be done. What of the size and shape of the room, its comfort, its ventilation, its light? Is there a speaker's stand? Are the listeners scattered about a large room or is it packed to standing room only? Is it relatively free from noise? You will adapt to such factors and modify them as you can to minimize distraction.

The success of your audience analysis as you speak will be influenced by your social sensitivity. Whereas many people consider themselves good judges of human nature, it is well known that people tend to overrate their abilities in this respect. Studies in social sensitivity have shown that this is a highly complex skill of many variables. Smith has shown that those people judge others best who tend to recognize and rate others at a level appropriate to their abilities, who spread their ratings of people in groups, who can empathize with the responses of others, who are observant of small and fleeting responses, who avoid the tendency to allow stereotypes to influence them, and who have had most experience with those being judged. T group procedures are often used as an educational device to increase social sensitivity.[1]

In an unpublished study by Knower and Smith students spoke impromptu to a familiar audience which, unknown to the speaker, had been instructed to respond in a manner suggested by one of

[1] Henry Clay Smith, *Sensitivity to People,* McGraw-Hill Book Company, New York, 1966.

six emotional categories. The speakers were able to identify the feedback after they had spoken in about 70 percent of the cases. Only about 17 percent accuracy could be expected by chance. This difference was significant at the 1 percent level of confidence. Speakers who got a highly favorable response were overstimulated to continue past their time limit. Speakers who were given an unfavorable response all cut their speaking short of their permitted time limit.

ADAPTING YOUR SPEECH TO YOUR SPECIFIC AUDIENCE

Although your preparation will provide for interpolations and cutting of your message as warranted, your first major art of adaptation will involve your introduction. A good start is often half the battle. Your introductory remarks should serve to orient your listeners to the tenor and substance of your message. Your task is essentially to create a speech situation. Unfortunately a speech situation does not consist merely of a gathering of people. Irving Lee once reported in a study of 200 audiences about 25 percent of the listeners were in attendance for some reason other than hearing the speaker. A speech situation has an audience which has been so polarized by events, the topic, or the speaker that they now want to hear the speaker through in what he has to say. When you have created this situation you are in your best possible position to achieve your purpose with your audience.

Your subject, its organization, and your illustrations, details, language, and delivery will depend upon the results of your analysis of your audience. In your choice of ideas, supporting details, language, and delivery, appeal to this particular audience's concern for security, freedom, material comfort, social approval, support of reference groups, popularity, pride, fair play, sympathy, adventure, escape from boredom, intellectual and aesthetic satisfactions, reverence, duty, and self-sacrifice. For a detailed discussion of motives and motivation, see Chapter 16, "Persuasive Speaking." Be considerate of their convictions and loyalties. Make it clear in your speech that you respect them as a group, or, at any rate, as individuals. If you are trying to make them change their minds, show your respect for them by giving them good arguments for doing so.

Beware of high-pressure techniques. Self-respecting persons shy away from overaggressive, blunt, and domineering speakers. Don't use your audience, don't trick them, don't get angry at them, don't stampede them. Little permanent satisfaction derives from "telling off" your audience. Avoid scolding, insulting, and sarcastic remarks. Shock and ridicule strike deep and are not easily forgiven. Those who use such techniques often have a mistaken sense of their own efficiency and importance. On the other hand, adjustment to your audience does not mean negating your convictions. It means trying to gain your ends as a speaker without sacrificing your integrity.

The more you expect from your audience, the more slowly you must move. If necessary, take your trip by stages. Do not expect to accomplish everything at once. Above all, cultivate your ability to sense the appropriate time to stop.

The principal dimensions of your audience are listed for you on the following pages. The first five may be referred to as primary dimensions of your audience. They are primary because they are the major functions of communication, and the kinds of behaviors involved are subject to modification through speech. They are measurable in various ways. The secondary dimensions of the audience consist of those variables which influence and may be influenced by communication but are not its primary objectives. Such variables as items 6 to 8 in the following list fall in this category. The ninth variable is considered a tertiary variable. The items such as age, sex, etc., may influence reactions and therefore require consideration although they are not generally subject to modification by communication.

Principal dimensions of the audience

You will want to check the following list of dimensions of the audience in planning your adaptation to them.

1. Size of the audience
2. Audience interests
  a. State of interest, expectations
  b. Mood, readiness to respond
3. Audience knowledge of the subject
  a. Informed or uninformed
  b. Experts or amateurs
4. Audience attitudes toward the subject
  a. Specific or general
  b. Favorable, unfavorable, or neutral
  c. Open or closed mind
  d. Current needs, wants, and desires
  e. General economic, social, political, religious, and other attitudes and interests

5. The potential active behavior of your audience relative to your subject

6. Audience attitudes toward the speaker

a. Impression of his knowledge, experience, and abilities

b. Impression of his social attitudes, humor, and goodwill

c. Impression of his moral qualities—honesty, integrity, and sense of responsibility

d. Reactions to his personality, mannerisms, and his style of speaking

7. The social and cultural orientation of the audience

8. The capacities and talents of the audience

9. Demographic characteristics of the audience which may influence reactions to the message

a. Age

b. Sex

c. Nationality of ethnic background

d. Occupation

e. Economic status

f. Cultural interests

g. General intelligence

h. Group affiliations

FEEDBACK—ONGOING ANALYSIS

From your analysis of your listeners in preparation of your message you will have anticipated some of their responses. If you can observe them as they react to a preceding speaker, this will help. If this kind of analysis is not possible, you may make some inquiries about them. Then when you speak watch their behavior. If you do not consider their response a favorable one, don't jump to conclusions. Speakers sometimes misinterpret the behavior of listeners. Experience will help you judge your audience more precisely.

PROJECTS AND PROBLEMS

Project 1 How good a people reader are you?

Study the reactions of people you observe in active conversation during a full day. Form some judgment as to their understanding and feeling in response to remarks. When you can, ask them to report their thoughts and attitudes to you. Check with your interpretation to see how frequently your interpretations were correct. Discuss the results of your experience in class.

Project 2 Adapting the speech to audiences with different degrees of understanding

For an informative speech, select a subject on which you may justly claim to be something of an expert, or about which you at least know more than many members of your audience. Prepare two short sets of speech notes on this subject. One speech should be to persons who know little or nothing about the subject. The other should be to those who know quite a bit about it. All the members of the class will be called on to present both sets of notes to the class. The class is asked to explain what adaptations were attempted, and to suggest other adaptations which might be made.

Project 3 Adapting argument to the attitudes of an audience

Prepare two short sets of notes for argumentative speeches on the same subject. In the first, try to convince an indifferent audience of the truth of your proposition. In the second, attempt to convince an antagonistic audience of the soundness of your belief. These speech notes are to be presented orally to the class. Discuss the differences in your speeches with your classmates.

Project 4 Adapting the speech to audiences of men and women

Select an interesting subject and discuss with the class the differences you would make in speeches on this subject to an audience of men and an audience of women.

Project 5 Adapting the speech to audiences of different ages

Prepare an informative speech to be presented to a group of adults. Then consider how you would explain the same subject to an eight-year-old boy. You will be asked to present the speech to the class and then report the changes you would make in explaining the subject to a child. Relate your ideas to the listener level of experience.

Project 6 Adapting the speech to the formality of the situation

Write out two versions of a part of a talk. One should be in informal and conversational style, as you would present it in a "bull session" to a group of friends. The other should be written for a conference—in more formal style.

Project 7 Adapting the emotional appeals to the audience

Select a subject for a persuasive appeal to action. Then select audiences of two different types. Prepare both speeches.

REFERENCES

Clevenger, Theodore: *Audience Analysis*, The Bobbs-Merrill Company, Inc., Indianapolis, 1900.

Davitz, Joel R.: *The Communication of Emotional Meanings*, McGraw-Hill Book Company, New York, 1964.

Eisenson, Jon, J. Jeffery Auer, and John V. Irwin: *The Psychology of Communication*, Appleton-Century-Crofts, Inc., New York, 1963, chap. 14.

Festinger, Leon, Stanley Schachter, and Kurt Bock: *Social Pressures in Small Groups*, Harper & Row, Publishers, Incorporated, New York, 1950.

Janis, Irving, Carl I. Hovland, et. al.: *Personality and Persuasibility*, Yale University Press, New Haven, Conn., 1959.

Maier, Norman R. F.: *Principles of Human Relations*, John Wiley & Sons, Inc., New York, 1953.

Newcomb, Theodore: *Social Psychology*, The Dryden Press, Inc., New York, 1950.

Sherif, Muzafer and Carl I. Hovland: *Social Judgment: Assimilation and Contrast Effects in Communication and Attitude Change*, Yale University Press, New Haven, Conn., 1961.

——— and Carolyn W. Sherif: *Reference Groups*, Harper & Row, Publishers, Incorporated, New York, 1964.

———, ———, and Roger E. Nebergold: *Attitude and Attitude Change*, W. B. Saunders Company, Philadelphia, 1965.

Smith, Henry Clay: *Sensitivity to People*, McGraw-Hill Book Company, New York, 1966.

Thibaut, John W., and Harold H. Kelley: *The Social Psychology of Groups*, John Wiley & Sons, Inc., New York, 1959.

Whiting, John W.: "The Cross-Cultural Approach," in Gardner Lindzey, *Handbook of Social Psychology*, Addison-Wesley Publishing Company, Inc., Cambridge, Mass., 1954, chap. 14.

5 LISTENING

There was a time when we studied communication as an art of expression. Today many scholars see it more as a social event. The speaker has a responsibility to adapt to his listener. The listener also has a responsibility to do his part to receive the message. The best listening can occur only if the listener lets himself get involved in the task. This does not mean that he must agree with the speaker. But unless he cooperates fully in trying to understand the message, he cannot know if he agrees or not, or to what extent he agrees.

Some listening is marginal or background listening although this is not the type from which one can expect to acquire useful information. Listening is not a process of abject submission, or the mediation of a stimulus which produces signal behavior—the instantaneous reflexive conditioned response to an order. Listening is not just a game people play.

Hearing is primarily a matter of a threshold of sensitivity. Although hearing is necessary, listening is more than hearing; it is a cognitive process. It has to do with perception, comprehension, and other mental reactions. It is not merely a matter of placing yourself within earshot. It is not waiting until you can get in your word. As we use the term here, listening includes visual perceptions that usually attend the listening situation. It includes watching the speaker, observing his actions and his use of visual aids, as well as hearing what he says. The observing process is included in listening because visible symbols are also ongoing confrontation communication behavior which may so dominate a communication act that they are the most important source of a message.

Listening is a term for a whole group of mental processes which enable us to interpret the meanings of messages. Of course one may listen to certain nonsymbolic stimuli such as the sounds of nature. These sounds may serve as signs to which we attribute meaning. If one is skilled in interpreting such sounds he will recognize much that the unskilled listener does not. Our main interest here is in increasing our skill in interpreting the symbols of man. As in reading we listen not only for what words may be used, we listen also for messages between, or underneath, the words in the voice; we listen for symbols of the message in overt behavior, in the climate, in the context, in the situation. We spend more time listening than in any other type of communication behavior. We have had many opportunities to practice listening, yet few people listen as well as they might.

Dale [1] says that there are a number of reasons why people don't listen. The speaker is hard to hear or understand. We are thinking about what we will say next. We have prejudged the speaker as unworthy of listening effort. We don't feel deeply enough involved. We don't listen because speakers we have heard haven't been helpful. Perhaps we are very tired. The room may be hot and stuffy. The speaker is arrogant, overly aggressive, unsure of himself, confusing, or unmotivated. Some other stimulus may be more attractive at the moment. Whatever it is, some appropriate action should be taken to correct it. If one is a part of an audience, he owes it to the speaker. You owe it to yourself. The best of speakers cannot do all your work for you. Your job here is to understand and develop the good listening habits which you should exercise all your life.

YOUR PURPOSE IN LISTENING

The development of good listening habits involves a recognition of your specific purposes in listening and adaptation of listening skills to each purpose. We listen for many purposes: (1) We listen

[1] Edgar Dale, "Why Don't We Listen?" *The News Letter,* The Ohio State University, Bureau of Educational Research, Columbus, vol. 22, 1957.

for enjoyment; (2) we listen for information, for inspiration, to understand the attitudes and feelings of people; (3) we listen in order to evaluate critically our own ideas and the ideas and communication processes of others. To be sure, one may listen with all three purposes in mind.

You should know what you are listening for. You may listen, for example, to observe the application of the principles of speech construction. If you are seeking information, on the other hand, the principles of speech in which you will be interested for the moment are the soundness and relationship of the facts and ideas presented; what you know otherwise about effective speaking should not be allowed to interfere with your getting those facts. If the speaker's feelings are an important aspect of those facts or reasons, you will want to be sensitive to those too. If you listen not only for information but for critical evaluation of ideas, you will be alert to test the accuracy of the speaker's facts and inferences.

Knowing what you are listening for will help you to organize your listening. If you hear in a vague, general way, you should not expect to get as much from your listening as you would if you did so for a specific purpose. Do not, however, fall into the error of hearing what you want to hear whether it has been said or not. Wishful listening is as harmful a psychological habit as wishful thinking. Knowing what you are listening for should help you not only to hear but to evaluate what you hear.

Your purposes in listening will be influenced by the situations in which your listening is done. Recreational listening may be casual or it may be highly focused and systematic. In informal social situations, for example, listening may not require concentration. On the other hand, even listening to a story for purposes of enjoyment may require concentrated attention; if you miss one point or are distracted, your enjoyment of the entire story may be spoiled. In listening to learn, you can never expect to achieve much satisfaction from incidental or irresponsible attention. It is in listening with a purpose that we may most truly make the important distinction between listening and hearing.

THE PROCESS OF LISTENING

Listening does not operate wholly independently of other higher mental processes. It is in many ways similar to reading with which it is moderately correlated. But reading is responding to words on a page; listening is responding to symbols as they are produced by a person. Listening is studying. Studying, Robinson tells us, is a

SQ3R process.[2] Listening is thinking. Listening is experiencing—a way of gaining information vicariously. Listening is perceiving, understanding, comprehending, gaining insight, decision making. The task of listening in short is to make sense out of what we hear. It is easy to misinterpret our senses. The sense we make out of the sensations we receive must be as close as possible to the real and total sense of the message.

Develop your sensitivities to people and messages

The first process in listening is sensitivity. The person who has perfect human hearing has the first requisite for good listening. However, one may have a low threshold for auditory stimulation, but still be lacking in sensitivity to people. Many of us aren't good people readers. This achievement appears to be correlated with persons who are high in other social habits and activities.

Listen with patience and consideration

People are most talkative with those in whom they have confidence. And confidence develops out of the respect and consideration which the listener exhibits. Try to hear the speaker out. Keep an open mind. Delay decisions. Do not disturb speakers with unnecessary noises or interruptions. Allowing the mind to wander is also disastrous. You can achieve alertness and concentration by taking personal responsibility for getting maximum benefit from what you hear.

Eliminate or ignore distracting elements

Eliminate wherever possible the many distractions in the environment which interfere with listening. Find a place where you can hear and see the speaker easily. Avoid putting yourself in a position where you might be disturbed by extraneous sounds and sights, drafts, and uncomfortable or too-comfortable chairs. If you expect to take notes, arrange a convenient place for writing.

Some factors in the speaker such as a physical deformity, a speech defect, or resemblance to a person with whom you have had an unpleasant experience cannot be eliminated by external control. Learn

[2] Francis P. Robinson, *Effective Study*, Harper & Row, Publishers, Incorporated, New York, 1941. [SQ3R stands for "Survey the material to be learned, stating objectives as Questions, Read, Recite, and Review."]

to dissociate the processes of communication from such distractions by concentrating on the subject under discussion.

Listen with attention

The first step in listening is always attentiveness. Keep your attention sharply focused on the ideas expressed. Try to develop your attention span. Don't worry about all the details. Be as alert and sensitive as possible to various stimuli. Seek optimal tonicity in your muscle system. Listen with an active mental attitude.

Try putting the idea in your own words. Ask yourself what it means. This means interpreting the speaker in terms of your own experience. We perceive by referring the incoming message to our own file of experiences. If you have difficulty doing this you may need to index better your own knowledge and understanding. Indexing of growing knowledge is a matter of constantly associating our ideas, sorting them, and selecting or rejecting meanings with discrimination.

In listening to learn, it is most important to make some mental-physical response to ideas. The right kind of note-taking provides this practice. However, one need not take notes; one can mentally relate the new ideas to what he knows, ask mental questions, make applications, provide examples, and reorganize what he hears to provide patterns easier to recall than the original.

Listen for message cues

To be a good listener one needs to listen to words and other symbols about the message as well as those which express it. Listen for sentences which predict, show development, relate, indicate transition, and summarize. Identify as you go along, but don't lag behind or you may get lost. Memory should help you here. Keep your associations active. Continually organize the message with the speaker. See the speaker's purpose and motivation. Differentiate main ideas from detail. Arrange in sequences which seem important to you.

To achieve these objectives you need to analyze the speech into its parts. Ask what can you forget? What must you remember? What does the speaker emphasize? What would you emphasize? The comprehension of the message may require detailed inspection, reflection, careful discrimination. Let your thoughts simmer, or perhaps incubate would be a better figure.

Critically evaluate ideas as you listen

Evaluate ideas in listening in the same way you evaluate materials for your own speeches. Examine the ideas for clarity, accuracy, logic, and relevance to the topic. Be alert to the sources of the material, for they may provide important cues in evaluation. Compare your frame of reference to that of the speaker.

We think more critically and independently when alone than when in the company of others. The social environment influences our evaluation of what we hear. Most people, for example, respond to humor much more vigorously in a crowd than alone, and some texts in public speaking advise the speaker on the methods of turning an audience into a crowd in order to render listeners less critical of suggestion. These methods include bringing the members of an audience together—getting them to rise and sit down together, to read aloud and sing in unison, and to applaud. Some speakers give the impression of gaining universal agreement by telling a joke which brings down the house or by expressing commonplace sentiments which evoke indications of widespread approval. The listener who wishes to maintain his independence of thought should be aware of these techniques for disarming critical reactions, and avoid them.

To listen well you will be continually exercising decisions, making judgments, evaluating. Evaluation means the application of standards. Select the standards for evaluating any communication with care. We don't judge all communication by reference to the same subjective anchors to value systems. Find the appropriate standards for this discourse and apply them tentatively.

Aristotle long ago said that there were three things which listeners ordinarily want to know about a speaker: the depth of his wisdom, the quality of his character, and the extent of his goodwill. How can we fairly test a speaker for these traits in order to avoid judging him merely through prejudice or bias?

As a listener, you must recognize the need for interpreting what is said in the light of the speaker's purpose in talking. Sometimes this purpose is stated; sometimes the listener must determine it for himself. Fairness and good sportsmanship are widely accepted mores of our society. Listening doesn't bind one to accept what he hears, but one cannot really know whether or not he accepts without careful listening. To fairly judge a man's wisdom, character, and goodwill requires that we hear him to the end of his discourses. Learn to delay judgment.

Recognize fallacies in logic and propaganda

A knowledge of the common logical fallacies and propagandistic tricks is especially important to the listener. To be forewarned is to be forearmed. Hasty generalizations, false analogies, arguing from questionable premises, and the *post hoc* argument—the assumption that because one event follows another it must have been caused by it—are some of the logical fallacies which the listener should guard against.

The Institute for Propaganda Analysis identifies a number of devices as propaganda techniques.[3] One such device is *name calling* which renders a person or subject undesirable by associating that person or subject with an objectionable name or classification, such as "Communist," "isolationist," "rabble-rouser," "yellow," and "traitor." The use of *glittering generalities* is a device for gaining acceptability for propositions by labeling them with approved verbal sanctions. Typical of such are the words "freedom," "progress," "democracy," "thrifty," "a balanced budget," and "investment." The technique of using sources of authority, prestige, respect, and reverence to create favorable attitudes toward a proposal is called *transfer*. The church, the flag, the home, educational institutions, the Rock of Gibraltar, and the red cross of mercy are examples of sources of emotional approval.

The *plain-folks* device expounds a proposal in terms of the simple, everyday experiences and personalities that make up our lives. Politicians delight in using this technique for showing that, after all, they are only one of our neighbors and therefore worthy of our trust in public office. *Card stacking* is a scheme used to deceive by means of carefully selecting only favorable evidence. Half-truths are used as a smoke screen to prevent the listener from really facing the facts. The *bandwagon* technique creates an expression of universal approval of an idea; the individual is supposed to consider himself an outsider if he does not approve: "Two million people can't be wrong." "I nominate the next President of the United States. . . ."

Other tricks of propagandists include appeals of fear, hate, anger, frustration, or discontent growing out of misfortune or lack of opportunity; the creation of scapegoats on which to place blame; threats of trouble, wishful thinking, rationalization, rumor, distrust, flattery, and repetition; and identification with the great, the beautiful, and

[3] Violet Edwards, *Group Leader's Guide to Propaganda Analysis*, Institute for Propaganda Analysis, Inc., New York, 1935.

the good; and prophecies and positive suggestion. The propagandist may be a head of state, or the man who sits beside you at lunch. The use of such techniques does not, of course, imply that the proposal is inherently unworthy. The listener must decide for himself whether or not the conclusions fit the facts.

LISTENING AND PERSONALITY

Begin your efforts to improve by testing your listening ability.[4] After you have obtained objective evidence concerning your efficiency as a listener, you can begin to make the psychological adjustments necessary for improvement. This means, first of all, that you must recognize your prejudices and understand their nature; we can interpret what we hear only against the background of our experiences and convictions. Our prejudices often act as unconscious earplugs to what we hear. Because what we believe profoundly influences our ability to listen fairly, we need to beware the common causes of prejudices. It is easy to make mistakes in listening when tense, in a state of conflict, or experiencing such emotions as irritation, anxiety, disappointment, grief. We may become better listeners by analysis and realization of personal motives, comparison of backgrounds and experiences, limitations and delays to our judgments, cultivation of an open-mindedness enabling us to look at conclusions from many points of view, and practice of the socialization techniques of empathy, role playing, and courtesy.

PROJECTS AND PROBLEMS

Project 1 Listening to instructions

Ask someone a question which requires instructions of at least three or four sentences. Then repeat the answer to see if you have understood it clearly. See how much of the answer you can repeat in the exact words used by the other person. If you do not do it correctly the first time, have him repeat the answer until you are able to recite it accurately. Then stand before the class and carry out this process with a new question. Such questions as the following may be asked: (1) How do you start a car in learning to drive? (2) How do you saddle and mount a horse? (3) How do you get to a distant place in a city? (4) How do you operate a

[4] For tests of listening, see James I. Brown and Robert G. Carlsen, *Brown-Carlsen Listening Comprehension Test,* World Book Company, Tarrytown-on-Hudson, N.Y., 1953, and Educational Testing Service, Princeton, N.J.

certain make of comptometer (or other machine)? (5) How do you handle a particular piece of sporting equipment? (6) How do you operate a specific laboratory apparatus? (7) What is to be done in a specific classroom assignment?

Project 2 Listening to evaluate argument

Listen to a radio, television, or platform public speech which is argumentative in nature. Make a report on the speech indicating (1) the central idea, (2) the main points in the organization, (3) the pattern of logical inferences, (4) the use of persuasive devices, (5) the techniques or propaganda devices used, (6) how the facts are differentiated from the opinions expressed by the speaker, (7) an evaluation of the speech content.

Project 3 Listening to restate an argument

Ask someone for his opinion on a certain proposition and have him elaborate in three or four sentences. Then ask him to listen to you as you restate the opinion in your own words. Try to do this fairly and completely, but avoid the language used by the other person. If you do not state the argument correctly at first, keep trying until you get his approval of your statement as the equivalent of his. Repeat this for the class.

Project 4 Listening to learn about speaking, reading, or plays

Listen to the speech performance of a public lecturer or entertainer, or go to a play. Evaluate the performance according to a systematic set of criteria for the type of activity involved. What was well done? What would have improved the performance? Report to the class, pointing out the principles of speaking involved.

Project 5 Listening to personal criticism

After you have finished speaking in a regular class project, ask some member of the audience for a criticism of your performance. When you have heard this criticism, repeat it carefully and completely. Try to avoid attitudes of apology, defense, or smugness.

Project 6 A programmed course of study on listening

Get the programmed instructional unit on listening published by McGraw-Hill and work through the course of study. Perhaps you have this material in your listening center. Your instructor may have some suggestions to make to you about this.

REFERENCES

Brown, Roger: *Social Psychology,* The Free Press of Glencoe, New York, 1965, chap. 2.

Bruner, Jerome: "The Perception of People," in Gardner Lindzey, *Handbook of Social Psychology,* Addison-Wesley Publishing Company, Inc., Cambridge, Mass., 1954, chap. 17.

Dale, Edgar: "Why Don't We Listen?" *The News Letter,* no. 22, 4 pp., Bureau of Educational Research, The Ohio State University, Columbus, 1957.

Dukor, Sam: *Listening: Bibliography,* The Scarecrow Press, Inc., New York, 1964.

———: *Listening: Readings,* The Scarecrow Press, Inc., New York, 1966.

Fries, Charles C.: *Linguistics and Reading,* Holt, Rinehart and Winston, Inc., New York, 1963, 265 pp.

Gibson, James J.: "The Useful Dimensions of Sensitivity," *American Psychologist,* 18:1–15, 1963.

Hartley, Eugene F., and Ruth E. Hartley: *Fundamentals of Social Psychology,* Alfred A. Knopf, Inc., New York, 1952, chap. 9.

Nichols, Ralph G., and Leonard A. Stevens: *Are You Listening?,* McGraw-Hill Book Company, New York, 1957.

Robinson, Francis P.: *Effective Study,* Harper & Row, Publishers, Incorporated, New York, 1941.

White, William H.: *Is Anybody Listening?,* Simon and Schuster, Inc., New York, 1950.

THE SPEECH

6
CHOOSING YOUR SUBJECT, PURPOSE, AND MATERIALS

CHOOSING YOUR SUBJECT

What should you talk about? The subject for your longer talk, or even for a dialogue or small group interaction, is apparently the most important problem for the beginning student. A series of scheduled talks with a deadline for each persists as an immediate threat to the well-being of anyone in an oral communication course.

"What shall I talk about?" can be dealt with by a postponement until inspiration arises, which result seldom occurs. Meantime intermittent worry helps to produce stage fright. More sensible is a systematic approach to your problem by asking: (1) What of my experiences and interests would furnish speech topics and materials? (2) What would my audience like to hear about? (3) What current situations of time and place give ideas for talks? (4) What topic has been assigned to me? Once we tap these speaker-audience-occasion sources a good deal of our difficulty in finding suitable subjects will disappear. Incidentally, your enthusiasm in the presentation, your delivery, and your speaking personality will all be helped by your selection of a topic that appeals to you and to others.

Select a subject appropriate to your interests and personality

All creative work should be first of all an expression of the person himself. You are your own best source of topics and ideas—unless you attempt merely to echo somebody else's clichés or profound compositions. Dip into your own career. It is the product of your total experience, your education in school and out, your occupation, your social relations, your attitudes, sentiments, so-called beliefs, your special experiences in reading, writing, speaking, listening, and the social system of culture that has produced you. Some of your recent or earlier experiences and ideas may seem to you trivial or too personal for revelation. But sometimes your familiar and routine recitals may engross others. Have you been a summer camper, the survivor of a cyclone, a worker in a steel mill, an explorer of Mt. Rainier or Mt. Washington, a fisherman in the Ozarks? You may have been a grocery clerk, news reporter, house painter, rancher, baby-sitter, dishwasher, golfer, baseball pitcher, chess expert, filling-station employee, secretary, nurse, member of the armed forces, or just a classroom student engrossed in history or physics.

What interests have you in sports, motorcycling, trout fishing, picture taking, gardening, waterskiing, coin collecting? What recent or older novels have you read? What is your reaction, if any, to Josephine Tey's *Brat Faraar*, Fitzgerald's *The Great Gatsby*, Dickens's *David Copperfield*, Fielding's *Tom Jones*, or Albee's *Who's Afraid of Virginia Woolf?*

What newspapers do you read? Do you specialize on women's columns, advertisements, comics, sports pages, editorials, advice to the lovelorn, local, state, national, and international issues? Aside from these general stimuli from your reading and observation, your campus newspaper will focus on college problems such as car parking, tuition changes, new and old dormitories, new courses, student elections, athletic and other events, parties, proms, and scheduled student recreation events to say nothing of sit-downs, teach-ins, and general rebellions against faculty-administration "restraints" on student freedoms.

What of your opinions, attitudes, reactions to political, educational, social, religious ideas and movements? Do you concern yourself with the problems of the hydrogen bomb, American space astronauts, landing on the moon, settlement of the Vietnam war, changes in the draft, compulsory arbitration, statesmanship of de Gaulle, student rights on college campuses, tightening marriage and divorce laws, closed-circuit teaching by television, further control of inflation (or deflation), upgrading the humanity studies, a minimum wage of 2 dollars per hour, abolishing capital punishment, voting for eighteen-year-olds, more rigid automobile driver tests, pop art, black power, joining picket lines, federal laws and local justice, expansion of medical hospitals, Medicare problems, and nursing as a profession?

These and similar topics and problems become a storehouse that may suggest to you lines of inquiry and later communication. Your review of your experiences, opinions, reading, listening, conversational exchange should send you on your way to the preparation and presentation of talks that possess some vitality and create interest in your coordinate communicators.

Select a subject appropriate to your audience

The suggestions above concerning your personal interests apply also to your audience. You are by turns speaker and audience. What appeals to you also often duplicates their drives and sentiments. Imaginatively you are to identify yourself with the role of the prospective listeners. Your business is to select topics that will grip your audience or at least will not bore them.

Their interests, especially if you are trying to put yourself in their place, will pretty much coincide with your own. In addition you and they are universal human beings with impulses common to the human race. They all want fresh light on facts and ideas already familiar to them. Also, they attend to glimpses and approaches that give their familiar views new perspectives.[1]

The subjects are usually informational or persuasive. Informational topics may be as wide as the audience's knowledge and interest. Illustrative topics include how to buy a common stock, an automated library service, rapid book reading, flying by instrument, Grant Wood as an artist, what is speech?, process of induction into the army, reporting for the college paper, radar and weather reporting, atomic structure of a chemical compound.

Problems that students and others have been recently discussing and arguing about include escalating the war in Vietnam, abandoning NATO, preventing the spread of nuclear bombs, providing further safety measures on automobiles as required by law, further legislation to deal with stream pollution, further legislation to prevent the fraudulent sales of pills, financial problems of landing men

[1] See Chaps. 4, 5.

on the moon, extension of pay television, strikes on airlines, and control of air pollution.

Audiences are thus interested in the many concrete subjects suggested by such general fields as family, inventions, marriage and romance, money, moving pictures, radio, music, atomic energy, politics, religion, health, personal appearance, smoking, drinking, gambling, sports, taxes, war, wealth, and friends.

In selecting a subject appropriate to the occasion, you are reminded that your classroom speeches in some way should be appropriate for a talk in an institution of higher learning. It is important that you select a subject worth the time your classmates and your teacher spend listening to you. You may not at times feel like an expert. You are interested in a serious idea of your own selection or someone helps you identify such a topic. It will take time to develop it. Most good subjects require effort even for an experienced speaker. Select your topic, organize what you know about it, and then go after that additional information or argument which makes the topic a learning experience even for yourself.

Select a subject appropriate to the occasion

Many subjects spring out of the immediate situation. Since the speaker and his group are obviously in the milieu of their time and place the audiences respond fully to these changing conditions, which often seem to them to be major crises. Campus situations, to begin with them, are continually challenging. There are campaigns for Red Cross donations or memberships; calls for talks appealing for support of "religious emphasis week," or welcoming freshmen or high school visiting groups; and there are student programs to honor the memory of John F. Kennedy, or to celebrate a major honor to your college, such as the completion of a drive for several millions.

Beyond these subjects that relate to campuses and student speaking occasions are those of the endless professional, social, parochial, and other meetings, each with its individual requirements for those who communicate. There are UN debates, congressional debates, political campaign speeches, educational or industrial or labor conferences, radio commentaries and talks at set times and under set sponsorship, commencement exercises, commemorative or dedicatory tributes and responses, judicial decisions, and civil rights demonstrations. Most of these occasions are led by a chairman who introduces the speakers, makes the concluding remarks, and sometimes calls for audience participation.

Limit the subject

Since it is impossible to deal adequately in a four-minute speech with all the arguments or information, you will cut your topic to the time. If, for example, you propose to talk about the attitudes of incoming students on American campuses, you will discuss one phase, such as "My first day on this campus." Suppose your subject is communications. You will limit it to public speaking, and further limit it to the study of debating in class and out, and finally to, "My intercollegiate debate two days ago at Whitford College." Or, your subject is professional football. You limit it to "strategy in football"; and also further reduce to "chief kinds of offense in football," and finally to "Bill Spaulding's kicking of a 40-yard field goal in yesterday's game."

One of the most obvious weaknesses of speechmakers (even mature speakers who should know better) is that they try to talk through a large subject in three, five, or six minutes. Your listeners will be much happier if you whittle out a segment and develop it concretely with illustration and summary.

The suggestions above will have further application if you are one of a small group discussion.

YOUR PURPOSES IN ORAL COMMUNICATION

Your specific purpose with the audience and in countercontribution is important. What do you wish your listeners to do? Add to their knowledge? Accept your point of view? Ask yourself what your aim is with any given audience.

More concretely the controlling purposes of a speaker will be:

1. To inform the listeners (add to their facts and ideas, increase their wisdom, strengthen their judgment, and enlarge their ways of looking at problems), primarily through expositional devices ("How the Xerox machine in my office works").
2. To interest or entertain them chiefly through narrative, dramatic, and descriptive devices ("My one day of house-to-house selling").
3. To arouse them to praise or blame, usually through your tribute to an individual, institution, idea, or attitude ("Why July Fourth is obsolete").
4. To convince them of the truth or falsity of an idea or attitude ("One suggestion for retaining your individual freedom and personality in a mass society").

5. To stimulate them to reflective thinking on a problem ("What is the problem of downtown parking in my hometown?").

6. To persuade them to follow a given course of action ("Vote for my candidate in the coming election").

7. To achieve some combination of these motives.

It is almost impossible and certainly unwise to confine your materials to one of these purposes exclusively. They support each other. To be sure, you must have a primary aim, such as to inform. But even a short talk will register more effectively if your participants inject elements of interest, inspiration, and even conviction.

Summarizing the subject and specific purposes

Once you have selected your subject and your aim, it is often to your advantage to combine them in a single specific sentence (even though this purpose is not stated directly to your auditors). For example:

Subject: Increasing the state sales tax
Purpose: To secure from my audience agreement with my proposition
Audience: College or university students
Purpose: I propose to convince you that our state should increase the sales tax by 1 percent.

Testing the subject

To test the ability with which you select a subject, you may ask yourself several questions. Check the success of your topic selection by a postmortem examination of the speaking performance itself.

1. Is the subject suggested by the interests, knowledge, attitudes, and needs of my hearers?

2. Is the subject appropriate to the occasion?

3. Is the subject timely?

4. Is the subject important?

5. Does the subject add to the listener's knowledge?

6. Does the subject grow out of my experience, interests, observations, or knowledge?

7. Do I have genuine enthusiasm for the subject?

8. Have I properly limited the subject?

9. Does the subject result from my purpose to explain, entertain, impress, convince, persuade, or deliberate with an audience?

FINDING MATERIALS

You are now well launched on your interesting and limited topic. How will you develop it? Will you look for concrete illustrations from your experience? Or turn to expositional details, or give two or three reasons for your thesis, or cite an authority or two, or turn to the citation of somebody's experience?

Certainly you want your talk to have substance as well as words. Four approaches or techniques will help you: systematic thinking, listening, talking (including interviewing), and reading (including note-taking). Your application of skill in these activities will provide you not only with general subjects but with interesting and convincing details.

Preliminary thinking. Try to do some thinking on your subject before you attempt a lot of reading. Often the student will pounce on an article in the *Reader's Digest* and hand it out in a speech with little modification of the printed material. Your own ideas are worthwhile and should prevent a wholesale absorption and later duplication of some article.[2]

How will you think? If your topic is informational, begin by concentrating on meanings. What does your subject mean? How does your device work? Is the topic studying for examinations, signs on superhighways, passing a driver's license examination, or vitamins? What do you understand by communism, political conservatism, liberal arts (an old term but still much ill-defined)?

Suppose your topic is more controversial. Begin by asking yourself: What is the problem? What facts led me to this topic? Why the trouble or difficulty? What general choices have I in solving this issue? What tangible proposition have I to offer in correcting the situation? This is the kind of reflective thinking that debaters and discussants use. Every speaker should ask himself such questions even though he may not think of tangible answers. Practice in seeking answers to such questions will greatly aid organization.

Other types of thinking are suggested to you. For example, how do you test the accuracy or falsity of an alleged fact? How dependable are the cases, illustrations, or other specific materials that you would include? If you take time to analyze your own ideas and thinking, you will find more points of view and questions than you yourself might have suspected. You are to think as well as read in preparation.

[2] See Chap. 8 on thought, facts, and inferences.

Listening. Stimulating ideas and facts are borne in upon you by speakers all through your waking hours. Jot down certain clue ideas or details from such sources, and you will have abundant materials for many a speech. Consider some speaking events which you attend as listener—lectures (in classroom or elsewhere on campus), radio and television broadcasts, business conferences, sermons, and other organized talks.

The art of listening is treated in detail in the previous chapter.

Conversation, discussion, and interviewing. If you want ideas or inspiration for your talk, just tackle somebody who is interested in the topic. He will quickly suggest points of view and information of value to you. Analyze at length a recent "bull session" or other conversation. Or review a more orderly discussion in which you and others have attempted to get at the bottom of some problem. Most good students of speech have made a point of discussing things with others as a means not only of practicing a speech but also of reporting points of view and facts to be appropriated (or bypassed) in later speeches.

Reading. A good deal of your preparation, we admit, may consist of following your topic through recent magazines, newspapers, and books. Your problem is how to read efficiently and how to take notes. If you are an effective reader, you will (1) approach your materials or ideas with an open mind, (2) read with a specific purpose related to your topic, (3) read to collect details, (4) read also for general ideas, (5) read also for definitions and the meanings of terms, (6) read to find both the causes of a problem and the solutions. How many of these reading practices do you employ? In so doing assert your personality: Raise questions about the biases of the writers and their possible tendency to unsupported assertions. If the book or magazine is yours, make marks in the margins so that you may refer back to given statements. Proceed with sufficient rapidity to comprehend and yet to assimilate a wide area under your examination.

Using the library. You must be able to find your way around the library; to know something of typical books and references and where they are located; to learn how quickly to use card files and other means (the librarian will help you) to get at the most helpful books, pamphlets, and magazines. For your more lengthy speeches you will need to compile a list of references and will take notes.

Use the card catalog; consult the indexes; refer to general reference works such as the *Encyclopaedia Britannica;* special encyclopedias, e.g., *Encyclopedia of the Social Sciences;* yearbooks, e.g., the *World Almanac;* directories and biographical dictionaries, e.g., *Current Biography.* You should learn how to find and use the appropriate newspapers and magazines, e.g., *New York Times, Saturday Review, Time, Newsweek.* You will make use of the index to *Readers Guide to Periodical Literature, New York Times Index, Education Index, International Index, Psychological Index,* and similar indexes. Sometimes you will need to tap the immense fund of information in government documents, e.g., the *Congressional Record.* Consult also the *Psychological Abstracts, Facts on File, Public Affairs Information Service, Bibliographic Index, Vertical File Service Catalogue, Year Book of the United Nations, Dictionary of American Biography, Vital Speeches of the Day, Price Lists of Public Documents* (U. S. Superintendent of Documents, Government Printing Office). You should be able to spot bibliographies and lists of references, to make one of your own, to read efficiently, and to take notes. We assume that you who study speech will know how to use the library card file and how to find your way to the sources pertinent to your topic.[3]

Prepare a list of references. If you intend to spend several hours reading in preparation for a speech of six or ten minutes, make use of bibliographical sources, including indexes, in order to avoid hours of partially wasteful rambling through stray books and articles. Using these sources, prepare a short working list of references of your own. Your list will be selective, accurately recorded, and thoroughly within the limits of your subject. You should include important books, magazines, pamphlets, reports, and newspapers, encyclopedias and reference books.

List your references systematically, using cards or slips of paper; place only one item on each card. Classify into sections, such as newspapers or magazines. In citing books and pamphlets, include the author's last name, also his first name or initials, the exact title of the book, the number of edition if more than one, the publisher, and the place and date of publication. For example:

> Kennedy, John Fitzgerald: *Profiles in Courage* (Memorial Edition), Harper & Row, Publishers, Incorporated, New York, 1964.

[3] For further suggestion of sources of reading, see Appendix C.

For periodicals and newspapers, list (for convenience in the order here suggested) the author's name, title of the article, title of the periodical, volume and pages, and date. For example:

> Eiseley, Loren: "Science and the Unexpected Universe," *The American Scholar*, 35:415–429, Summer, 1966.

Use a file box with suitable guide cards. Aim at accuracy in your references so that anyone can quickly use your list. Debaters often cooperate in drafting and using such references.

Note-taking. The final step in collecting ideas and details for your own speaking is taking notes of what you read and jotting down original ideas apart from your experiences with books. Two objectionable kinds of notetakers are among those who pursue oral communication: those who eschew the whole mechanical process as a bore and a waste of time and those ultraconscientious copyists who put down almost everything. Mere reliance on your memory is insufficient, if you wish to classify many details. Voluminous reproduction without discrimination is also unfortunate. A more sensible procedure is somewhat as follows:

1. Aim to get the gist of an idea or an article. Read discriminately.
2. Use cards or papers of a uniform size. Your notebook recordings are inconvenient if you intend to shuffle the items into any order.
3. Place one fact on a card.
4. Tag each card at the top with the topic or division under which the statement or date may fall.
5. Cite at the bottom the exact source. Be accurate and complete in the citation. You will later appreciate your meticulousness here.
6. Quote accurately, but avoid long quotations.
7. Get facts mainly rather than broad opinions.
8. Start out with a general scheme for your reading and for the classification of your notes. Later you can modify it.

It is advisable to take seriously this method of note-taking. You will apply it more and more efficiently as you attend classroom lectures and engage in your general or required reading. The habit will become more profitable to you in your total educational development. More to the point as far as this course is concerned, you will have a systematic procedure for preparing your speeches.

PROJECTS AND PROBLEMS

Project 1 Selecting and limiting the subject

Purposes of this assignment: To select a satisfactory subject for a speech, to limit it, and to frame it in a purpose sentence.

Procedure: Present to the instructor, on a paper, (1) a subject you have selected for a four-minute speech, (2) your purpose, (3) your purpose sentence, (4) your testing of the subject as suggested by the nine criteria listed at the end of this chapter. Deliver your talk before the class. Sample general topics from which concrete subjects might be suggested: art, aviation, automobiles, superhighways, books, crime, communication, education, food, physical health, family, friendships, inventions, love, mental power, marriage, money, television, music, politics, races, religion, smoking, drinking, sports, taxes, travel, war, national budget, population explosion, poetry, novels.

Project 2 Purposes in speaking

Purposes of this assignment: Analysis and criticism of your purpose in your speech as assigned for project 1.

Procedure: As your classmates speak, make brief notes of their evident purposes and the success of such purposes. Cooperate in the postmortem comments by instructor and students on the presentations, including your own speech.

Project 3 Reading as a source of materials

Purposes of this assignment: To provide training in intelligent reading.

Procedure: Read an article in a recent magazine or a reprint of a recent complete speech. Present to the class in not more than four or five minutes a brief summary and interpretation of the speech or article. For your reading follow closely the suggestions given in this chapter.

Alternate procedure: Discuss your methods in your reading of this speech text, for example, the first three chapters. Comment on such details as (1) preliminary skimming, (2) careful rereading, (3) mental absorption of the principal ideas, (4) marginal notes, (5) review of author's headings, your marked passages, your marginal questions.

Project 4 Library reading and note-taking

Purposes of this assignment. To provide further training in the use of the library, the preparation of references, and note-taking.

Procedure: Select a subject which requires some library reading but which is limited in scope and difficulty of investigation. Get your instructor's approval of your topic. Prepare a list of about ten references on 3- by 5-inch cards. Take at least fifteen systematic notes from several sources, according to the suggestions in this chapter. Be prepared to submit your notes for inspection by your instructor and by two or three classmates appointed for this purpose. Retain these references and notes, to be supplemented and used later in a talk of five or ten minutes.

For the instructor: Assign questions for review in the *Teacher's Manual* under Choosing Your Subject and Purpose, and Finding Materials.

REFERENCES

Arnold, C. C., D. Ehninger, and John Gerber: *The Speaker's Resource Book,* Scott, Foresman and Company, Chicago, 1961.

Baird, A. Craig, and Lester Thonssen: *Representative American Speeches,* The H. W. Wilson Company, New York, 1938–1968.

Berquist, Goodwin F.: *Speeches for Illustration and Example,* Scott, Foresman and Company, Chicago, 1965.

Black, Edwin, and Harry P. Kerr: *American Issues: A Sourcebook for Speech Topics,* Harcourt, Brace and World, Inc., New York, 1961.

Daly, Thomas F., Jr. (ed.): *Vital Speeches of the Day,* City News Publishing Company, Pelham, N.Y. Twice a month since 1934.

Friedman, Edward L.: *Speechmaker's Complete Handbook,* Harper & Row, Publishers, Incorporated, New York, 1955.

Linkugel, Wilmer A., et al.: *Contemporary American Speeches,* Wadsworth Publishing Company, Inc., Belmont, Calif., 1965.

Reid, Loren: *American Public Address,* University of Missouri Press, Columbia, 1961.

St. Onge, Keith R.: *Creative Speech,* Wadsworth Publishing Company, Inc., Belmont, Calif., pp. 203–464.

Sutton, Roberta Briggs: *Speech Index,* The Scarecrow Press, Inc., New York, 1966.

Thonssen, Lester, and William L. Frankel: *Ideas That Matter: A Sourcebook for Speakers,* The Ronald Press Company, New York, 1961.

Wrage, Ernest J., and Barnet Baskerville: *Contemporary Forum,* Harper & Row, Publishers, Incorporated, New York, 1962.

7 ORGANIZING AND OUTLINING

ORGANIZATION AS AN AID TO EFFECTIVE SPEAKING

The organization of ideas serves many functions. First, your listeners must be oriented to your message. In your introduction to a conversation or a speech, you give the new member of your group some cue to the ongoing line of thought. As the thought develops you call attention to main ideas and details. This speech keeps the listeners aware of the relationship of facts to the whole.

Perhaps a major function of organization is that it is the soundest of preparation for any discourse. Much of the meaning we wish to communicate, as well as the meaning others derive from our communication, involves a process of categorizing our thoughts.[1] The way we organize suggests the way we categorize ideas. Sequence is also important at times. The meaning of the sentence "The boy hit the ball" differs from the meaning of the sentence "The ball hit the boy." One sequence of main ideas sometimes conveys a different meaning from another.

[1] Jerome S. Bruner, Jacqueline J. Goodnow, and George A. Austin, *A Study of Thinking*, John Wiley & Sons, Inc., New York, 1966.

Our categories of ideas must represent our subject fairly. We arrange material to achieve an appropriate emphasis. Our organization provides an opportunity of pretesting our logic. It is an appropriate time to consider psychological implications and to select points and lines of development in light of probable audience interpretation. Organization time is also a time for decisions about the style of one's speech. The style to be used may determine your organization.

Audiences respond more completely to speeches that are organized. The well-structured speech holds better attention and helps listeners to comprehend more easily.[2] So important did the classical rhetoricians regard organization that they stressed it as one of the five major components of oral communication: *inventio, dispositio, elocutio, memoria,* and *pronunciatio.*

What then is the concept of this second part of ancient rhetoric? Organization comes closest to a satisfactory translation and modern interpretation, but the connotation implies commitment to plan or outline. According to Russell Wagner, *dispositio* means "the functional selection of and use of materals for a partcular purpose." According to him, *dispositio* is "planned adaptation." The audience-adjustment factor heavily affects and determines (1) the selection of materials with the communicative ends in view, (2) their adaptation applied in the relevancy of materials, the order of their unfolding, and the massing of the points for impressiveness.[3]

Disposition (or arrangement) serves both the listeners in their understanding and reactions to the message, and the speaker in his own thinking and effective preparation and presentation of his talk. The clear framework will aid you in recalling your ideas and will increase your fluency. It may also enhance your credibility as a speaker. It will above all help you in your preparation by pretesting the relationship of the details you select to your purpose and to the time limits of your remarks.

Systematic steps in organization will guide you in an effective pattern of your ideas.

[2] The testimony that audience reaction is more favorable to well-structured materials than to the unorganized ones is overwhelming. See, for example, E. Thompson, "An Experimental Investigation of the Relative Effectiveness of Organizational Structure in Oral Communication," *Southern Speech Journal,* 26:59–69, Fall, 1960; and F. H. Knower, "Studies in the Organization of Speech Material," *Journal of Educational Research,* 39:220–230, 1945.

[3] Russell H. Wagner, "The Meaning of *Dispositio,*" in Herbert A. Wichelns (ed.), *Studies in Speech and Drama in Honor of Alexander Drummond,* Cornell University Press, Ithaca, N.Y., 1944, pp. 285–294.

1. Decide upon the objective of your speech—the audience reaction you hope for.

2. Express your purpose in a topic or thesis sentence.

3. Divide your subject into a few main points (this step is analysis and division).

4. Organize your material so as to ensure audience adaptation, unity, desirable sequence, and the massing or emphasis of the points.

5. Organize the introduction to ensure orientation of your subject and the interest and attention of your audience.

6. Organize the main body so that you move forward from one aspect of your subject to another.

7. Organize the conclusion so that it reinforces your initial speaking purpose.

SPECIFIC PURPOSE—THE BASIS OF ORGANIZATION

With your subject selected and materials under way, you will need to understand audience motives, attitudes, and sentiments. Are you there primarily to entertain them? Or to add to their knowledge? Or to persuade them to elect a course in computer training? Or to accomplish other communicative purposes?

Whatever your aim, you will frame it for your private guidance as well as for occasional insertion in your talk. Thus: "My purpose is to persuade my audience to support the Red Cross in its current drive for funds." You hope that *circular response* will occur and that they, too, will talk and act in unison with your appeals to them.

METHODS OF DIVIDING THE SUBJECT

Once you have selected your subject, adapted to your hearers, collected and selected your materials, and framed a purpose sentence, you will divide your central subject into two or three main divisions and perhaps into subdivisions. This analysis is the selection of main points to be developed in the body of your speech.

Such analysis and division applies even though your speech may be brief—with a single point. The single idea of a three minute talk may consist almost entirely of a supporting illustration. Nevertheless, you are here to survey the subject in its limited scope. You will thus focus on one phase of the broader division, with the more complete treatment if more time is allowed for your talk.

The application of a number of well-known principles of analysis or division will help you to arrange your ideas satisfactorily.

1. Divide the materials according to a consistent thought pattern and method of classification. Types of approaches fall roughly into several groups, any of which you may adopt as means of sorting your subject into details.

a. The *time-order* approach arranges the materials in chronological sequence.

b. The *space-order* focuses on space relations rather than on chronology. The pattern may be from local to national and international; from front to rear; from bottom to top; or from near to far (or the reverse). For example:

Our general library is arranged at three levels.

(1) The central reading room and special references are on the first floor.

(2) Classified literature and magazines are on the second floor.

(3) Government documents and archives are on the third floor.

c. The *classificational* or *topical* pattern calls for the grouping under economic, literary, scientific, religious, and similar categories.

Subject: The profession of the teaching of speech is to be recommended.

(1) Communication is important in national life.

(2) The salaries are promising.

(3) The subject itself is highly interesting.

d. The *logical* (cause-and-effect) order of division traces the causes and/or results of a given agent, situation, or condition. To illustrate:

Subject: The race riots in the Watts section of Los Angeles in 1965 were a national disturbance.

(1) The alleged causes of the riots lay in slum housing, unemployment, social and political discrimination.

(2) The alleged results were deterioration of interracial forebearance and progress.

(3) The political factors fostered bigotry.

(4) The moral results were deplorable.

e. The *problem and solution* method, akin to the causal pattern, analyzes the disturbing situation and offers remedies. This is the typical debating-discussional procedure. To illustrate:

Subject: The traffic problem in my city must be settled at once.

(1) The congestion, confusion, delays, and mounting traffic violations work against municipal progress.

(2) To help solve the problem, much more parking space must be immediately provided, more one-way streets established, an added police force assigned, and municipal voters' opinions in support of these programs must be further organized.

These and other modes will be illustrated in the section below, "Organization of the body."

2. Divide so that you usually have at least two chief divisions, but not more than three or four. In a short speech, you may say to yourself, and to your hearers, "I have time to develop only one main idea." But you should make clear to your audience that you are selecting a limited part of a more comprehensive subject.

3. Divide so that points of your two or three chief ideas do not obviously overlap.

4. Select those ideas that will be most informative and interesting to your audience.

THE INTRODUCTION, MAIN BODY, AND CONCLUSION

Speeches, as teachers have reminded us, should have at least three well-defined divisions or parts: an introduction, main body, and conclusion. Plato, of the fourth century B.C., stated that a speech should have a beginning, middle, and end. It should be put together like "a living creature." Aristotle, also of the fourth century B.C., stated that ideally a speech should have only two parts: (1) statement of the case and (2) proof of it. Usually, however, as he explained, a speech should contain (1) an introduction, (2) statement of the case, (3) central idea, (4) partition of main points, (5) proof or refutation, and (6) peroration or conclusion. This elaborate division applied to courtroom pleas. Modern rhetoricians have reverted to the simple structure suggested here, with recognition of subdivisions that would somewhat echo this classical Roman approach.[4]

The simple distinction of parts here recommended parallels the steps you as speaker take. First you will introduce yourself and your

[4] Lester Thonssen and A. Craig Baird, *Speech Criticism*, The Ronald Press Company, New York, 1948, chap. 14, "The Structure of Oral Discourse"; A. Craig Baird, *Rhetoric: A Philosophical Inquiry*, The Ronald Press Company, New York, 1965, chap. 9, "Structure"; Donald K. Darnell, "The Relation between Sentence Order and Comprehension," *Speech Monographs*, 30:97–100, June, 1963; Halbert E. Gulley and David Berlo, "Effect of Intercellular and Introcellular Speech Structure on Attitude Change and Learning," *Speech Monographs*, 23:288–298, November, 1956.

ideas to the group; then you will provide an elaboration of your ideas so that they are established and emphasized; finally you will climax the whole with a summary or appeal. The creation of goodwill for the speaker and his thinking is the aim of the introduction. The successive marshaling of the ideas to be implanted is the work of the main body. The final effort to consolidate these impressions makes up the conclusion.

How much further should you go in dividing and subdividing? It is hard to say. Flexibility of structure is the rule; follow common sense. Overelaboration of structure may be as bad as disorganization. A purely mechanical effect may bore or even annoy those trying to look interested. The constant recurrence of "my next point is" and "the six phases of the second inquiry will not be treated in detail" is a good way to deaden your performance.

Organization of the introduction

How long or short should your introduction be? Its length, content, and general effect will depend on your speaking aims, the character of your audience, and the time at your disposal. Your single-point speech should move at once into your topic. In practically every case you hope to (1) establish goodwill between your audience and yourself, (2) give some explanation of what your subject is about, and (3) make clear your theme and purpose.

Enlisting attention and goodwill. Your initial job is to enlist the attention and goodwill of listeners, whether they are a face-to-face group or a radio or television audience. At the start they may be curious about you and your topic, indifferent, prejudiced against your subject, or prejudiced against you because you are a Scotsman, a Methodist, a girl, or a mere youth. Cicero's advice to the young men of Rome was to "render auditors well disposed, attentive, teachable." James Winans, in his *Public Speaking* (Century Company, New York, 1915), H. W. Hollingworth, *The Psychology of the Audience* (American Book Company, New York, 1935), and a long list of other recent writers also stress enlisting attention.

1. *You may begin with a personal reference.* President Dwight Eisenhower did so on February 29, 1956, when he told the nation that he would be a candidate for the presidential nomination in 1956.[5]

[5] A. Craig Baird, *Representative American Speeches, 1955–56,* The H. W. Wilson Company, New York, 1956, p. 102. By permission.

My fellow citizens:

I wanted to come into your homes this evening because I feel the need of talking with you directly about a decision I made today after weeks of the most prayerful and devoutly careful consideration. I made that decision public shortly after ten this morning. Immediately I returned to this office. Upon reaching here I sat down and began to put down on paper thoughts that occurred to me which I felt might be of some interest to you in connection with that decision. This is what I wrote. . . .

I have decided that if the Republican party chooses to renominate me I shall accept that nomination.

2. *You may begin by reference to the importance of the occasion.* Chief Justice Earl Warren in the rotunda of the Capitol at Washington, D.C., on November 24, 1963, opened his address on the assassination of President John F. Kennedy, November 22, as follows: [6]

There are few events in our national life that unite Americans and so touch the heart of all of us as the passing of a President of the United States.

There is nothing that adds shock to our sadness as the assassination of our leader, chosen as he is to embody the ideals of our people, the faith we have in our institutions and our belief in the fatherhood of God and the brotherhood of man.

We are saddened; we are stunned; we are perplexed.

3. *You may begin with a humorous or mock-heroic reference.* Note the opening of Governor Mark Hatfield's address at Philadelphia, May 27, 1964: [7]

A recent theater production carried the title, "Stop the World, I Want to Get Off." From what I read about the national debates on foreign policy, there are quite a number of Americans who wish it were possible.

For them, the title of a TV play of some years ago may provide the proper answer: "You Say Good-by But It Doesn't Go Away."

4. *You may begin by citing a striking fact or giving a condensed narrative.* President Franklin D. Roosevelt on December 8,

[6] *Congressional Record,* 109:21592, Nov. 25, 1963.
[7] *Vital Speeches of the Day,* 30:533, June 15, 1964. By permission.

1941, began his appeal to Congress for a declaration of war against Japan thus: [8]

> *Yesterday, December 7, 1941,—a date which will live in infamy—the United States of America was suddenly and deliberately attacked by the naval and air forces of the Empire of Japan.*

Supplying explanations and background of the subject. Along with this inclusion of material to promote goodwill and interest, the introduction should contain such explanations and facts as may be needed for the unfolding of the subject. Expository speaking, for example, almost invariably begins with an explanation of the terms or processes to be treated in detail. If you intend to talk about a radio transmitter system, or the ballistics of military rifles, or the handling of infantry mortars, you will naturally begin with a preliminary description of a radio transmitter, or a definition of the term *ballistics* or *infantry mortar.*

Especially in argumentative or discussional speaking you will need to explain terms. If you discuss Medicare, you will explain specifically what you mean by that term as related to socialized medicine. Usually speakers supporting such proposals have in mind the extension of social security to provide full medical care for millions of older citizens. Much confusion by the speakers and by the audience will be avoided if the debaters, discussants, and others clarify what the terms are before the speechmaking develops.

Stating the specific purpose. A third function of your introduction is to state your specific purpose. Such a statement usually comes at the end of the introduction. It may, on occasion, comprise the opening sentence. Its purpose is obviously to clarify what is to be said. Its disadvantage is that it may lead to audience boredom or hostility if the opening statement is objectionable.

This central idea or purpose sentence may be briefly stated, such as, "I propose to tell you about a play, *The Snob,* that I attended last night at the university theater." "May I give my version of the best way to avoid a wreck when you have a sudden tire blowout on a throughway?" A more elaborate statement, sometimes stated as a question or series of questions, may comprise the final section of your introduction.

Robert Oliver, on "Education in the year 2000 A.D.," at the Speech

[8] A. Craig Baird, *American Public Addresses: 1740–1952,* McGraw-Hill Book Company, New York, 1956, p. 266. By permission.

Association of the Eastern States, New York City, April 10, 1964, stated: "The question we must ask ourselves is whether we are preparing a new generation of graduate students to meet the problems and use the resources of the new era that is coming, or whether we are nostalgically sharing with them the pleasant reminiscences of our own intellectual past." [9]

The methods of getting under way in your talk are obviously varied. Only a few of the standard ways of treating your introduction are here listed. All depends on the time limits of your talk, your purpose, and the conditions of time and place that affect your mood and methods and especially those of the listeners. Thus you may stress the immediate interest of your topic, its background, the preliminary definitions, your stated purpose, the divisions of your subject, as well as your use of narrative, humorous references, questions, quotations, and so on. But your aim is to let your audience know at once what you are trying to say, and to capture their attention and interest—however you do it. But since all talks are short, or should be, you are advised usually to cut short any extended introduction and to move at once to the main body of your remarks.

Organization of the body

If the introduction has been well designed and if the division of the subject, based upon the specific purpose, has been clearly done, the problem of organizing the main body of the speech is mostly taken care of. Your job is to state clearly the essential ideas or propositions that make up your subject division and to relate those ideas in the best order. First and last you will continue to select and arrange these divisions with an eye to their acceptability to your listeners. Here selection, audience adaptations, order of development, and proposition of ideas are applied in detail as they were in the introduction.

Selection of ideas. You may wonder, in view of the audience and the limited time at your disposal, what two or three main points of your topic you should stress. It may perhaps be wisest to talk mostly about one point and to only illustrate others.

In the body of your talk you will continue to make clear your specific purpose. You will see that the statements or ideas representing your division of the subject are clearly enunciated throughout. You will not make the customary mistake of trying to cover every-

[9] *Vital Speeches of the Day*, 30:399, Apr. 15, 1964. By permission.

thing in three minutes. Furthermore, you will insert enough repetitive, transitional, summarizing, and topic-introductory sentences to make the listener see the relevancy of the materials and the significance of your structure.

Order. Arrange your material and subject ideas in that order most appropriate for securing both logical sequence and audience acceptance. Refer again to your plans of analysis or division. You may use the chronological, topographical, definitional, logical, problem-solution, psychological, or other procedure.

The treatment thus may be that of the historian or biographer. Or the material may be developed according to space relations, from the near to remote (Report of an astronaut space flight); the definitional method (What is jazz? Moonlighting?); classificational or topical [Rhetoric draws on various areas of learning for its method and substance: (1) logic, (2) psychology, (3) language, (4) ethics, (5) literature]; cause-and-effect method [Urbanization of our society is steadily increasing: (1) The demand for industrial jobs is expanding; (2) the mechanized farms and size of the agricultural units are increasing]; the problem-solution method (The number of automobile deaths as a result of drinking drivers is increasing. The more rigid policy of canceling driving licenses is necessary). Any one of these or any combination of methods may be used.

Within such framework the order may be inductive or deductive or a combination of these two logical approaches. If you use concrete objects, details, or cases, and show that they support a wider conclusion, your method is inductive. Of course it is immaterial whether you state the generalization first or last. It is the use of examples, cases, and illustrations to support a general contention, not the time sequence of the argument, which makes the approach inductive.

The alternative method is deductive. You concentrate on a general proposition and then show that this generalization applies to a particular or specific contention. Or you may make a statement about a particular conclusion you want your audience to reach and show that this conclusion is warranted because it is merely a case which is supported by an accepted generalization.

Induction and deduction are obviously different in the relation of the evidence to the point it supports, and not obviously different in their time sequences. For example, if I want to gain acceptance of the proposition "Communists cannot be trusted," I may begin with this statement and proceed to cite cases showing Stalin could not be trusted, Khrushchev could not be trusted, Castro cannot be trusted, etc. Or I may begin with these cases without stating the generalization until I have finished. In either case I am arguing inductively because I use specific cases to support the generalization. Now if I want to gain your acceptance of a specific contention by showing that the declaration belongs to a general class of declarations you accept, I argue deductively. Let us say I want to convince you that "Mao cannot be trusted." I might begin with this statement and argue that it is believable because Mao is a Communist, and "Communists cannot be trusted." Conversely I may begin with the last statement and end up with the conclusion that "Mao cannot be trusted." When we look at induction and deduction in this way, we see that there is no inherent sequence for either form of argument.

Inductive reasoning, as we have said, seeks support for general hypotheses or assumptions. Deduction, though it uses premises as evidence, takes for granted that these, too, are checked and verified by inductive testing.

Shall you proceed from the limited to the more general? It all depends. Often you gain your point by moving from several concrete items to a wider statement of principles until the logical goal is accepted. On the contrary, when you want your audience to accept a belief about a particular case, when your time is limited, and when your audience wishes the most rigid logic, your treatment may well begin with the generalization.

The problem of selecting the order for presentation of topics constantly arises, and their relative importance and appeal must be considered. Should the strongest proposition be placed first, last, or in a medium position? What of the climax and the anticlimax order? Gulley and Berlo in their investigation of speech structure in relation to attitude change concluded: "The best advice the rhetorician can give the speaker is that the climactic order seems slightly preferable. Yet this advice must be qualified inasmuch as one can not 'guarantee' more effective results." [10]

It is impossible to answer this question of most effective order without an understanding of each audience (and the requirements of the same group will vary from meeting to meeting).[11]

[10] Gulley and Berlo, *op. cit.*, pp. 288–297.

[11] See A. Craig Baird, *Argumentation, Discussion and Debate,* McGraw-Hill Book Company, New York, 1950, pp. 227ff., 229; Ray Ehrensberger, "An Experimental Study of the Relative Effectiveness of Certain Forms of Emphasis in Public Speaking," *Speech Monographs,* 12:94–111, 1945; L. W. Doob, "Effects of Initial Serial Position and Attitude upon Recall under Conditions of Low Motivation," *Journal of Abnormal and Social Psychology,* 48:199–205, 1953; Harold Sponberg, "The Relative Effectiveness of Climax and Anti-climax Order in an Argumentative Speech," *Speech Monographs,* 13:35–44, 1946.

On other occasions you may wish to offer your chief idea first. Your approach here may be somewhat like that of the newspaper reporter who attempts to put forth in his opening sentence the gist of his story. Effective speakers like Dr. Harry Emerson Fosdick may offer their strongest idea at the outset. Wherever you place your prominent point, and however much or little time (or space) you give to it, your aim is to linger sufficiently over a major idea to drive it home; you are to present it where it will have maximum reception.

Preparation. Since your function in building your plan is not only to make clear but to impress, you will naturally give proper position and time to the important ideas. This principle is an old one. Your problem of structure, then, is to decide both where you should put your most important idea or ideas and how much of your five-minute speech you should give to them as we have stated above. We cannot decide these things without knowing your subject, your knowledge of it, and the occasion.

Organization of the conclusion

The conclusion, like the beginning, may have a function other than that of adding to the listener's knowledge of the topic. The final sentence, or perhaps paragraph, should probably summarize what is said, especially if your remarks have been rather complicated. If your subject matter is in special need of repetition, a somewhat longer summary may be in order—perhaps a recapitulation in slightly different language. In general, good advice is for any speaker to stop when he is done.

The function of the conclusion, however, is often more than that of making clear what has been said. You must also impress your audience and inspire them to action. Your conclusion may end with a challenge, an applicable quotation, a summary, a prophecy, an appeal, a series of questions, or other material and techniques to enforce your purpose. Examples of some of these types of conclusions follow.

1 ***Summary.*** Note how Charles W. Eliot concluded his address on "Five American Contributions to Civilization": [12]

> *These five contributions to civilization—peace keeping, religious toleration, the development of manhood suffrage, the welcoming of*

[12] Charles W. Eliot, *American Contributions to Civilization,* The Century Company, New York, 1897.

> *newcomers, and the diffusion of well being—I hold to have been eminently characteristic of our country, and so important, that, in spite of the qualifications and deductions which every candid citizen would admit with regard to every one of them, they will ever be held in the grateful remembrance of mankind. They are reasonable grounds for a steady glowing patriotism. They have much to do, both with causes and as effects, with the material prosperity of the United States; but they are all five essentially moral contributions, being triumphs of reason, enterprise, courage, faith and justice, over passion, selfishness, inertness, timidity, and distrust. Beneath each one of these developments there lies a strong ethical sentiment, a strenuous moral and social purpose. It is for such work that multitudinous democracies are fit.*

2 ***Prophecy.*** Winston Churchill concluded his address before the American Congress, December 22, 1941, as follows: [13]

> *It is not given to us to peer into the mysteries of the future. Still I avow my hope and faith, sure and inviolate, that in the days to come the British and American people will, for their own safety and for the good of all, walk together in majesty, in justice, and in peace.*

3 ***Personal appeal.*** Woodrow Wilson concluded his first inaugural address, March 4, 1913, by a personal appeal for support of his national program: [14]

> *This is not a day of triumph; it is a day of dedication. Here muster, not the forces of party, but the forces of humanity. Men's hearts wait upon us; men's lives hang in the balance; men's hopes call upon us to say what we will do. Who shall live up to the great trust? Who dares fail to try? I summon all honest men, all patriotic, all forward-looking men, to my side. God helping me, I will not fail them, if they will but counsel and sustain me!*

4 ***Quotation.*** Judge Learned Hand concluded his address on "A Fanfare for Prometheus" at a dinner of the American Jewish Committee, New York City, January 29, 1955, as follows: [15]

[13] A. Craig Baird, *Representative American Speeches: 1941–42*, The H. W. Wilson Company, New York, 1942, p. 29. By permission.

[14] A. Craig Baird, *American Public Addresses: 1740–1952*, McGraw-Hill Book Company, New York, 1956, p. 224. By permission.

[15] A. Craig Baird, *Representative American Speeches: 1955–56*, The H. W. Wilson Company, New York, 1956, p. 45. By permission.

Borrowing from Epictetus, let us say to ourselves, "Since we are men, we will play the part of a Man"; and how better can I end than by recalling to you the concluding passage of Prometheus Unbound:

To suffer woes which Hope thinks infinite;
To forgive wrongs darker than death or night;
To defy Power, which seems omnipotent;
To love, and bear; to hope till Hope creates
From its own wreck the thing it contemplates;
Neither to change, nor falter, nor repent;
This, like thy glory, Titan, is to be
Good, great and joyous, beautiful and free;
This is alone Life, Joy, Empire, and Victory.

THE OUTLINE

The purpose of an outline is to enable you to survey your case as a unit, to note digressions, to size up the major and minor divisions of your analysis, to evaluate the order of your topics, to gauge more carefully the length of your speech, to take a second look at your definitions, and to inspect your illustrations and other facts which should be inserted in your outline. This blueprint will aid you in assimilating more easily the talk itself. In short, the outline, if properly used, should make you a better speaker.

Principles and rules for outlining

For your convenience in constructing the outline, we suggest that you apply standard principles and rules. The suggestions given below will be modified or interpreted to suit your own needs. The instructor sometimes has decided views about methods of outlining; his advice concerning these mechanics will be important. Most of these rules are those which speakers have consistently followed. They are based upon the experience of many speechmakers.

1. *Prefix to the outline a clear statement of your subject.* Use as few general terms as possible. Knock out the ambiguous words. Be sure that the statement represents a careful limiting of the general field you have chosen for your talk. Be sure that your subject statement (topic sentence) reveals clearly and concisely the content and direction of your discourse.

2. *Generally organize your outline into introduction, discussion, and conclusion.*

3. *Use complete sentences throughout.*

4. *See to it that your statements of main ideas say exactly what you mean.* Be sure that they are the main ideas, that they do not overlap, and that they are arranged in the sequence which facilitates their understanding or support for your purpose.

5. *Use suitable symbols and indentations.* The customary system of numbering, lettering, and indenting is as follows:

I. ______________________________

  A. ____________________________

    1. __________________________

      a. ________________________

        (1) ______________________

          (a) ____________________

6. *Where logic is an issue give each division at least two heads.* Where one subpoint is adequate for support or illustration, a single subdivision may suffice. Have few main headings in your outline. Otherwise your division may represent no division at all. Keep the wording short.

7. *See that each subtopic is logically subordinate to the topic under which it is placed.* See that the entire framework, both in its larger elements and in its minor statements, is a logical unit. If you have placed ideas together with care, each subhead will support a more general proposition.

8. *Include in your introduction those steps necessary to secure a proper unfolding of your subject.* Usually include some of the following: (*a*) reason for the speech or other data that identify you and your topic with the audience and the occasion, (*b*) explanation of terms, (*c*) the purpose sentence (often in the form of a question), and (*d*) a statement of the topics you propose to develop.

9. *In your conclusion include a summary or any other material necessary to reinforce or apply the ideas previously developed.*

10. *On the margin or in the body of the outline, insert at the appropriate point the exact source of any material quoted or cited from printed sources.*

11. *Include the concrete materials composing your speech, but in the outline avoid undue personal comment (make an outline, not an essay).*

Types of outlines

Speech outlines are here suggested with some differences in outlining indicated, determined by whether the speech is to inform, entertain, or persuade.

Outline for an informational speech. Outlines for the short informative, or expositional speech, are comparatively simple. The subtopics provide further details about the main topics rather than, as in the case of the typical argumentative outline, give reasons for the support of propositions. For example of the outline for an informational speech, see Chapter 13.

Outline for an argumentative or persuasive speech. The outline for an argumentative speech is more elaborate. Although much exposition is included, the framework of the outline consists of a series of reasons. *For* or an equivalent word is used in such an outline to link main and sub-ideas to demonstrate the reasoning process. Thus:

- I. Wider support of educational television is needed, *for*
  - A. The claim that the educational needs should be handled exclusively by commercial stations is not justified, *for*
    - 1. Few commercial stations can afford to devote much of their daytime service and best evening hours to nonprofit educational shows, *for*
      - a. (Further subtopics)

A full outline of this argumentative type is a *brief*.[16]

Outline for a panel discussion. The discussion outline varies somewhat from the expositional or argumentative form. Its pattern usually includes (1) cause for discussion, (2) definitions, (3) goals to be considered in any solution of the problem, (4) a diagnosis or analysis of the problem corresponding to the step, in the argumentative brief, that examines the need or necessity for the proposed change, (5) examination of representative solutions, and (6) arguments to support the solution that is chosen by the group.

This individual outline, converted from a series of declarative statements to one made up of impartial questions, then becomes a *group outline* for use by the members of the panel, who set out to answer these questions.[17]

Outline and the speaker's notes

Once you have assembled a satisfactory outline, you question what is to be done with it. Should you carry it with you to your feet

[16] For example of an argumentative outline, see Chap. 15, "Persuasive Speaking, Logical Techniques."

[17] For example of a discussional outline, see Chap. 14, "Discussional Speaking."

and speak directly from it? Certainly not; it will cramp your speaking style. Should you memorize it as it stands? This would probably not be too helpful. Should you write a full speech from it and recite the results verbatim? You may write out the speech, but you will not have time to memorize it nor should you do so. The more practicable procedure is to draft a few *speaker's notes* from your material—catch phrases that will guide you in the speech itself, if you feel you must have such support. These notes are for you alone. Your aim in such preparation is to develop skill as an extempore speaker. You will make both an outline and speaker's notes; the latter you will regard as much more abbreviated, informal, and private than the former. And you may easily disregard any such "props" in your short speech.

PROJECTS AND PROBLEMS

Project 1 To identify and word main ideas in a speech you are assigned

Read one of the speeches in the Appendix of this text which has been assigned by the instructor. Select and word the speaker's main ideas. Bring these to class in written form and compare your analysis with the analyses of other members of the class.

Project 2 To apply the principles of dividing a subject

Purposes of this assignment: To prepare and present a speech in which the main divisions of the topic will be according to a time sequence.
Procedure: Each will prepare and present a five-minute speech in which the two or three main headings are in chronological order.
Subjects for this speech (to be limited further):

1. The development of communism in Russia
2. The civil rights struggle for the Negro
3. The development of professional football in America
4. Production of a printed book
5. The process of a bill through the state legislature (or through Congress)
6. The Telstar operation
7. Early Bird
8. The early life and speech education of John F. Kennedy (or any other important speaker)
9. The United Nations during the past year

10. America's latest space flight
11. The Soviet Union's latest space flight

Project 3 To apply the principles of dividing a subject by classification

Purposes of this assignment: To prepare and present a speech in which the main divisions will be classificational or topical.
Procedure: Each will prepare and present a five-minute speech in which the two or three main headings will be classificational.
Subjects for this speech (to be limited further):

1. The qualifications of a good speaker
2. The qualifications of a good listener
3. Factors in highway safety
4. Production of a play
5. The advantages of living in New England (or any other section of the United States)
6. Characteristics of a satisfactory television talk
7. Labor-management relations
8. The Alliance for Progress

Project 4 To apply the principles of dividing a subject by logical order

Purpose of this assignment: To prepare and present a speech in which the main divisions will be those of cause and effect (logical order).
Procedure: Each will prepare and present a five-minute speech in which the two or three main headings are in logical order.
Subjects for this speech (to be limited further):

1. The economic threat from a European Common Market
2. Smoking and lung cancer
3. National scholarships for students in colleges and universities
4. Our antiquated county government system
5. Railroad economic woes and proposed consolidations
6. Jet plane landing strips
7. Channels for commercial and military flight in the United States
8. Educational television
9. Prohibition of nuclear explosions in space
10. Automation and employment

11. Racial equality and desegregation in housing
12. Black power
13. Black Africa and the threat to whites there
14. The ecumenical movement
15. Birth control
16. American foreign aid without military elements

Project 5 To study and apply methods of systematic outlining

Purposes of this assignment: To review the methods of systematic outlining and apply them to the outlining of a speech.
Procedure: Outline, in accordance with the rules suggested in this chapter, a representative speech as printed in a recent issue of *Vital Speeches of the Day*, or in the most recent edition of *Representative American Speeches*,[18] or reprinted in a recent newspaper or pamphlet.

Project 6 To study and apply methods of systematic outlining

Purpose of this assignment: To apply to your own speeches systematic methods of outlining.
Procedure: Prepare and deliver a short speech based upon one of the topics and methods of dividing the subject as suggested in projects 1, 2, and 3 above. Accompany your talk with a full-sentence outline, to be handed to the instructor before the delivery of the speech. At the following class period the outlines will be returned to the students, with comments on methods of outlining. At the discretion of the instructor all subsequent classroom speeches will be accompanied by satisfactory outlines.

For the instructor: Assign the questions under "Organization and Outlining" in the *Teacher's Manual*.

Project 7 To study organization in cognate fields

Organization is a popular word in many fields of learning today. A team of class members may be assigned the last seven books in the reference list which contain articles or chapters on organization of ideas, language, human behavior, business enterprises, social participation, and programmed learning. Report back to the class as a briefing team on concepts of organization in the study of other topics which might be useful for better organization in speaking.

[18] Published annually by the H. W. Wilson Company, New York.

REFERENCES

Bruner, Jerome S., Jacqueline J. Goodnow, and George A. Austen: *A Study in Thinking*, John Wiley & Sons, Inc., New York, 1966.

Deese, James: *The Structure of Associations in Language and Thought*, The Johns Hopkins Press, Baltimore, 1965.

Etzione, Amitar: *Complex Organizations*, Holt, Rinehart and Winston, Inc., New York, 1961.

Hebb, D. O.: *Organization of Behavior*, John Wiley & Sons, Inc., New York, 1949.

Johnson, Falk: *How to Organize What You Write*, Houghton Mifflin Company, Boston, 1964.

Letterer, Joseph A.: *Organizations: Structure and Behavior*, John Wiley & Sons, Inc., New York, 1964.

Mills, Glen E.: *Message Preparation*, The Bobbs-Merrill Company, Inc., Indianapolis, 1966.

Sebeok, Thomas A.: *Style in Language*, The M.I.T. Press, Cambridge, Mass., 1960.

8
FACTS, THOUGHT, AND DETAILS OF DEVELOPMENT

FUNCTION OF THOUGHT IN SPEECH

Speech is primarily concerned with ideas. Ideas are the sphere of the cognitive system. Although ideas are or should be the central core of all talks or series of talks, we do not dismiss the affective or emotional-imaginative qualities that should always be present in informative-persuasive oral exchange. We do assume that thought is the key to all worthwhile communication. As Norwood Brigance, a contemporary authority on speech, stated: "Reason's basic use, then [in speech], is to show men how to fulfill their needs and how to solve thought problems." [1]

The individual, we agree, is a "bundle of emotions" and the purists' concept of "man as a thinker" is misleading. Reaction is the product of complicated cognitive, affective, and motor activity. We describe some tendencies as primarily intellectual and logical and others as largely emotional. The assumption of most contemporary authorities of speech, nevertheless, assumes that speech involves a logical movement; that this method tends to minimize haphazard

[1] William Norwood Brigance, *Speech: Its Techniques and Disciplines in a Free Society,* Appleton-Century-Crofts, New York, 1952, p. 147.

trial-and-error and the disorganized types of some emotional activity of communicators; and that cognitive perceptions, under the speaker's control and guided by his skill, lead to dependable conclusions and to desirable audience behavior.

Representative processes of thought, then, are involved in every speech. What are these processes? They have to do with (1) initial and basic reactions to external and internal stimuli, (2) the inferences that lead to a pattern of ideas and relevant conclusions, (3) the crystallization of these sensory experiences and inferences in communicative language.

FACTS IN COMMUNICATION

The basis of all good communication lies in the experience of the communicator with events, situations, "felt difficulties," and the appropriation of facts. First is the event itself—the source of stimulation—external to the sensory organs of the speakers or writers. We speak of this initial source or sources as the *thing itself* or the *referent*. This referent philosophically and practically cannot be verified, but we assume it.[2]

This external stimulation continues within the organism. "Once a sensory receptor has been stimulated, nerve currents travel quickly along the spinal cord and normally up through the base of the brain to the higher reaches of the cortex, out again along efferent tracts to muscles and glands."[3] These contractions and secretions, further sensory stimulation reverberating to the cord and brain, effect further changes. This sensory reaction thus may come from immediate contact with the "thing itself" (the so-called "external object") or from earlier experiences that through recall are again vivified and made active.[4]

What are these *facts* that are the recordings directly or indirectly of stimuli, internal or external? They are the concrete or abstract materials out of which we try to interpret relationships or from which we try to draw conclusions. "They have to do with the existence of things, the occurrence of events, and the character of phenomena."[5] They are the laboratory material assembled for ex-

[2] Harold A. Larrabee, *Reliable Knowledge* (rev. ed.), Houghton Mifflin Company, Boston, 1964, chap. 4.

[3] Wendell Johnson, "The Spoken Word and the Great Unsaid," *Quarterly Journal of Speech*, 37:419–429, December, 1951.

[4] A. Craig Baird, *Rhetoric: A Philosophical Inquiry*, The Ronald Press Company, New York, 1965, p. 147.

[5] John Dewey, *How We Think*, D. C. Heath and Company, Boston, 1933, pp. 71–78, 91–101.

perimental hypotheses. For the historians they are the record of careers and of local and national movements to be verified by every research means. So educators, psychologists, political scientists, microbiologists, and all others try to relate their thinking and utterances to facts. To the semanticist a fact is that which deals with the thought-word-thing relationship. The referent (*Ding an sich*), however we describe or assume it, is the source of stimulation. Through sensory reactions—including sound, sight, and temperature—we become aware of the original thing represented by the sign or symbol. According to Susanne Langer in her *Philosophy in a New Key*, the fact is "that which we conceive to be the source and context of the signs to which we react successfully." [6]

Our symbols are the representative kinds of facts that speakers and writers and all investigators use in the development of their discourses. The uses may be informational, argumentative, discussional, persuasive, descriptive, narrative, or some combination of such purposes that clarify, vivify, or otherwise influence the receiver of the message.

Perception

Since we are concerned with ideas and facts in speech, it will be well to take a brief look at what we learn about man's thinking in the communication process from studies in perception. The meanings others derive from our communicative thinking are subject to a number of hurdles. The first of these hurdles is man's tendency to filter out or misinterpret what he does not want to hear or what is contrary to his best judgment. Secondly, speakers and listeners trying to interpret a stimulus will add those features to the stimulation necessary for it to make sense in their thinking. The thoughtful communicator, in the third place, will avoid that signal response tendency which causes him to bypass important parts of his mediational thought about and judgment of his ideas. We must always exercise our utmost care to select those response patterns which are the most fair and realistic we can make. Finally the meanings we give to and get from a communication often depend upon the way we organize it. Perceptual responses will be different for different people. A communicator and the communicatee alike have a responsibility to know of the possibilities of distortion and misinterpretation of thought through the perceptual mechanisms and to take every possible precaution to avoid them.

[6] Susanne Langer, *Philosophy in a New Key*, Mentor Books, New American Library of World Literature, Inc., New York, 1948–1962, p. 225.

Development by particulars and instances

Instances or examples are probably the most frequently used form of development. Thomas J. Watson, Jr., chairman of the International Business Machine Corporation, discussing "Self Protection-Individualism," at Lafayette College, Easton, Pennsylvania, June 5, 1964, stated that the great men of history each had to choose between the safe protection of the crowd or the risk of standing up and being counted. Said Watson: [7]

> *You can find no truly great men who took the easy way.*
>
> *For their courage some suffered abuse, imprisonment, or even death. Others lived to win the acclaim of their fellow men. But all achieved greatness.*
>
> *Through history, examples are abundant:*
>
> *—Columbus*
>
> *—Charles Darwin*
>
> *—Galileo, who confirmed the theory that the earth traveled about the sun, and who for his affirmation became a prisoner to the inquisition.*
>
> *—Socrates, who told his judges at his trial: "Men of Athens, I honor and love you; but I shall never cease from the practice and teaching of philosophy."*
>
> *If we turn to our own times, we can all of us recall other men of other lands who refused to take the easy way out, who stood up against the current for what they believed right and just. Nehru in India, de Gaulle in France, Churchill in England.*
>
> *And in our own country, it wasn't easy in 1956 when the British, French and Israeli forces invaded Egypt—in the midst of an American presidential election—for the President of the United States, Dwight D. Eisenhower, to condemn the use of force and to call upon the aggressors to get out. But he did it—and the electorate overwhelmingly upheld his courage.*
>
> *And it wasn't easy for another American President of a different political party—John F. Kennedy—to take an unequivocal stand on civil rights, when that stand might have cost him the votes of the South, which in the 1960 election gave him his tiny margin of victory. But he did it and thereby added a post publication chapter to* Profiles in Courage.
>
> *All these men, despite their great variety, had something in common. Every single one of them put principle first, safety second; individuality first, adjustment second; courage first, cost second.*

[7] *Vital Speeches of the Day,* 30:599, July 15, 1964.

Such cases are actual and are to be presented accurately. Hypothetical or imaginative instances may also be presented. But no matter how imaginary the cases, such as *Gulliver's Travels* or the *Hans Christian Andersen Tales,* the details nevertheless originate in actual sensory experiences that later through recall are given either with approximate representation of the initial stimulus or with perceptive coloring.

Similar instances are the details that comprise a section of some object or situation under examination. These details are the parts that together make up the whole. A technical description is an obvious case in point. You describe a camera, television set, or spectroscope in general terms; then you follow with particulars—a detailed description of the portions, sections, or parts, such as shape, size, materials, finish, and connections. Since your enumeration is never complete, these details or particulars serve to suggest or represent the whole.

Robert S. McNamara, the Secretary of Defense, before the National Security Industrial Association in Washington, D.C., March 26, 1964, gave details of war-torn Vietnam.[8]

> *My purpose this evening is three-fold. After recalling some facts about Vietnam and its history, I want: first, to explain our stake and objectives in South Vietnam, second, to review for you the current situation there as General Taylor and I found it on our recent trip, and finally, to outline in broad terms the plans which have been worked out with General Khanh for achieving our mutual objectives in South Vietnam.*
>
> *Let me begin by reminding you of some details about South Vietnam—that narrow strip of rich coastal mountain and delta lands running 900 miles in the tropics along the South China Sea to the Gulf of Siam.*
>
> *It contains the mouth of the Mekong River, the main artery of Southeast Asia. It has a population of about 14 million—almost that of California—in an area slightly larger than England and Wales.*
>
> *South Vietnam does not exist by itself. Mainland Southeast Asia includes Laos, Cambodia and the two Vietnams, together comprising former French Indochina. It also includes Thailand, Burma and part of Malaysia.*

Anecdote, even though not significant as logic, has distinct value in injecting life and movement in your talk. You may make such detail personal or biographical. A brief story, although often in-

[8] *Vital Speeches of the Day,* 30:394, Apr. 15, 1964.

corporated in a dinner speech, is pertinent for almost any kind of give-and-take speaking and for almost any occasion.

LeRoy Collins, then president of the National Association of Broadcasters, at Los Angeles, December 8, 1963, began as follows:[9]

> *When I received the Center's invitation, I asked my good friend Harry Ashmore about the role in which I was being cast. He assured me that I would not be expected—because I am from the South—to come on with a rebel yell and wind up with an impassioned defense of states' rights.*
>
> *The truth is, the South has never enjoyed any monopoly in championing the sovereignty of states. Bruce Catton tells this mordant anecdote to illustrate the point:*
>
> *General Thomas, the phlegmatic Union commander, rode to the rescue of the Yankee troops at Chicamauga, and finally carried the day after some of the heaviest casualties of the war. After the battle, he went out, according to custom, with his quartermaster to pick the burying ground for the Yankee dead.*
>
> *"Shall we do it the way we always do, General?" the quartermaster inquired. "Put the Illinois men together over there, and the Iowa men next, and the New York men over yonder . . . ?"*
>
> *"No," the General replied. "Mix 'em all up. I'm getting pretty damned sick of states' rights."*

The use of figures and statistics

In developing a topic, either for information or for more argumentative purposes, figures to illustrate or establish a point of view are often most effective. President Lyndon B. Johnson, addressing the Iowans at Des Moines on June 30, 1966, discussed the subject of agricultural prices to show that the Washington, D.C., policy had been to support farm prices—while at the same time attempting to control inflation here as in the rest of the economy. Stated he: "It is the story of a successful farm policy unparalleled in the world." He then cited many figures.[10]

> *The record shows that net farm income rose from $11.7 billion in 1960 to $14.1 billion in 1965, and is headed for over $15 billion this year; that the income of the average farm rose more than $1200 between 1960 and 1965; that net income on individual farms right here in Iowa climbed 47 percent between 1960 and 1965; that farm exports were up from $4.8 billion in 1960 to $6.2 billion last year.*

[9] *Vital Speeches of the Day*, 30:369, Apr. 1, 1964.
[10] *Des Moines Register*, July 1, 1966, p. 4.

There are people who want you to forget that cattle are bringing $1.30 more a hundred-weight than they were six years ago, that hogs are up $6.90 per hundred-weight, that corn is up 12 cents per bushel, grain sorghum 25 cents a hundred-weight, soybeans 90 cents a bushel, and milk 56 cents a hundred-weight.

Is this administration oblivious to the farmers' needs? FHA farm loans in 1965 totaled $798 million. In 1960 they were $309 million. REA loans totaled $477 million. In 1960 they were $325 million. Crop insurance totaled $593 million. In 1960 it was $266 million. Last year 635 watersheds were approved. In 1960 there were 264 approved. Government payments to farmers in 1965 reached two and a half billion dollars, more than three times the total in 1960.

I do not see the future of agriculture as a great battlefield—where warring armies of farmers stand ranged against consumers. With the farm legislation we have won through Congress during the past four years, I believe we have the tools to make good on the promise we made to ourselves at the beginning of this decade: plentiful food at fair prices for the consumer and full parity of income for the American farmer in the 1960's.

Statistics are figures so grouped as to bring out their comparative significance. They are arrangements of facts systematically collected and classified so that one group may be compared with another and an inference or interpretation made. In your talk, quote the source of your statistics. What were President Johnson's sources? Inquire whether the sampling was systematic. When you refer to an average student or an average college, be sure you know the basis for that classification. Is the college classed as average on the basis of its enrollment, the sex of its students, its endowment, its athletic teams, its age? Is the student based on freshmen only, or seniors, or even on a limited number of athletes and scholars?

To give vividness to your statistics, translate or interpret them for audience understanding and interest. Use approximate figures where they are appropriate. Where they are interestingly explained and applied, figures are a valuable aid in developing ideas, especially argumentative propositions.[11]

Development by definition and explanation

Definition or explanation of the symbols (words) is the necessary means of clarifying the concept or reactive process as it passes

[11] Ernest C. Bormann, *Theory and Research in the Communicative Arts,* Holt, Rinehart and Winston, Inc., New York, 1965, chap. 13.

through the spectrum of the person's experiences from the preverbal activities and is transformed into words or equivalent symbols. The speaker here delves into his latent or active vocabulary and attempts to reduce the mental flow to the actual language directed to a specific audience.[12]

Stokely Carmichael, at that time national chairman of the Student Nonviolent Coordinating Committee, advocated that Negroes support *black power*. He was asked, "What is your definition of the concept?" His answer was:

> *Black power seems to me a number of things. Number one, that black people in this country are oppressed for one reason—and that's because of their color, and that's what this country has to face. Their rally cry must be the issue around which they are oppressed, as it was for unions. The workers came together. They were oppressed because they were workers. And we must come together around the issue that oppresses us—which is our blackness. Unions—they needed power to stop their oppression. We need power to stop ours. So it's black power. And black power just means black people coming together and getting people to represent their needs and to stop that oppression.*

Barry Schweid, in an Associated Press report from Washington ("The World Today," July 7, 1966) commented:

> *Black power. It defies definition. But its impact on the civil rights movement and on American society promises to be profound.*

Unlimited confusion results when basic terms are unexplained. In the presidential campaign of 1964, for example, Senator Barry Goldwater in his acceptance speech at San Francisco, July 15, stated, echoing the party platform, "I would remind you that extremism in the defense of liberty is no vice. And let me remind you also that moderation in the pursuit of justice is no virtue." Many critics, including Governor Rockefeller of New York, denounced this definition of extremism. It was variously explained as radicalism, the utmost end or border, having the greatest degree, immoderation, a condition or state of danger, distress; a state of greatest need or peril. Its legal, political, moral, and constitutional aspects and interpretations were variously interpreted and certainly needed clear explanation. Entire debates, editorials, and speeches during that summer were based on the confused meanings of *extremism*.

[12] Baird, *op. cit.*, p. 44.

The orderly process of definition consists of two steps: first, establishing the class to which an idea belongs, and second, indicating the difference between the given idea and others of a similar class. Definitions must be inclusive as well as exclusive. A good definition not only tells us what something is; it also tells us what it is not. Some recent examples of definitions which are ambiguous in this respect are "Communication is culture," "Communication is a discriminative response to a stimulus." You may define *oligarchy* as a form of political society and set it off from *monarchy* or *democracy*. You may define literature as the kind of writings, prose or poetry, that is distinguished by imaginative-emotional character. These associational or even dictionary distinctions are often insufficient. *Extremism, democracy, communism,* or any other often-used word will need to be described as it is used in the given context.

To minimize confusion in a given usage and to help with the further clarifications by the audience, you will apply specific methods of definition, such as (1) an enumeration of the details that compose a term, (2) a description of the operation of your term if it is an object, agency, or institution, (3) an explanation of its purpose, (4) a placing of the term in a continuum, (5) a review of its origin and history including the etymology of the word or words, (6) a comparison and contrast between it and other closely related concepts, (7) a review of the steps in an operation.

Another feature of a good definition is that it focuses our attention on the important features of the word or concept defined. Many concepts such as *communication* have been defined in many ways. The definer of a term from a certain point of view will identify the features of the term he deems important. These may be far from the important features of the concept from the point of view of others. You as the user of a word will know what meaning is important to your understanding. See to it that your definition focuses attention on that meaning.

REPRESENTATIVE MODES OF INFERENCE

Inference is the ability to observe the connection between personal experiences, data, facts, and related phenomena, and the process of describing and evaluating such relationships. Focusing on the broader relationships of these instances, particulars, testimony of witnesses, and incidents is the inferential activity of all who sooner or later have the urge and necessity to communicate.

This movement from fact to fact and from fact or event to wider associations is often explained psychologically and logically as the experience of the human being attempting to adjust to his environment or to maintain equilibrium in a world of constant change. The impelling nature may be curiosity, fear, or other primary reaction. John Dewey has described this process as *thinking*. The reflection is thus grounded in perplexity and conflict. With no perplexities, Dewey would say, man is thoughtless. "Men do not in their natural state think when they have no troubles to deal with, no difficulties to overcome." [13]

This kind of thinking has led in modern psychology to *consonance* and *cognitive dissonance* learning and attitude change theories. Just as change brought about by personal problem solving has its beginning in a state of doubt, uneasiness, and conflict to be resolved, the communication intended to produce change must give attention to that dissonance in the listener's thinking which is perhaps necessary to get him to give any attention to your argument.

The mental grappling with the problem and the more systematic examination of the way out is the design of thinking and the inferential procedure. The thinker's internal and external drives and the motivative activity thus quickened produce a chain reaction of reflective materials. The more specific reaction to phenomena is supplemented by an attempt to decipher the relatively unknown. This movement from the known to the unknown, the leap in the dark, is inference.

What are these representative modes of inference? They are reasoning or inferring from (1) specific instances and details leading to generalizations, (2) analogies, (3) causal relations, (4) authorities, (5) general propositions (deduction).

Inference from specific instances and details

Reasoning from specific instances (labeled variously as inferences from generalization, induction, example) relates the specific cases to a general field in which they occur. You thus speculate or guess about the broader area. (See the illustration above of Thomas J. Watson and his examples of "truly great men" and their common elements of courage.) But your guess, if a properly reflective one, should be reasonably successful.

How do you check these generalizations from details and instances? (1) Are the examples sufficient in number to warrant the conclusion? (2) Are the general statements so framed as not to claim too much? (3) Are the cases typical or representative of the

[13] John Dewey, Edward C. Lindeman (ed.), in *Reconstruction in Philosophy*, Mentor Books, New American Library of World Literature, Inc., New York, p. 13.

field? (4) Are contrary cases noted? (5) Are the cases you use well-authenticated and reliable? (6) Does common sense confirm your general statements?

Inference by analogy

Analogy (comparison and contrast) is a form of inference by likenesses and differences. We match one situation, person, or event about which we know a good deal with another about which we would like to know more, in order to throw light on the less well known. The method proceeds from the known to the unknown, from the well-known to the strange, from the like to the unlike.

The comparison may be direct and literal: "Baseball is a great game in this country. Why should it also not become a national sport of Great Britain?" "The two national candidates of the major parties for the Presidency of the United States debated each other in the campaign of 1960. Why should not the candidates for the Presidency in 1964, Johnson and Goldwater, also have debated?"

Often the similarities are comparatively remote: We may compare a forceful public speaker and a dive bomber (in their devastating results); a huge air armada and a dike (each protects the country). Churchill used comparison subtly in his address of September 11, 1940, suggesting that Germany might invade England: "The next week or so will be a very important period in our history. It ranks with the days when the Spanish Armada was approaching the Channel."

Comparisons and analogies will make your expositions much clearer and more interesting. When properly interpreted and backed by other types of argument, they serve the same purpose as proof. In using comparisons, ask yourself: (1) Is the comparison clearly and interestingly stated? (2) Is the comparison logical? That is, do listeners accept it as plausible and pertinent? (3) Are the facts which you state or imply in your comparisons true? (4) Is your comparison trite and therefore boring ("ship of state," for example)?

Contrast is merely comparison in reverse; opposites are contrasted to point up their differences. Any object or quality becomes more vivid and dramatic when seen in juxtaposition with others: white and red, democracy and dictatorship, free enterprise and socialism, Mississippi and Minnesota. Use contrasts that are genuine and logical as well as vivid. Be sure that the two things discussed belong to the same class.

Brooks Atkinson, in a series of articles on "Polluted America" contrasted the early Hudson with the polluted river of today.

In the spring of 1965, I rode up the river from New York City to Glens Falls and back again in a helicopter with a director of the New York State Regional Development Office. From a helicopter, the configuration of the Hudson is a natural masterpiece—broad bays of open water shining in the sun, the dramatic stone wall of the Palisades, the narrow trench of the Highlands, the noble mound of Storm King across the river from the steep pitch of Breakneck ridge, green hills, smooth croplands, charming islands.

No wonder Henry Hudson admired it. When he was there, the bays contained whales and bred shellfish, and the river was full of sturgeon. Sturgeon still abounded in the Nineteenth Century and were known as "Albany beef" because of their food value.

A helicopter journey today, however, discloses the negative aspects of this glorious waterway. It is a sewer and a dump. One sees oily scum, garbage dumps, sewage outlets that stain the water along the shore, ragged plumes of smoke from industrial plants, white and yellow waste fluids pouring out of factories and spilling into the river, decaying piers, capsized barges, abandoned buildings without roofs or windows. Given time, the Hudson will be a wasteland.[14]

Inference by causation

Explaining the factors that produce a given situation or condition is a logical procedure. You may develop your talk by lining up the causes and results of a given situation or proposal. You thus ask, "Why has this situation occurred?" "What have been the results or outcomes, or what will probably be the results?" Such reasoning may be illustrated from your own experience and from that of other speakers.

In 1966, and later, conservative Americans were concerned by the apparently rampant instability of the business cycle. One argument ran: "Unless we resist, more than we have, the increase in prices and wages and easy credits [cause], we are in for headlong inflation and another 1929 crash [results]."

Senator J. W. Fulbright argued before the Senate on March 25, 1964, that agreements with the Soviet government concerning trade, nuclear controls [cause] and other issues would result in the "alleviations of the extreme tensions and animosities that threaten the world with nuclear devastation [results]." [15]

[14] *Des Moines Register,* July 1, 1966, Reprinted by permission from the 1966 *World Book Year Book.* Copyright 1966 by Field Enterprises Educational Corporation.

[15] *Vital Speeches of the Day,* 30:390, Apr. 15, 1964.

The American automobile tire, according to the critics, has been unsafe at any speed. What are the causes? According to Walter Rugaber, of the *New York Times* News Service, the policies of the rubber and automobile industries have minimized proper control over tire safety.

> *(1) Prior to this year's models, it was difficult for a motorist to find out how much weight he could carry in his car without overloading it and placing a dangerous strain on the tires. (2) Before a hasty change in the load figures, a number of American autos—especially station wagons—were overloaded even when standing empty. (3) Detroit's interest in a soft, quiet ride has produced a tire that critics insist lacks the traction and maneuverability crucial in emergencies. (4) Poor materials and lax quality controls in the construction of certain cheaper tires, some selling for less than $8, mean poor wear and dangerous failures. (5) The presence of at least 250,000 retail dealers and about 950 different tire names often makes the task of choosing a new tire hopelessly confusing.*[16]

Ask yourself these questions as you use the cause-and-effect method:

> **1.** Have I described clearly and accurately each event which I have attempted to arrange in a causal sequence?
>
> **2.** Is my assumption justified that a cause-and-effect relationship exists in this case?
>
> **3.** Have I overestimated the influence of a given cause over a given effect? [17]

Inference by testimony or authority

Audiences often silently refuse to accept our word but react favorably if we quote an authority or cite a source for our facts. We want to know the "truth," and the best evidence of the truth is confirmation by other scholars of ability and repute. Although quotations are sometimes used for their happily effective style, or the prestige they might reflect upon a speaker who seeks their reflected glory, the major use of this device is strengthening of the credibility of argument. If some speaker asserts that the national income in 1958 was 300 billion dollars, you as a critic should check the validity

[16] *Des Moines Register*, July 5, 1966.

[17] For further discussion of cause-and-effect sequences, see Chap. 13, "Informative Speaking," and Chap. 15, "Persuasive Speaking, Logical Techniques."

of this statement by reference to the *Statistical Abstract of the United States* for that year.

G. Allan Yeomans, speaking before the Virginia Speech Association at Charlottesville, February 15, 1964, on "Speech Education," cited some fifteen outstanding business leaders, industrialists, scientists, and educators concerning the value of their speech training. He quoted at some length statements from Philip Abelson, director of the Geophysical Laboratory of the Carnegie Institution of Washington; John D. Wilson, vice-president of the Chase Manhattan Bank, New York; and a dozen others concerning their speech experience. Carl H. Hanson, superintendent of schools, Rock Island, Illinois, for example, was cited as stating:

> *I have had much formal instruction in speech. Course work in it began in high school and continued through college. . . . I feel that instruction and experience in speech activities were among the most valuable of all of my course work. It is that* (*instruction*) *which has made it possible for me to communicate. If the program in speech is reasonable, I believe that it should be required of all who expect to teach—not only in the secondary schools, but any place. I do believe that speech education is an essential part of the well developed secondary school curriculum.*[18]

In order that the testimony you cite be accepted without question by your hearers, ask yourself the following questions concerning the authority you are quoting:

1. Does he have special training in the field in which he is alleged to have authority?

2. Is he free from prejudice?

3. Is his testimony accurately reported, and is it specific? Be sure that you have not unintentionally misquoted your source. Do not make vague references to authorities, such as: "A prominent member of a college faculty denounced the 'one-hundred-best-books' type of higher education"; or "One of the student speakers contended that movies are a menace to higher education."

4. Is the authority or source well known and acceptable to the audience?

5. Is his testimony corroborated by that of others?

6. Have you cited too many sources? Quote sparingly. Two or three apt references in a five- or ten-minute talk should be adequate.

[18] *Vital Speeches of the Day*, 30:348–352, Mar. 15, 1964.

Development by quotation

In addition to citing authorities and witnesses to confirm your points, you may also insert quotations of poetry or prose for added interest and impressiveness. Lionel Crocker, a speech specialist, quoted Edmund Burke:

> *Edmund Burke, the greatest political scientist the English speaking peoples have produced, knew a thing or two about getting along with others. He was surrounded by such talents as Richard Brinsley Sheridan, Charles James Fox and William Pitt. He left us the aphorism, which is inscribed on one of the monuments in Washington, D.C., "Magnanimity in politics is not seldom the wisest policy." This statement about generosity in politics can be applied to every walk of life.*[19]

Inference from general propositions

Inference moves by the inductive method toward general conclusions or by the deductive method from general statements to more inferences; only a combination of the induction-deduction generalization from specific materials assumes some broader view into which they try to fit their concrete examples (the scientific method of hypothesis). Similarly, inference from analogy always involves general propositions under which the more specific comparisons are made. Causal inference, too, assumes and implies basic propositions that provide logical foundations.

Deductive inference, to logicians, is illustrated by syllogism, in which the major proposition is labeled major premise; the related or more specific proposition is the minor premise; and the connecting proposition is framed as the conclusion. A typical categorical proposition follows:

> **I.** Whatever policy the United States follows in helping to preserve peace between the Soviets and Western Europe should be endorsed.
>
> **II.** The United States advocates continued support of NATO as a policy to preserve peace between the Soviets and Western Europe.
>
> **III.** This policy of the United States should be endorsed.

Seldom is this expanded form of logic used. Hypotheses, assump-

[19] *Vital Speeches of the Day,* 30:538, June 15, 1964.

tions, and similar general positions are often used—though not always directly stated. The deductive development sometimes helps to give, in a brief statement, the essence of the speaker's ideas. The procedure fails logically unless the speaker carefully explains and expounds whatever step his listeners may question. In the deductive pattern it is important to frame and examine the assumptions of hypotheses if they have not been so treated by the communicator.

Each premise needs to be tested for its reliability—with due examination of the instances and other inferential materials that justify the proposition. All ideas need to be verified by induction, causation, testimony, and authority. Each proposition in the syllogism above needs detailed examination.[20]

In conclusion

Each of the methods of inference may be used with equal effectiveness in each of these distinct types of speeches—those that inform, convince, move to action, and entertain. Obviously, the devices used in exposition are *mainly* definition, particulars, and instances. In argumentative and persuasive speeches, instances, statistics, analogies, cause-and-effect sequences, and testimony are frequently used. Speeches in which entertainment is an important purpose make use of concrete details, short narratives, anecdotes, quotations, and references to the speaker, the audience, and the occasion. But no particular type monopolizes any of these modes of treatment.

The various forms of development outlined in this chapter by no means exhaust the list. You may add others, or you may suggest a somewhat different grouping of these elements. The methods here stressed are those which effective communication have long used. If your talk is to be comparatively free from unsupported assertions, from vague thinking, and from dull, uninteresting treatment, you will develop your ideas by these concrete, particular, factual, analogical, and causative techniques.

PROJECTS AND PROBLEMS

Project 1 The study of examples of failure to develop an idea well

Bring to class a report on one or more instances in which a speaker failed to make adequate use of evidence or reason to make his point, or committed some error in the use of logic or common sense.

[20] See Chap. 15, "Persuasive Speaking, Logical Techniques" for further explication of induction and deduction.

Project 2 Relate the principles of perception to the meaning derived from the same experience

Did you filter, add, bypass, and organize your perceptions to resist a useless change or to facilitate a major event later?

Project 3 The development of a talk by the use of specific facts and figures

Purposes of this assignment: To study and apply the use of facts and figures as the main material in the development of a speech.
Procedure: You will concentrate on figures and specific facts as the backbone of your three-, four-, or five-minute talk. Cite on the margin of your outline the exact source of your figures. For statistical examples, consult the bulletins of learned societies (e.g., *Speech Monographs,* for facts concerning experimental data in speech studies), the *Congressional Record,* or speeches as reported in *Vital Speeches* or elsewhere.
Subjects for this speech:

1. The trend in the stock market will probably be upward (or downward)
2. We are in for a period of inflation (or deflation)
3. The college student enrollment has been steadily increasing and will continue to do so
4. The Medicare program assures improvement in American health

Project 4 The development of a speech by the use of comparison and contrast

Purposes of this assignment: To study and apply the use of comparison (including analogies) and contrast as the main material of your speech.
Procedure: Proceed as in project 1. Stress analogies and contrasts.

Project 5 The development of a speech by the use of causes and results

Proceed as in projects 1 and 2.

Project 6 The development of a speech through incidents and authorities

Purposes of this assignment: To study and apply the use of incidents and testimony by authorities in the development of your speech.

Procedure: Proceed as in the projects above. Incorporate as the main elements of this speech either incidents, anecdotes, questions, authorities, or some combination of these methods. Be sure to limit the subject. Subjects for this speech (any other subject to be chosen):

1. The argument for (or against) mercy killing
2. Franklin D. Roosevelt was a "great man"
3. We are heavily influenced by environment
4. The spirit of intolerance is rising in the United States
5. My experience in Australia
6. A universal language
7. America 100 years from now
8. If I were a Communist
9. If I were a labor leader
10. College disillusionments
11. Americans are succumbing to the "mass mind"
12. National advertising methods should be condemned

REFERENCES

Allport, Floyd H.: *Theories of Perception and the Concept of Structure,* John Wiley & Sons, Inc., New York, 1955.

Anderson, Richard C., and David P. Ausubel: *Readings in the Psychology of Cognition,* Holt, Rinehart and Winston, Inc., New York, 1966.

Bartlett, Sir Frederic: *Thinking,* Basic Books, Inc., Publishers, New York, 1958.

Bormann, Ernest G.: *Theory and Research in the Communicative Arts,* Holt, Rinehart and Winston, Inc., New York, 1965.

Brembeck, Winston L.: "The Effects of a Course in Argumentation on Critical Thinking Ability," *Speech Monographs,* 16:177–189, 1949.

Brigance, William Norwood: *Speech: Its Techniques and Disciplines in a Free Society,* Appleton-Century-Crofts, Inc., New York, 1952.

Creelman, Marjorie B.: *The Experimental Investigation of Meaning,* Springer Publishing Company, New York, 1966.

Deese, James: *The Structure of Association in Language and Thought,* The Johns Hopkins Press, Baltimore, 1965.

Dember, William N.: *Psychology of Perception,* Holt, Rinehart and Winston, Inc., New York, 1965.

Fearnside, W. Ward, and William B. Halther: *Fallacy,* Prentice-Hall, Inc., Englewood Cliffs, N.J., 1959.

Glazer, Edward M.: *An Experiment in the Development of Critical Thinking,* Teachers College Press, Columbia University, New York, 1941.

Hovland, Carl I., et al.: *The Order of Presentation in Persuasion,* Yale University Press, New Haven, Conn., 1957.

Howell, William S.: "The Effects of High School Debating on Critical Thinking," *Speech Monographs,* 10:96–103, 1943.

Johnson, Alma: "An Experimental Study in the Analysis and Measurement of Reflective Thinking," *Speech Monographs,* 10:83–96, 1943.

Larrabee, Harold A.: *Reliable Knowledge,* rev. ed., Houghton Mifflin Company, Boston, 1964.

McKellar, Peter: *Imagination and Thinking,* Basic Books, Inc., Publishers, New York, 1957.

SOCIAL PROCESSES OF SPEECH

9
LANGUAGE

IMPORTANCE OF LANGUAGE IN SPEECH

Language, in speaking, is more than a demonstration that you know the English language, more than a superfluous bit of preparation for a public speech. It is an element with which the major fundamentals of speaking—the thought or ideas, organization, specific detail, personal adjustment, phonation, articulation, and bodily activity—are all interwoven.

The importance that classical rhetoricians and present-day speech authorities attach to language is reflected in the space and value they give to this factor in communication. Aristotle in his *Rhetoric,* Cicero in his *De Oratore,* Quintilian in his *Institutes of Oratory,* George Campbell in his *Philosophy of Rhetoric,* Hugh Blair in his *Lectures on Rhetoric and Belles Lettres,* Richard Whately in his *Elements of Rhetoric,* and recent writers on rhetoric and public address, including N. W. Brigance, Waldo Braden, Stuart Chase, Wilbur Howell, Donald Bryant, James McBurney, Horace Rahskopf, Karl Wallace, and almost all other twentieth-century writers on communication give prominence to language or style (*elocutio*, to use the classical term).[1]

There are scholars in many other disciplines who are studying language today. We will refer to many of these sources of information as we move through this chapter. The student of speech can profit from learning what they have to contribute to speech. For the moment we may be content to recognize that the business of speaking is not a mere matter of learning to vocalize words. The voice and behavior of the speaker as we shall see in later chapters do not merely deliver the message. Although the voice carries the word forms in speech, voice and action also possess symbolic features and meaningful messages on their own.

Language, we agree, is a code of symbols which has many useful functions for the individual. Language, as we use the term here, however, consists of words, combinations of words in phrases, clauses, sentences, and larger units; and other symbol systems we use to send and to receive messages. It is the verbal component in your communication. This chapter, then, deals with your use of language in speaking.

The character of the response to this verbal intercourse is influenced by the character of the words and combinations of words you are able to marshal for your task. Words are a class of symbols by which objects, experiences, ideas, feelings, and emotions are represented.

Thus words are to be understood as representing and substituting for the objects, events, experiences, and concepts that give rise to the initial meaningful association with the stimulus. These sources are the referents. We apparently cannot philosophically discern these referents, but at least we assume their reality as the original source of stimulation through our common sense and experience. The referent leads to the *thought* or *reference* and in turn to the word itself, the symbol. Thus we note the word-thought–referent relationship.

The map, to use the familiar illustration of the semanticists, is not the same as the country itself; the word *book* is not identical with the collection of printed pages you are now reading. The word is a *symbol*, composed of the signs and sounds by which we echo or represent our own meanings and stimulate the listener to create his own representation of what we talk about. This link between the

[1] See Lester Thonssen and A. Craig Baird, *Speech Criticism*, The Ronald Press Company, New York, 1948, chap. 15, "The Style of Public Address"; A. Craig Baird, *Rhetoric: A Philosophical Inquiry*, The Ronald Press Company, New York, 1965, chap. 8, "Language and Style."

referent and the word or symbol is the thought or mental process (the reference). The referent, then, stimulates the brain to perform a mental process, which calls up the appropriate word to name or describe that experience. This reference is "a set of psychological contexts by which we link a mental process and referent."

C. K. Ogden and I. A. Richards in *The Meaning of Meaning* illustrate the relationships of the (1) word or symbol, (2) the thought or reference, and (3) the referent or thing itself:

Thought (Reference)

Word (Symbol) .... *Referent* (Thing itself)[2]

Your language should be both concomitant with and reflective of the thought which precedes and accompanies the formulation of the words and their expression in the speaking itself. These words should be selected to reveal your thinking. The comment "Her mind never knew what her mouth would say next" is a description of what unfortunately prevails in many conversations and sometimes in more formal speaking. When the political speaker proclaims, "I believe in the equality of the races," a sentiment that may be contrary to his real thinking and feeling, we need to be able to detect the lack of character in his communication.

Your words are one of the instruments by which your communication itself succeeds or fails. You may use a vocabulary largely unintelligible to your audience. Your terms, for example, may be accurate but technical. Or your words in the discourse may be quite simple but may not accurately convey your meaning. Or the arousal of meaning you hope will take place in your listener may be blocked by unhappy syntax, by dangling participles, misplaced antecedents, or involved sentence structure. Language, properly used, translates ideas; unfolds them with sequence, relevance, impressiveness; enforces logical and persuasive (emotional) elements in the speech; and furnishes the symbols by which the act of speaking itself, including voice, articulation; and gestures, is facilitated. Thus your language is associated with the other processes of speech.

[2] C. K. Ogden and I. A. Richards, *The Meaning of Meaning*, Routledge and Kegan Paul, Ltd., London, 1923, p. 11. For further review of this topic see Wendell Johnson, "The Spoken Word and the Great Unsaid," *Quarterly Journal of Speech*, 37:419–429, December, 1951; Baird, *op. cit.*, pp. 44, 145–153; Daniel Fogarty, *Roots for a New Rhetoric*, Bureau of Publications, Teachers College, Columbia University, New York, 1959, chap. 2, "I. A. Richards' Theory," pp. 28–56.

FUNCTIONS OF LANGUAGE

Language symbols serve many functions of man. To be sure, language is not the only symbol system or form of stimulation which serves these functions, but it plays its part. It is some of these parts with which we are concerned at the moment. What are some of these functions?

1 ***Language as used in speech serves a function of practical economy in social interaction.*** To learn, for example, by being told may be much easier than it is to learn the hard way. An organization such as the United Nations which operates primarily through communication has shown many times that it can be "the moral equivalent of war." Such examples are legion. They run the whole gamut of communication purposes, from attention to the motivation of the muscular system in action.

2 ***Language is a form of social behavior.*** Indeed "language is culture" according to many sociologists and anthropologists. We prefer to think of language as that set of symbols which binds us tenuously to our heritage, which provides those commonalities in experience which enables persons at a distance to share their experiences symbolically. It is a humanizing agency among men.

3 ***Language is closely related to and is a facilitator of thought: reflective, manipulative, critical, and creative.*** Many of man's mistakes in thought are mistakes arising from his weakness in the use of language. Improvement in thought is to be undertaken as a series of exercises in the improvement of the use of language, and vice versa.

4 ***Just as language which malfunctions may produce a distortion of mental activity, language scientifically formulated and pursued may function as a mental cathartic; a builder and maintainer of mental health.***

5 ***Language is not only a link with the past; it is by its very nature a creative force among men.*** Since meanings are developed out of personal experience and no two people ever have exactly the same experience, every communication forces the receiver to create the meaning of the communication for himself. It is only the broad overlapping similarities of our experiences which enable a communicator

to so stimulate a communicatee that the messages he receives approximate the messages sent. To the extent that each person creates his own meanings out of communication, the possibilities of the creative uses of language are virtually infinite.

There are other functions of languages such as entertainment, ritual, problem solving, etc. Since these are considered more fully in other chapters of this book we shall not dwell further upon them here.

There are many standards by which language, and indeed all communication, must be judged. The standard of first importance is a pragmatic one—Is the goal attained? Of course it may not succeed 100 percent, and nevertheless be considered successful. In this sense standards are relative. Another standard is the standard of accuracy: accuracy of grammar, of statement of fact, of representation of the reality which is the referent. Again absolute accuracy may be so difficult to determine that we must be satisfied with or accept a relatively accurate statement of conditions. We also apply standards of fairness and goodness to communication. A subject of communication must be represented fairly and realistically if it is to be ethically acceptable. We know that a particular communication may meet certain standards and not meet others. A communication can be effective but not good in the philosophical sense. We must learn to apply whatever standards are applicable to a communication event. But above all, the standard of ethics or character stands supreme. If a message violates ethical standards, it is unworthy of the application of any other standards to it.

SOME RHETORICAL AND SEMANTIC GUIDEPOSTS

Although you as speaker are by no means interested in high literary style, you want your words to contribute to the total pattern of your ideas, organization, language, voice, etc. Your want is not decorative but practical language that will secure for you from your listener-observers responses of importance to them and, you hope, favorable to your purposes.

Certain language principles, ancient yet modern, with their specific applications, you will follow or at least keep in mind. These basic attributes of "good" language include the principles of (1) adaptation, (2) accuracy and clearness, and (3) interest and vividness.[3]

[3] Thonssen and Baird, *op. cit.*, pp. 410–416; Baird, *Rhetoric*, pp. 156–162.

I Adaptation of language

Adapt your language to your audience, the occasion, your subject, your speaking purpose, and your own personality. Just as such adaptation is necessary for efficient organization and speaking, so adjustment of language obviously helps in communicating and obtaining the response you want.

Adapt your language to your audience. Visualize to yourself their individual and collective personality, their probable attitudes toward you and your ideas, their interests, experience, knowledge, and thinking habits. Adjust your language according to what you know about your audience. You can probably make an accurate guess as to their general perceptions and the experience will no doubt lead you to make satisfactory adaptations. More and more experience should lead you to make more satisfactory adaptations. Such audience *rapprochement* will affect your language; it will be bookish or idiomatic, formal or informal, colloquial or even slangy, national or regional, humorous or solemn, technical or popular, according to audience analysis.

Adapt your language to the immediate occasion. Usually your understanding of an audience will be sufficient for you to adjust to the specific occasion. Different occasions obviously affect your language. It may be ordinary conversation, more formal dialogue, colloquy, symposium, informal discussion, open forum or "Oregon style" debate, greetings at some get-together, or at a farewell dinner, or at any one of the scores of other occasions where interpersonal or more formal talking occurs.[4]

Adapt your language to your communicative purpose. If your aim is to inform and if your student audience is reasonably interested in your topic as announced, you can concentrate on clarity and accuracy. Your words may be largely denotative in their effect. If, however, your aim is to communicate your feelings, or to convert, or to stimulate, you will no doubt find yourself using more connotative symbols. The extent to which your purpose is informative or, on the other hand, persuasive, like the demands of audience and occasion, should partly explain the character of your oral expression.

[4] Baird, *op. cit.*, p. 156.

Adapt words to your personality. The audience wants contact with you as an individual rather than with an unknown person masquerading in the language of some professor, radio or television personality, or in that of some article or book that has caught your fancy. Then, if you are naturally formal or informal, you will remain so, except that you will eliminate from your language the words that call undue attention to themselves. Capitalize to the best of your ability on your own personality. There is point to Buffon's statement that "*Le style est L'homme même*"—Style is the man. Your language should be the expression of your own experiences, attitudes, interests, intellectual and emotional activity, and of similar factors that account for your individuality. Cicero suggests that a speaker's or a writer's language is normally identified with his profession. The philosopher, historian, poet, soldier, lawyer, and other representative groups all had certain language marks of their trade or profession [5] and they still do today.

These classical approaches as they deal with personality apply to our present-day speakers and writers. The columnists, editorial writers, college professors, businessmen, labor leaders, preachers, radio and television talkers, college women, college men, young talkers out of gangs in Chicago, Los Angeles, or New Orleans—each has a vocabulary that identifies him with his group as well as his own individuality within that group.

It is important to know that at times one's purpose is to communicate a scientifically replicable description or inference. Under such circumstances we must use linguistic and other symbolic behavior which encourages our listener to focus on the ideas. At other times the communication of feelings and emotional attitudes is more important than the specific facts and ideas which are the rational foundation of the feeling. People probably communicate their feelings less efficiently than they communicate their ideas, although there is evidence that feelings can be communicated through nonlinguistic symbols with considerable accuracy.

II Accuracy and clearness

Accuracy or correctness in word usage calls for close correspondence between the symbols and the realities they represent. The first requirement, then, is that the speaker or writer report as accurately as he can the happening, scene, person, situation, event,

[5] Cicero, *The Orations of Marcus Tullius Cicero*, C. D. Yonge (tr.), H. G. Bohn, London, 1852, vol. 4.

article, or concept that he would incorporate in his discourse. In a sense every speaker is a scientific reporter. His purpose is to repeat with fidelity the referent or source and character of the stimulus or idea. This application means care in definition and reproduction of the original even if technical language is used. One of the problems of present-day communication is the difficulty of professional groups in talking to those of other professions. Some sophisticated teachers of communication in their explanation of communication may refer to *encoding* (the problem of the message sender), nonverbal signs, *decoding* (the problem of the message receiver), *dyad* (the two-party, face-to-face interview), the *communication nets,* and similar terms. The concept of encoding, so useful in engineering communication, does not do justice to the problems of a speaker's use of reinforcing simultaneous multisymbolic symbol systems of a complex nature used in speaking.

Accuracy and clearness call for absence of ambiguity, archaisms, slang, localisms, foreign terms, exaggerated or all-inclusive language, or emotional distortions. The requirement is for both the applications of grammar, syntax, linguistic acceptability, and the adaptation of ideas and other supports to audience comprehension.

Avoid ambiguity and inconsistency of meaning. As this paragraph was written, a few political leaders of this country were denouncing the sacrifice of "national sovereignty" in our international commitments to the United Nations. Almost every speaker used "national sovereignty" in a different sense. One word, as your dictionary will remind you, may easily list five or ten well-recognized meanings, as well as many slang, personal, and regional interpretations.

Avoid exaggerated or hasty generalizations in language. This is illustrated by such statements as: "Englishmen have no sense of humor." "College education serves no useful purpose." "Middle Westerners are isolationists." "The churches have sold out to the capitalists." "Latin Americans hate the Yankees." "Practically all Americans are morons." What we really mean is that *some* Middle Westerners are isolationists, *some* preachers have been unduly influenced by the wealthy members of their congregations, *some* Latin Americans dislike certain traits of the citizens of the United States, and so forth.

To correct such immaturity of thinking and expression, examine your own attitudes and prejudices; check your assertions against the facts; treat most statements as relative rather than absolute. Although you need not bore others by protesting every generalization they offer or by making a show of your own precision, you should avoid the practice of verbal looseness.

Avoid barbarisms and improprieties. Barbarisms are those words which by general consent have no place in formal or informal vocabulary. Improprieties are reputable words used incorrectly in a sentence. To illustrate the latter: One should say, "I agree *with* (not *to*) the proposal." "I differ *from* (not *with*) you concerning the merits of Daniel Webster." "He proved to be superior *to* (not *than*) the other speakers." "He lives quite a *way* (not *ways*) from New York." "A large *number* (not *amount*) of people are interested in the proposal." Such usage generally reflects lack of educational background or sophistication and may cast doubt on the credibility of your message.[6]

Avoid emotional distortions. Your language in speechmaking should be free from emotional distortions.

Name-calling, the device of destroying an argument by attacking a person or institution, is perhaps as popular today as in Greek and Roman legal and popular-assembly speaking. "Communist," "Red," "pink," "imperialist," "capitalist," "atheist," "crook," and their equivalent *ad hominum* arguments have been hurled back and forth as substitutes for analysis and appraisal of the ideas for which those so labeled may stand.

Heightened language, we agree, is not inconsistent with correctness and clearness. Although your vocabulary should not be stripped of emotional language, you should weed out those terms that carry obvious biases.

Use concrete and specific language. Many abstract words have emotional appeal, but their connotations for each individual may be so varied as to produce little reaction. The expression "life, liberty, and the pursuit of happiness" vaguely suggests an American ideal, but the words hardly evoke precise denotative meaning in the minds of listeners. For abstract terms, substitute concrete or specific ones that readily call up in the minds of your audience common pictures, associations, and experiences. Contrast the examples of abstract statements in the first column with the concrete illustrations in the second:

[6] Stanley Harms, "Listener Judgments of Status Cues in Language," *Quarterly Journal of Speech*, 47:164–169, 1961.

Abstract	*Concrete or Specific*
Communication is today a multidisciplinary field of study.	We are learning about communication today from linguistics, psychology, sociology, biology, and electronics, as well as the communication behavior disciplines such as speech, theater, broadcasting, and journalism.
The United Nations has done much to keep the peace of the world.	Action taken by the United Nations has worked to keep the peace in such places as Greece, Korea, the Congo, Egypt, Israel, Jordan, and Cyprus.
In 1965 most American car manufacturers brought out new sports car models.	1965 saw the advent of new sports car models in the Mustang, the Barracuda, and Corvette.
In the Vietnam war, helicopters have been extensively used.	In the Vietnam war in 1966–67, more than 8,500 helicopters were used, including Bell's Huey cobra, Hughes's XV-9A, and Sikorsky's Skycrane.

For concreteness, substitute individual names for general classes (Jones$_1$, Jones$_2$ versus men); use specific dates, days (stock market, 1965, stock market, 1966, stock market, 1967); give specific figures, usually in round numbers; include instances, illustrations, dialogue, direct quotations, and brief anecdotes. In general, test each word and term for precise associations.[7]

Use concise language. Wordiness is an unfortunate habit of most amateur and of many experienced speakers. Good speaking is often marked by an economy of words. Elmer Davis, director of the Office of War Information, achieved fame largely through broadcasts that were only five minutes long. Conciseness does not necessarily mean brevity; rather it means the avoidance of superfluous words. Express your idea in the fewest possible words without sacrificing the essential thought and without ignoring rhetorical principles. A statement of 300 words may be concise. A sentence of twenty words may be annoyingly diffuse. Edward R. Murrow who delivered the com-

[7] See S. I. Hayakawa, *Language in Thought and Action,* George Allen & Unwin, Ltd., London, 1965, including chap. 12.

mencement address at Grinnell College in June, 1958, was rated excellent for several reasons including the fact that his speech was just twenty minutes long.[8]

Use oral style. The language of most speech today calls for a lively style. When you compose a speech, you should hear the sounds and orally test the words for their effect. Although your language must in some measure be adapted to the audience, it should be largely the language of good idiomatic conversation. Conversational speech is elliptical; we say *phone* instead of *telephone, co-ed* instead of *woman student in a college which both sexes attend,* and *movie* instead of *motion picture.* We use contractions such as *isn't, didn't,* and *can't.* Short words are preferable to polysyllabic synonyms. If a short and simple word can carry your meaning, use it.[9]

Avoid pretentiousness and indirectness. Winston Churchill, probably the greatest speaker of this generation, used simple Anglo-Saxon and Biblical words. Note these illustrations:

> *The day will come when the joybells will ring again throughout Europe, and when victorious nations, masters not only of their foes but of themselves, will plan and build in justice, in tradition, and in freedom a house of many mansions where there will be room for all.*—January 20, 1940.
>
> *Let us therefore brace ourselves to our duties and so bear ourselves that, if the British Empire and its Commonwealth last for a thousand years, men will say, "This was their finest hour!"*—June 18, 1940.

Substitute original for hackneyed and trite terms. Public speakers in general, especially campaign orators and the speakers who introduce them, often use such hackneyed phrases as: "it gives me great pleasure," "we are assembled," "it is an honor for me to address you," "my friends," "last but not least," "in conclusion let me say," "this is a new day," "the immortal Bard," "the Good Book," "our distinguished guest," "in the last analysis," "youth has its responsibilities," "it is of vital importance," "the postwar world," "this is an age of transition," "my worthy opponent."

[8] See Herbert Spencer, "The Philosophy of Style," *Westminster Review,* new series, 58:436–437, October, 1852.

[9] James Gibson, Charles Gruner, Robert Kibler, and Frances Kelly, "A Quantitative Examination of Differences and Similarities in Written and Spoken English," *Speech Monographs,* 33:444–451, 1966.

Some of these sentiments are highly patriotic, philosophical, or religious. But can they not be put in slightly different words? Use Roget, Fernald, and Webster for ideas. Read aloud again Winston Churchill and Woodrow Wilson. Become more critical of your own vocabulary. Doing these things will enable you to give a more effective three-minute extempore speech.

III Interest and vividness

To hold attention and sustain interest you will need to be vivid. Vividness will add impressiveness to your remarks. Adopt the language of emotion and imagination—but do not overdo it. Friendliness and respect also stimulate attention.

Figurative language. Appropriate figures of speech are almost indispensable elements in lively oral composition. Ineptly used, they fall flat. Rightly expressed, simile, metaphor, personification, and analogy make ideas clear and emphatic and, in addition, sometimes furnish convincing evidence. Note the figures of speech from talks made in recent years:

> *We Americans have learned that we cannot dig a hole deep enough to be safe from predatory animals.*—F. D. Roosevelt
>
> *The United Nations, as it is doing, may scurry about valiantly with its firefighting machinery and put out a war-fire in Indonesia today, in Palestine tomorrow, and in Korea and Kashmir or Greece the next day. But new war-fires will continue to flare up and one day one of them, fanned by a furious windstorm of human conflict, may very well get out of hand.*—Ralph Bunche
>
> *From Stettin in the Baltic to Trieste in the Adriatic an iron curtain has descended across the continent.*—Winston Churchill

Sophisticated writers have no monopoly over good metaphorical (figurative) language. "Hold the line," "breakthrough," and a long list of other terms of ordinary language heard on campuses have these figurative identifications.

Although our standard advice is to avoid much worn clichés there are times when such figurative terms are still justified. Joseph Wood Krutch lists the use, sometimes effective, of comparisons, such as "quick as lightning," "crazy as a loon," "eat like a horse," "drink like a fish," and "brave as a lion." Mr. Krutch cites many words that are a part of the standard vocabulary that, traced back, were originally metaphors, such as *astonish* (struck by thunder), *lunatic* (struck by the moon).[10]

Vividness through structure of language. Use strong words at the beginnings and ends of sentences. Avoid the colorless "There is . . . ," "It is . . . ." Use a balanced structure to heighten contrast of ideas. For example: "He talks intervention: he votes isolation." "If we continue making hydrogen and A-bombs we invite war; if we cease doing so we invite surrender."

Rhetorical questions. Spoken language uses more questions than does the written form. To hold attention, to point forward to other ideas, to create suspense, to challenge thinking, and to evoke constant response, interrogations are important. A quick check of any animated conversation will illustrate this constant resort to interpersonal exchange of questions. In more formal speaking, the more persuasive purposes and methods lead to more formal use of questions.

President Edward M. Eddy, Jr., of Chatham College, Pittsburgh, in discussing "Our Common Denominator—the Student," asked six questions and dealt with each:

> *First: Are we willing to be realistic about education?*
>
> *Second question: Are we willing to call a halt to senseless collegiate comparisons?*
>
> *Third: Are we willing to believe in the diversity of students within the college as well as the diversity of the colleges themselves?*
>
> *Fourth: Are we willing to make the mighty effort to achieve genuine democracy in higher education?*
>
> *Fifth: Are we willing to encourage the judgments and selection of colleges as criteria which are in keeping with academic aims?*
>
> *Finally, question number six: Are the colleges ready to adapt themselves to a different sort of student who is ready for a higher level of achievement all along the line?* [11]

Parallelism. The recurrent use of the parallel structure of phrases and sentences is effective if not overdone.

Winston Churchill often used such impressive phrases, as for ex-

[10] Joseph Wood Krutch, "The Great Cliché Debate," *New York Times Magazine,* Sunday, June 10, 1953, p. 13, 32ff.

[11] Edward D. Eddy, Jr., "Our Common Denominator—the Student," in Lester Thonssen (ed.), *Representative American Speeches: 1960–61,* pp. 130–140.

ample, his address to the British people when invasion threatened in 1940:

> *"We will fight them on the beaches. We shall fight them on the landing field. We shall fight them in the fields and streets. We shall fight them in the hills. We shall never surrender."*

President Kennedy, in his important public utterances, often used such language structure. In his inaugural address, for example, he phrased his suggestions of pledge:

> *"To those old allies whose cultural and spiritual origins we share. . . .*
> *To those new states whom we welcome to the ranks of the free. . . .*
> *To those people in the huts and villages of half the globe. . . .*
> *To our sister republics south of the border. . . ."*

Like all compositional devices parallelism is to be used only as it grows out of the composer's feelings and out of his spontaneous usages rather than from some artificial effort to duplicate the grand manner of some orator.

Suggestions for improvement in language usage

What specifically can you do to have at your disposal an ample vocabulary? Your problem, first of all, is to become more familiar with a considerable number of the thousands of dictionary words, and, second, to assimilate enough of them to give you readiness in extempore speech. Groping for words in conversation or other oral situations no doubt diminishes your effectiveness. Ease with words will clarify ideas for the audience, reassure them, and sustain their interest. More important, your own thinking will be organized and clarified.

Readability. Test a written sample of your speaking for its readability or listenability. Use the Flesch formula, the Dale-Chall formula, or some other formula to determine the estimated difficulty level of your use of language.[12]

[12] See Rudolph Flesch, *How to Test Readability,* Harper & Row, Publishers, Incorporated, New York, 1951; or Edgar Dale and Jeanne Chall, *A Formula for Predicting Readability,* Educational Research Bulletins, Bureau of Educational Research of the Ohio State University, Columbus, 1952, 31:43–47.

General Reading. This suggestion for wide reading as an agency for the development of your command of words is standard advice, confirmed by the practice and testimony of many learners past and present. Find time for reading biographies, histories, science, politics, psychology, sociology, semantics, and literature. Read silently and aloud, both for content and for the language usages.[13]

Study of representative oral and written communication sources. Read speeches and articles in collections: Carrol Arnold, Douglas Ehninger, and John Gerber: *The Speaker's Resource Book,* Scott, Foresman and Company, 1961; A. Craig Baird: *American Public Addresses: 1740–1952,* McGraw-Hill Book Company, 1956; Edwin Black and Harry P. Kerr: *American Issues: A Source Book of Speech Topics,* Harcourt, Brace & World, Inc., 1961; A. Craig Baird and Lester Thonssen: *Representative American Speeches,* The H. W. Wilson Company, annually since 1937; Ernest J. Wrage and Barnet Baskerville: *Contemporary Forum: American Speeches on Twentieth Century Issues,* Harper & Row, Publishers, Incorporated, 1962; Mayland Maxfield Parrish and Marie Hochmuth: *American Speeches,* Longmans, Green & Co., Inc., 1954; *Vital Speeches,* fortnightly; current speeches in the *New York Times* and other newspapers. Outline the speeches or articles, note methods of supports, study the vocabulary.

Listening. Listen to superior radio-television speakers and to visiting lecturers on your local radio and television station, or to the educational broadcastings of classroom curricula. Check with the printed versions or copies supplied to you by the stations or the speakers. Various series of programs, for example, religious and educational, are available. Consult your radio-television guide.

Viewing of films. Attend documentary and other films. Note the language of those involved.

Study of words. Study synonyms, antonyms, and the history of words. Roget's *International Thesaurus,* already mentioned, is excellent. Crabb's *English Synonyms, Antonyms, and Prepositions,* Smith's *Synonyms Discriminated,* Soule's *Dictionary of English Synonyms,* H. W. Fowler's *Dictionary of Modern English Usage* have long been recognized as important helps. But above all, get a good dic-

[13] See Appendix C for suggested readings. Also review Chap. 6 for material on sources of materials.

tionary and use it at every turn. The results should tell favorably in your speaking skill.

Oral and written composition. Frequently write speeches, but by no means memorize the manuscripts or follow them closely in your oral communication.

PROJECTS AND PROBLEMS

Project 1 To review the principles of effective use of language in speech

Purposes of this assignment: To review the principles and methods of language usage in speech composition and presentation.
Procedure: Present a three- or four-minute talk on some phase of one of the suggested topics. Use illustrations. Draw on the suggestions of this chapter and the references cited at the end of the chapter for sources.
Subjects for this speech:

1. What is the evidence to support the conclusion that "oral language is essentially different from the written form"? Cite any sources.
2. "Your thinking is just as wide as your vocabulary." Discuss.
3. Explain the thing-thought-symbol relationship. Cite any sources.
4. Explain the semantic interpretation of "levels of abstracting." Cite any sources.
5. Discuss: "The word is not the thing."
6. Expound: "Extensional and intensional meaning."
7. Explain: "Two-valued orientation." See S. I. Hayakawa, *Language in Thought and Action*, or any other book on semantics.
8. Slang of college students.
9. Radio-television policies relating to length of individual talks.
10. Clichés in recent political speeches.
11. Local characteristics of Maine (or other region) vocabulary.
12. What are "loaded words"?

Project 2 To increase insight into the theory and criticism of oral-language usages

Purpose of this assignment: To analyze the language techniques used in typical speechmaking.
Procedure: Each student will analyze one of the following speeches, or a representative section of the speech, to comment on typical language

elements. Note especially concreteness, conciseness, oral style, triteness or originality of phrasing, colorful and figurative usage, and the features of sentence structure. Confine your written report to not more than two pages. Do not attempt to treat in detail all the language elements, but treat those features that impress you as effective or otherwise. Be prepared for a brief oral report of your short paper. Consult *Index to International Periodicals; New York Times Index; Representative American Speeches,* and similar references for sources for these speeches.

1. Loren Eisley, "Science and the Unexpected Universe"
2. J. Bronowski, "The Logic of the Mind"
3. Walter Rosenblith, "On Cybernetics and the Human Brain"
4. C. P. Snow, "The Moral Un-neutrality of Science"
5. Willy Ley, "The Conquest of Space"
6. Albert L. Elder, "A Chemist Looks at the World Population Explosion"
7. Glenn T. Seaborg, "The Scientist as Human Being"
8. Robert T. Wert, "The Restless Generation and Undergraduate Education"
9. Robert F. Goheen, "The Library and the Chapel Stand Side by Side"
10. W. W. Taylor, "Civil Rights and Federal Responsibility"
11. M. L. King, Jr., "I Have a Dream"
12. Ernest Wrage, "Antidote to Anonymity"
13. J. W. Fulbright, "Old Myths and New Realities"
14. J. F. Kennedy, "Address to the Nation, October 22, 1962"
15. Adlai Stevenson, "Eulogy of Eleanor Roosevelt"
16. R. W. Sarnoff, "Television's Role in American Democracy"
17. Walter Lippmann, "The Frustrations of Our Time"
18. John H. Glenn, Jr., "Address before Congress, February 26, 1962"

Project 3 To apply the principles of effective oral language

Purpose of this assignment: To provide experiences in language usage in your own speaking.

Procedure: Write in full a four-minute speech on some informational or argumentative topic. Be sure to limit your subject. Check to note whether you conform reasonably well to satisfactory standards of language usage. On the margin of your composition, note any sections that fully meet the requirements for satisfactory language usage. Deliver your speech to the class without reference to your writing. Avoid direct memorizing of the words. Join in the class comment on the various speeches with respect to the problems of composition.

For the instructor: Show to your class the film *Say What You Mean* according to the instructions of the *Teacher's Manual.* For objective tests, see Using Effective Language in the *Teacher's Manual.*
Suggested topics for this project: Limit further or select another topic.

Should the streams in my state be purified?
How should we make the superhighways safer?
Is the three-semester college plan preferable to the two-semester or three-term plan?
Should the use of motorcycles be more strongly controlled by law?
Should avowed Communists be prohibited from enrolling in American colleges and universities?
How a space vehicle is launched
Buying a common stock in the stock market
How Medicare works
The leading American living poet
America's leading living novelist
Rhodesia and the race problem

REFERENCES

Black, Max: *The Importance of Language,* Prentice-Hall, Inc., Englewood Cliffs, N.J., 1962.

Bram, Joseph: *Language and Society,* Random House, Inc., New York, 1955.

Carroll, John B.: *Language and Thought,* Prentice-Hall, Inc., Englewood Cliffs, N.J., 1964.

Chall, Jeanne: *Readability,* The Ohio State University Press, Columbus, 1958.

Condon, John C., Jr.: *Semantics and Communication,* The Macmillan Company, New York, 1966.

Deese, James: *The Structure of Associations in Language and Thought,* The John Hopkins Press, Baltimore, 1965.

Estrich, Robert M., and Hans Sperber: *Three Keys to Language,* Holt, Rinehart and Winston, Inc., New York, 1952.

Hall, Edward: *The Silent Language,* Doubleday & Company, Inc., Garden City, New York, 1959.

Hayakawa, E. I.: *Language in Thought and Action,* George Allen & Unwin, Ltd., London, 1965.

Jones, L. V., and L. B. Thurstone: "The Psycho-physics of Semantics: An Experimental Investigation," *Journal of Applied Psychology,* 39:31–37, 1955.

Katz, Jerold J.: *The Philosophy of Language,* Harper & Row, Publishers, Incorporated, New York, 1966.

Klare, George R.: *The Measurement of Readability,* The Iowa State University Press, Ames, 1963.

Lasswell, Harold D., et al.: *Language of Politics,* George W. Stewart, Publisher, Inc., South Norwalk, Conn., 1949.

Martin, Richard R.: *Intension and Decision,* Prentice-Hall, Inc., Englewood Cliffs, N.J., 1963.

Morris, Charles: *Signification and Significance,* The M.I.T. Press, Cambridge, Mass., 1964.

Ogden, C. K., and I. A. Richards: *The Meaning of Meaning,* Routledge and Kegan Paul, Ltd., London, 1923.

Osgood, Charles E., et al.: *The Measurement of Meaning,* University of Illinois Press, Urbana, 1958.

Saporta, Sol: *Psycholinguistics,* Holt, Rinehart, and Winston, Inc., New York, 1961.

Sebeok, Thomas A.: *Style in Language,* The M.I.T. Press, Cambridge, Mass., 1960.

Shaw, George B.: *On Language,* Philosophical Library, New York, 1963.

Thorndike, Edward L., and Irving Lorge: *The Teacher's Word Book of 30,000 Words,* Teachers College of Columbia University, New York, 1944.

Weaver, Carl H.: "Measuring Point of View as a Barrier to Communication," *Journal of Communication,* 7:5–13, 1957.

10 THE SPEAKING VOICE

The human voice is a most interesting characteristic of man. Your voice serves you in many ways. It is first of all a channel of communication. The airwaves, which when heard are the voice, carry many messages. First, they carry the modulations representing the sounds which make up the words and sentences we speak. The voice also is subject to variations in the form of resonance, loudness, rate, pitch, and inflectional patterns which cue such additional messages as the age, sex, state of energy or health, degree of emotional tension, and other features of the personality of the speaker.[1,2,3]

[1] See Delwin Dusenbury and Franklin H. Knower, "Studies in the Symbolism of Voice and Action," *Quarterly Journal of Speech,* 24:424–436, 1938, and 25:67–75, 1939; and Franklin H. Knower, "Analysis of Some Experimental Variations of Simulated Expressions of the Emotions," *Journal of Social Psychology,* 14:369–372, 1941.

[2] Franklin H. Knower, "The Use of Behavioral and Tonal Symbols as Tests of Speaking Achievement," *Journal of Applied Psychology,* 29:229–235, 1945.

[3] Melba Hurd Duncan, "An Experimental Study of Some of the Relationships between Voice and Personality among Students of Speech," *Speech Monographs,* 12:47–60, 1945.

When we talk in the dark, the voice must carry the meaning which functions for both ears and eyes. To those who are familiar with your voice, it carries your name. When you talk with members of your family or with friends, it isn't necessary for you to say, "This is Mary" or "John speaking." With your first utterance they will know that.

Whatever vocal skills you possess are skills you have learned. Whatever the quality of your voice, you tend to use it in a reflex manner. Most of us have little idea of what our voice sounds like to others. To improve one's voice this reflex behavior must be raised to the level of consciousness. We must know not only what we want to change, but also what we want to change it to. Such learning typically takes desire, work, guidance, and time. Since our voices serve us in so many ways, it is well that we have the best possible voices and that we learn to use them to their fullest for each of their functions. That many of us have voices which can be improved is evident from much research.

How effective is your voice?

According to Harry Barnes, who analyzed the voices of 1,661 beginning students in a required speech course at the State University of Iowa, "Sixty percent of the group were not classed as effective in the control of their voices during their speaking performance. Forty-seven percent were marked poor or below in their voice and voice control." [4]

Moser [5] found that air traffic control operators showed voices with the following faults or weaknesses in the order of frequency listed:

Too fast	Anger or irritation in the voice
Weak	Poor quality
Hesitant	Too slow
Too loud	Trailing off
Poor phrasing	Monotone
Pitch too high	Vocalized pauses

[4] Harry G. Barnes, "A Diagnosis of Speech Needs and Abilities of Students in a Required Course in Speech Training at the State University of Iowa," unpublished doctoral dissertation, State University of Iowa, Iowa City, 1932, p. 231.

[5] Henry Moser, *A Voice Training Manual,* Federal Aviation Agency, Washington, 1962.

Workers at other jobs might show faults in a different order of frequency. The point is that many people do have voice faults of which they are unaware. Such weaknesses need correction.

Many beginners in speech have weak, indistinct voices. Others, on the contrary, artificially declaim or orate. Many are unable to project and seem to ignore their audience. Some are breathy, speak too fast, or have a toneless style of speaking.

A few persons have organic difficulties, such as a cleft palate, poor teeth, and vocal paralysis. No attempt is made in this book to analyze or treat such problems. Many of these defects are remediable, but they require the attention of a specialist. The student who finds that he is in need of this type of speech correction should consult a speech pathologist for guidance in work with his problem.

Other vocal deficiencies are caused by personality problems involving nervousness, irritability, and lack of confidence. Inadequate preparation also causes poor vocal control. Quite apart, then, from serious organic handicaps, many speech students need to give serious attention to voice production both in conversation and in more formal speaking.

What constitutes a good voice?

Audibility. When you speak, you must be heard without strain upon yourself or your listeners. Many persons who are accustomed only to the soft and moderate tones of informal speech do not make themselves clearly heard even in a small room. On the other hand, a voice which is too loud is also objectionable, for it not only hammers the eardrums but also shocks the social sensitivities. Beginners in speech more often have weak voices than loud. The degree of loudness you need depends, of course, upon the size of the group and the acoustics of the room as well as the audience situation. The skilled speaker has sufficient control of loudness to project his voice adequately in all ordinary speech situations.

Pleasantness. Your voice must not only be clearly audible but also be reasonably pleasant. Of course, voices which are so loud that they irritate or so weak that one must strain to hear are unpleasant. But unpleasantness is more commonly associated with vocal resonance than with loudness. Voices that are harsh, guttural, raspy; metallic, shrill, or nasal; wheezy or breathy; too soft and formless—all are unpleasant for listeners. Tempo that is too fast or too slow is also unpleasant.

Fluency. This is essentially a problem of rate, which should vary with the types of material you present, your mood and personality, and other factors in the speech situation. The ideas of your speech should be presented as rapidly as the audience can grasp them. Most beginners, however, tend to speak too rapidly. If you fill your pauses with *ah, er,* or *uh,* the rate is slowed down and the listener is distracted. Such excess vocalization represents an unconscious attempt to keep the attention of your listeners while you are searching for a word or an idea. The severe stutter provides an extreme example of lack of fluency.

Flexibility. Ideas should be expressed in a variety of tones and at a variety of rates to achieve meaningfulness. These vocal variations should not occur in a regular stereotyped pattern, as in chant and singsong speech, but should depend upon your thought and reflect your attempt to adjust your communication to ideas and your particular listeners.

Improving your voice and voice control

At least four steps are involved in voice improvement: first, a clear understanding of the elements of voice production, including breathing, phonation, resonance, articulation, loudness, rate, pitch, and quality; second, a clear understanding of your own vocal skills and limitations; third, systematic practice in voice improvement; fourth, systematic evaluation of your progress.

It is a common occurrence for a student hearing the playback of the first record of his voice to exclaim: "Do I sound like *that?*" Most of your friends would recognize your recorded voice as they do your telephone voice, and they do not criticize because they have become accustomed to it. You are surprised because the sound comes to you in a different way than the way you customarily hear yourself. For the first time you are in a position to hear your voice the way others hear it. If you do not like it, you should work at improving it. Even if you do like it, you should listen carefully to the criticisms of others who can judge it more objectively.

An important factor in voice improvement is the development of an ear for effective voice production. Playing and replaying your recording may be helpful in developing your ear. Do not stop at one or two playbacks. Play the record many times; then play others. Get the feeling or sensations involved in producing standard tones. A competent critic who listens, advises, and points out differences is a great help in guiding the speech student to the development of new voice standards.

When you have clearly distinguished between old vocal habits and those you must work to develop, the next step is systematic and persistent practice. Practice at first on material planned to make the new forms of expression easy. Drill materials are commonly of this type. (See, for example, the projects at the end of this chapter.) As soon as possible, you should practice with materials and in situations in which the new habits are expected to function. You cannot expect the speech-laboratory voice drills alone to be sufficient to fix the new habits of voice in daily speech. Although mechanically formed habits may at first seem artificial, they should function quite naturally when the skill is thoroughly developed.[6]

For the remainder of this chapter, let us focus on the first step in voice improvement—understanding its elements.

1 ***Cultivate proper breathing.*** Good breathing in speech depends upon three factors. First, the lungs must retain enough air to make it unnecessary to pause within a phrase to breathe. Second, the muscles which regulate expiration must be sufficiently controlled to exert strong and steady pressure upon the breath stream. And third, this pressure must be exerted without causing undue tension in other muscles involved in voice production, particularly the muscles of the larynx.

The development of good breathing habits for speech is a process of modifying reflexive and accidentally acquired habit patterns of muscular action so as to achieve the necessary supply of controlled air pressure with the least exertion and superfluous tension. The fact that adults employ different patterns of muscular action for breathing is sufficient evidence to indicate that breathing habits are acquired. And evidence that many speakers have improved their breath control indicates that the early, accidentally acquired habits can be profitably modified.

2 ***Cultivate proper phonation.*** The second element of voice improvement is phonation—literally the process of uttering voice sounds. When the vocal folds of your larynx (voice box) are brought closely together and set in vibration by the force of the breath stream, a vocal tone is initiated. The pitch and some other characteristics of your tone are the result of the nature and operation of

[6] Charles H. Woolbert, "The Effects of Various Modes of Public Reading," *Journal of Applied Psychology*, 4:162–185, 1920.

the vocal folds and other muscles of the larynx. Whispered speech and unvoiced or voiceless sounds, as we shall see later, are produced without the vibration of the vocal folds. The fundamental pitch of the voice is determined by the rate of vibration of the vocal folds as a whole. The overtones are produced by the segmented vibration of the folds, and the rate at which the folds vibrate is dependent upon their length, thickness, and tension. The quality of your voice is influenced by the capacity of the folds to set up vibrations of the frequency that can best be reinforced by your vocal resonators (air chambers in the head and throat). Many persons have not learned to speak at the pitch level which will produce their best possible voice. Your study of voice should include an evaluation of your most satisfactory pitch.

3 ***Work for satisfactory resonance.*** The third fundamental vocal process is resonance. Resonance, or the lack of it, is responsible for the relative pleasantness and strength of the voice. Voices that are hoarse, raspy, metallic, nasal, cramped, or mouthy are the result of the poor functioning of resonators. The main vocal resonators are the pharynx, the mouth, and the nasal cavities.

Changes in resonance produce changes in the meaning communicated by the voice. Qualities of voice which suggest personality traits, moods, and emotional conditions are often determined by the ways in which tones are resonated. The vowel sounds of speech are strongly influenced by resonance.

Quality is that characteristic which makes one voice differ from another as to harshness, huskiness, guttural quality, nasality, and richness in tone. Quality is one of the most complex of the physical attributes of the speaking voice. It is influenced by, and influences, each of the other elements we have studied. Even more than other characteristics of your voice, it reveals your personality and your frame of mind. Pleasing vocal quality equips the speaker with a considerable vocabulary of tonal qualities to reveal emotional variations.

Improvement of vocal quality depends upon (*a*) the elimination of bad muscular habits in the resonance chambers, as exemplified by nasality, muffled tones, metallic tones, or aspiration, and (*b*) variation of muscular tensions in the resonance cavities of the throat and head. Many characteristic defects in vocal quality can be eliminated simply by learning to respond effectively to the ideas expressed.

Improvement in vocal quality requires analysis of personal problems and practice in the new pattern of resonance until it becomes a skill. Work to sharpen your ear for changes in quality of voice. Free your neck, throat, and mouth muscles of interfering tensions. If you speak too fast, slow down by giving duration to speech sounds. Practice to develop a vocabulary of tones.

The skills you acquire by drill or in isolated projects must be exercised in the pattern of speech activity as a whole if they are to be of much value to you. Only perpetual attention to voice development in the normal social uses of speech over a long period of time will produce lasting results. If you develop vocal skills in isolated situations, however, you may with effort transfer these skills to your everyday speech.

4 ***Articulate properly.*** Articulation, the fourth of the physiological processes of voice, will be discussed in greater detail in Chapter 11. We shall limit ourselves here with the statement that the major articulators include the lips, tongue, jaw, and soft palate.

5 ***Cultivate control of loudness.*** The voice should be sufficiently loud to be heard easily. Loudness is technically known today as sound pressure level. Variation in vocal intensity is necessary to emphasize and subordinate ideas, to give words acceptable pronunciation by stressing certain syllables, and to make speech interesting. A voice which is uniformly too low or too high does not permit adequate variety. Listeners easily tire of uniform loudness. They are irritated by inaudibility.

You need not shout to achieve force in speaking. But your voice must be firm, vigorous, and well-controlled. Obviously you will need more force to be heard by a large group of listeners than to be heard by a small group; speaking outdoors or in the presence of competing noises and other distractions requires more force than speaking indoors and in places where there are no distractions. Physically energetic people like a more vigorous speaker than do people who lead sedentary lives. Forceful ideas uttered in an indifferent manner lose some of their vigor. A speaker who cannot suit the vigor of his voice to the vigor of his ideas seems insincere.

6 ***Control your speech rate.*** Another characteristic of the speaking voice is speech rate. Direct your study of rate control in speaking toward the development of a rate slow enough to be easily understood and fast enough to sustain the audience's interest and avoid the appearance of hesitant or drawling speech. In speaking, this is

ordinarily between 130 and 150 words a minute, and in oral reading it is between 150 and 175 words a minute.[7] The presentation of light subjects, simple narrative material, and exciting ideas can be carried on at a faster rate than difficult and instructional material in unfamiliar subject-matter areas. When a number of listeners are included in the discussion (other things being equal), the speech rate should be slower than when there are only one or two persons. Situations involving distraction require a slower rate than situations which are free from distraction. Sight-reading is ordinarily slower than the reading of familiar material. Speech that is too fast is characterized by the shortening of vowel and continuant consonant sounds and of pauses.

Rate variation is an effective way of suggesting the nature of the thought being expressed and the relative emphasis to be given it. The timing of the punch line, for example, is very important. Practice to determine your most effective rate in speaking and oral reading. Your speaking rate should vary with the relative importance of the ideas, and it should never be so fast that your phrasing or emphasis suffers. Nervous speakers frequently give the impression of trying to express what they have to say before they forget it. Mumbling sometimes gives the erroneous impression of a rapid rate, whereas drawling of continuant sounds, long pauses, vocal stumbling, repetition of words, and intrusion of *ah, uh,* and *and ah* result in a slow rate. Rates that are too fast or too slow do not permit normal variation in speeding up or slowing down for expression. The absence of variation in rate produces monotony, and an arbitrary pattern of rate variation that does not accurately suggest or reflect the ideas discussed confuses listeners.

The task of controlling speech rate appears to be relatively simple, but it may require considerable practice. First, learn to vary the length of time required to articulate vowel and other continuant sounds. Second, learn to vary the duration of interphrasal and intersentence pauses. Third, eliminate stumbling and useless sounds. If your speech is too fast, slow it down by increasing the duration of sounds and the frequency and length of pauses. If it is too slow, speed it up by reversing these techniques and eliminating the excess vocalizations. Mechanical practices in developing rate control should be considered as only a step in habit formation, and the student should always remember that his essential purpose is to make rate the servant of the meaning to be communicated.

[7] Ernest Fossum, "An Analysis of the Dynamic Vocabulary of Junior College Students," *Speech Monographs,* 11:88–96, 1944.

7 ***Develop satisfactory pitch control.*** The pitch of your voice is an important signal of your intentions. It communicates to the listener as much as rate and loudness do.

Your pitch should not be too high or too low. A pitch that is habitually too high produces a piercing, metallic quality suggesting strain and discomfort; a pitch that is too low produces hollow, hoarse tones that are often inappropriate and unpleasant. The best pitch level for your normal speech is determined by the structure of your larynx and by your resonators. It may not be the pitch which you have developed by habit. Test your voice at various levels to determine whether or not you habitually speak at your best pitch level. If you do not, find the pitch level your resonators reinforce most effectively. It should be high enough to permit lowering and low enough to permit raising for contrast. Inflectional slides, steps, and patterns are useful in communication. Remember, however, that regular pitch changes which disregard meaning and produce singsong effects are confusing and distracting.

PROJECTS AND PROBLEMS

Project 1 Analysis of skills in using the voice

Purposes of this assignment: (1) To obtain a systematic evaluation of your vocal skills; (2) to obtain guidance in the development of vocal skills.
Procedure: Find a part of an article, a book, or a speech which you think might be interesting to your listeners. It should take at least three and not more than five minutes to read. Then prepare a three-minute speech about the subject. Present your speech to the class, and then read the selection to the class. Have your speech and your reading recorded on a tape recorder or record-cutting machine. Your instructor and classmates will rate you on use of voice.

Project 2 Development of loudness control

Do the following exercises as directed:

1. To learn how to inhale by active use of the diaphragm and exhale by active use of the waist muscles, stand erect with shoulders back, open your mouth, and pant like a dog. Place your hand across your diaphragm and note the action of the diaphragm. This is the first step in developing tone control.

2. Simulate a yawn by standing erect, taking a deep breath, throwing your arms up, and stretching. Then relax and expel the air from your

lungs as vigorously as possible. Note the feeling of vigorous contractive action of the waist muscles in this process.

3. Stand erect in a place where you can push against a wall with one hand. Count to ten in a normal voice, taking a separate breath for each count. Then repeat the exercise while pushing vigorously against the wall with one hand, allowing the waist muscles to contract vigorously on each count. Can you get a stronger tone by exerting pressure as you push?

4. Read the following sentences, using a single breath for each sentence. Do not lower vocal intensity at the end of the longer sentences.

a. I don't want to go.
b. The engineer cautioned us to drive slowly.
c. Deep, well-controlled breathing is required to read a long sentence on one expiration.
d. Scarlett O'Hara, the heroine in *Gone with the Wind,* was a Southern beauty of great personal pride, ambition, and willpower who would make almost any sacrifice to achieve her ends.

5. Try to read the first part of the following sentences normally and the last part forcefully without raising the pitch.

a. You must not come in here; please move along.
b. If we win that victory, what a celebration we shall have.
c. I believe in a program for the preservation of peace, but certainly not peace at any price.

6. Read the sentences in exercise 5 again, and this time raise the pitch of the last phrase to increase intensity of the voice.

7. Read the following paragraphs [8] in a forceful voice and at a rapid rate. Then read them slowly. Listen to the difference in general effectiveness and intensity at the two rates of speed.

> *No man can speak for the South. No one man can—by himself alone—define the beliefs of the people of this great region. But all of us and each of us must assume and exercise some degree of responsibility for persuading this nation to heed what we have to say.*
>
> *We must make clear what we believe.*
>
> *We must set the record straight.*
>
> *We must, finally, stand together in unity and pursue with determination a course to victory.*
>
> *That is our outline of duty.*
>
> *At the outset, let us establish one fact firmly.*
>
> *Gathered here tonight, we are Texans, we are Louisianans, we*

[8] From Alan P. Shivers, "The South Must Be Admitted to Full Partnership," *Vital Speeches,* 21:972, 1955.

are Southerners. Of these allegiances we are proud. We are honored by the heritage with which we are endowed.

But, in our hearts, we are—first and last—Americans. When we speak of duty, we speak of duty to our country. We acknowledge no loyalty greater than our loyalty to America. By that standard, we regard no principle as worthy, and we accept no cause as just unless it will contribute to the lasting strength of America, our America. It is our love for our country—not our pride in our region—which impels us to undertake this fight for principle.

8. Read the following sentences, giving considerable force to the italicized phrases and normal force to the phrases not italicized.

a. I know not what course others may take, but as for me, *give me liberty, or give me death.*

b. This is the last time I shall request that *those in the back row keep quiet.*

c. We shall make our preparation; *then we shall bomb, and blast, and burn them into surrender.*

d. *Though the mills of God grind slowly,* yet they grind exceeding small.

9. Read the following sentences without, then with, vigorous stress on the italicized words.

a. He who laughs last laughs *loudest.*

b. It's a *marvel* to me that she stays with it.

c. "*Mister,*" he said, "you dropped something."

d. The boys in North Africa *certainly* didn't agree with him.

e. Sarcasm is a *woman's* weapon.

f. If *I* were in his place, I wouldn't stand for it.

g. The only thing we have to fear is *fear* itself.

Project 3 Rate control

Practice the following projects:

1. Read the following sentences rapidly or slowly as the meaning suggests:

a. Watch out! It's hot.

b. Please let me do it.

c. They trudged wearily up the trail.

d. Come as quickly as you can.

e. The fried pheasant is delicious.

f. What a beautiful view you have from this window.

g. Bowed by the weight of centuries, / He leans upon his hoe. —*Markham h.* The day is cold, and dark, and dreary.—*Longfellow*

i. And slowly answered Arthur from the barge, / The old order changeth, yielding place to new.—*Tennyson*

j. And next comes the soldier, / Sudden and quick in quarrel.—*Shakespeare*

2. Read the following selection as rapidly as you can without mumbling or falling into a staccato pattern of articulation.

Speak the speech, I pray you, as I pronounced it to you, trippingly on the tongue; but if you mouth it, as many of your players do, I had a lief the town-crier spoke my lines. Nor do not saw the air too much with your hand, thus; but use all gently: for in the very torrent, tempest, and, as I may say, whirlwind of passion, you must acquire and beget a temperance that may give it smoothness. O! it offends me to the soul to hear a robustious periwigpated fellow tear a passion to tatters, to very rags, to split the ears of the groundlings, who, for the most part, are capable of nothing but inexplicable dumb shows and noise: I would have such a fellow whipped for o'erdoing Termagant; it out-herods Herod: pray you, avoid it.—Shakespeare

3. Read the following paragraph as slowly as you can without drawling: [9]

During the whole of a dull, dark, and soundless day in the autumn of the year, when the clouds hung oppressively low in the heavens, I had been passing alone, on horseback, through a singularly dreary tract of country, and at length found myself, as the shades of the evening grew on, within view of the melancholy House of Usher. I know not how it was—but, with the first glimpse of the building, a sense of insufferable gloom pervaded my spirit. I say insufferable; for the feeling was unrelieved by any of that half-pleasurable, because poetic, sentiment, with which the mind usually receives even the sternest natural images of the desolate or terrible. I looked upon the scene before me—upon the mere house, and the simple landscape features of the domain—upon the bleak walls—upon the vacant eye-like windows—upon a few rank sedges—and upon a few white trunks of decayed trees—with an utter depression of soul which I can compare to no earthly sensation more properly than to the afterdream of the reveller upon opium—the bitter lapse into everyday life—the hideous dropping off of the veil.

[9] Edgar Allan Poe, "The Fall of the House of Usher," *The Works of Edgar Allan Poe,* P. F. Collier & Son Corporation, New York, 1903, vol. II, p. 145.

4. Try reading the selection in exercise 2 slowly and the selection in exercise 3 very rapidly. Report on the differences in effect of rate of reading on the moods of these selections.

5. Read the following selection, using duration of vowel sounds to slow down the rate.[10]

This brave and tender man in every storm of life was oak and rock, but in the sunshine he was vine and flower. He was the friend of all heroic souls. He climbed the heights and left all superstitions far below, while on his forehead fell the golden dawning of the grander day.

He loved the beautiful, and was with color, form and music touched to tears. He sided with the weak, and with a willing hand gave alms; with loyal heart and with purest hands he faithfully discharged all public trusts.

He was a worshipper of liberty, a friend of the oppressed. A thousand times I have heard him quote these words: "For justice all places a temple, and all seasons summer." He believed that happiness was the only good, reason the only torch, justice the only worship, humanity the only religion, and love the only priest. He added to the sum of human joy; and were every one to whom he did some loving service to bring a blossom to his grave, he would sleep tonight beneath a wilderness of flowers.

Life is a narrow vale between the cold and barren peaks of two eternities. We strive in vain to look beyond the heights. We cry aloud, and the only answer is the echo of our wailing cry. From the voiceless lips of the unreplying dead there comes no word; but in the night of death hope sees a star, and listening love can hear the rustle of a wing.

6. Time yourself in reading the following passage.[11] A good reading rate is 150 to 175 words per minute. Does your rate approximate this speed?

I should like to discuss with you today a central question—one which rightfully looms large in the concern of the American people about foreign affairs. What is the policy of this government toward international communism?

[10] Robert Ingersoll, *The Works of Robert C. Ingersoll*, Dresden Publishing Company, New York, 1900, vol. XII, pp. 389–391.

[11] From a speech by Dean Rusk, "Communist Countries: The Difference in Treatment," *Vital Speeches*, 30:354–355, 1964.

At the present time, as throughout the postwar period, there are some who, for political or other reasons, deliberately sow confusion about our real intentions. Also, both at home and abroad, puzzlement may arise on more legitimate grounds.

We are asked how we can object to other free countries selling goods to Cuba when we are willing to sell wheat to the Soviet Union. We are asked why we refuse to recognize the Peiping regime when we recognize the Soviet Union. We are asked why we have treated Yugoslavia and Poland somewhat differently from other Communist states in Eastern Europe. We are asked why we enter into cultural exchange agreements, or a test ban treaty, with a government whose leader has continued to boast that he will "bury" us.

If the Communists, as a group, have as their aim the destruction of our way of life, how is it that we can treat one Communist country differently from another? And why do we enter into an agreement or understanding with a Communist government over one matter, while accepting the hard necessity of continued hostility and conflict over other matters?

Before answering those questions, let me make one point clear. We, in this Administration, and in this country, are under no illusions as to the designs of the Communists against us and the entire Free World. No one needs to tell us that the Communist menace is deadly serious, that the Communists seek their goals through varied means, that deception is a standard element in their tactics, that they move easily from the direct attack to the indirect, or to combinations of the two.

To know what the Communists are up to, and to understand their varied techniques, is a major order of business with us in the State Department and other branches of the government. It is an order of business we do not neglect.

We are fully aware that Moscow, as well as Peiping, remains committed to the Communist world revolution. Chairman Khrushchev tells us bluntly that coexistence cannot extend to the ideological sphere, that between him and us there will be continued competition and conflict. We hope this will not always be so. But as long as Mr. Khrushchev says it is, and acts accordingly, we must believe him, and act accordingly ourselves.

The first objective of our policy toward the Communist states must be, and is, to play our part in checking Communist imperialism. This Administration will vigorously oppose the expansion of the Communist domain, whoever the Communists in question may be, by force or the threat of force, whether directly or indirectly applied.

Project 4 Development of pitch control

1. Sound the vowel *a* or *ah* at your habitual pitch level. Vary the pitch upward, then downward, a half step at a time until you have gone as far as you can toward either extreme. Try to find the pitch level at which you get the strongest reasonance for your fundamental pitch. Is it higher or lower than your habitual pitch? Repeat the sound five times at the level at which you get the best tone.

2. Read the following stanza from Wordsworth's "I Wandered Lonely as a Cloud" twice. Read it once with marked emphasis on the mechanical rhythm of the verse. Read it a second time with changes of inflection to bring out the meaning of the verse but with subordination of the pitch changes to the pattern of rhythm.

> *I wandered lonely as a cloud*
> *That floats on high o'er vales and hills,*
> *When all at once I saw a crowd,*
> *A host, of golden daffodils;*
> *Beside the lake, beneath the trees,*
> *Fluttering and dancing in the breeze.*

3. Read the following sentences with an upward or downward step in pitch as indicated. When the arrow points upward, utter the words following at a higher pitch; when downward, at a lower pitch.

   a. Come ↑ here.
   b. How ↑ much?
   c. It's ↑ nonsense.
   d. Strike ↓ hard.
   e. You may pick it up, ↓ but handle it with care.
   f. I loved the excitement, ↓ but I am very tired.
   g. The plan of the attack, ↓ because of the presence of mines, was changed at the last moment.
   h. If any of you are doubtful, ↑ and I suspect some of you are, here is the proof.

4. Read the following sentences with an upward or downward slide as indicated.

   a. Isn't that a beautiful sight? ↓
   b. He doesn't know the meaning of ethics. ↓
   c. I have tried everything. ↑
   d. Is that what you mean? ↑
   e. I've never doubted it for a moment. ↓
   f. Now, what do you say to that? ↑

g. Now, what do you say to that? ↓
h. How do you do this? ↑
i. How do you do this? ↓
j. Drive to the end of Summit. ↓
k. He won't believe it. ↑
l. I simply will not permit it. ↓

5. Bring to class a poem or piece of emotional prose of your own choosing and demonstrate the use of pitch variation in communicating the meaning of the passage. Listen to the reading of others to develop an awareness of pitch changes.

Project 5 Development of vocal quality

1. Loosen up any tension in the muscles interfering with effective resonance by the following exercises:

a. Drop the head forward as if you had fallen asleep sitting up. Relax the neck muscles until the head seems to bounce. Try letting it drop backward in the same way.

b. Let the jaw muscles relax and drop the jaw in a relaxed manner, opening the mouth as far as possible. Start slowly and then increase the rapidity with which you say the word *bob*. Relax and let the air push the lips out from the teeth as far as possible in this exercise.

c. Relax the cheek muscles and blow out the cheeks as far as possible. Start slowly and then increase the rapidity with which you say the word *bob*.

d. Repeat the word *who* three times (1) with high pharyngeal resonance as when you yawn and say *ho hum*, (2) with relaxed pharyngeal resonance, and (3) with a definite attempt to get resonance from the oral cavities.

e. Repeat the sentence "It's a very fine thing" twice, first tensing the muscles of the soft palate, then relaxing them.

f. Say *ah*, beginning with a whisper and gradually phonating the tone until it is fully resonant; then gradually aspirate the tone until the sound is whispered.

g. Push against the wall and practice relaxing the muscles of the neck and mouth until you can say with a clear tone, "I am working to control relaxation of my speech muscles."

2. Develop resonance in your vocal attack by use of the following exercises:

a. Count to ten:
(1) As if counting out pennies on a table
(2) As if giving telephone numbers to a receiver with difficult telephone connections

(3) As if counting with difficulty the numbers of persons in a party barely visible in the distance
(4) As if "counting off" in doing setting-up exercises
(5) As if "counting out" a man in the ring

b. Utter each of the following statements in a fully resonated, positive tone:

(1) We came, we saw, we conquered.
(2) We have met the enemy and they are ours.
(3) I have not yet begun to fight.
(4) Ship ahoy! Ship ahoy!
(5) Open—'tis I, the King.
(6) Stand, the ground's your own, my braves!
(7) Roll on, thou deep and dark blue ocean—roll!

c. Read a passage of ordinary prose, carrying into it the pattern of sharp vocal attack that was necessary for the foregoing sentences. Learn to make the voice forceful without shouting.

3. Work on the following exercises for the development of a tonal vocabulary.

a. Pronounce the word *well* to indicate the following meanings:

(1) I never would have thought it possible!
(2) What do you want? I am very busy.
(3) That's a small matter.
(4) Now let me think a minute.
(5) So you thought you could get away with it!
(6) I am very pleased to see you.

b. Read the question "What are you doing?" as it would be expressed by the following characters:

(1) A burly policeman
(2) An old man or woman
(3) A half-frightened child
(4) An ignorant, shiftless tramp
(5) A fond young husband

c. Read each of the following sentences twice, first in a monotone and then with a tonal quality suggested by the emotional mood of the sentence.

(1) It's a beautiful night.
(2) I wish I could remember where I have seen that face.
(3) Say that again, and smile when you say it.
(4) My! You think you're smart, don't you?
(5) I never thought you would sink low enough to do a trick like that.
(6) We'll have dinner at the Ritz, see a show, and dance all night.

(7) So sorry. There are no more tickets for tonight. Next! What can I do for you?
(8) I never want to see your face again. Now get out.
(9) Isn't he a cute little thing! And he's only five.
(10) I have never known anyone who seemed to be such a thoroughly good man.
(11) There doesn't seem to be any use trying. I'm thoroughly beaten.
(12) Watch out! You'll hit that car!
(13) I am so full that I feel as if I'll burst; and it was all so good.
(14) We're so proud of Steve. He takes his honors like a man.

4. Select a poem that expresses a mood with which you sympathize. Read it for the class in a vocal tone which expresses the mood. Listen critically to the vocal quality of your classmates when they read their poems.

REFERENCES

Anderson, Virgil: *Training the Speaking Voice,* Oxford University Press, New York, 1942.

Black, John B., and Wilbur E. Moore: *Speech, Code, Meaning, and Communication,* McGraw-Hill Book Company, New York, 1955.

Bronstein, Arthur J., and Beatrice F. Jacoby: *Your Speech and Voice,* Random House, Inc., New York, 1967.

Eisenson, Jon: *The Improvement of Voice and Diction,* The Macmillan Company, New York, 1958.

——— and Paul H. Boose: *Basic Speech,* The Macmillan Company, New York, 1964.

Fairbanks, Grant: *Voice and Articulation Drillbook,* Harper & Row, Publishers, Incorporated, New York, 1960.

Grasham, John A., and Glenn G. Gooder: *Improving Your Voice,* Harcourt, Brace & World, Inc., New York, 1960.

Gray, Giles W., and Claude M. Wise: *The Bases of Speech,* Harper & Row, Publishers, Incorporated, New York, 1959.

Hahn, Elsie, Donald E. Hargis, Charles W. Loomis, and Daniel Vandragen: *Basic Voice Training for Speech,* 2d ed., McGraw-Hill Book Company, New York, 1957.

Hanley, Theodore D., and Wayne L. Thurman: *Developing Vocal Skills,* Holt, Rinehart and Winston, Inc., New York, 1963.

Rahskopf, Horace G.: *Basic Speech Improvement,* Harper & Row, Publishers, Incorporated, New York, 1965.

Van Riper, Charles, and John V. Irwin: *Voice and Articulation,* Prentice-Hall, Inc., Englewood Cliffs, N.J., 1958.

11 ARTICULATION AND PRONUNCIATION

Articulation and pronunciation consist of the production of the sounds of the language and their acceptable usage in the words of the language. A person is said to have an articulation difficulty if he does not properly produce one or more sounds of the language. When he can produce all sounds properly but does not produce them acceptably, including accents, in particular words, the difficulty is said to be one of pronunciation. Acceptable pronunciation is pronunciation without substitutions, additions, omissions, inversions, or misplaced accents.

Two criteria of satisfactory articulation

The most significant criterion of satisfactory articulation is intelligibility. Many words in our language differ from others only in the articulation of a single sound. Failure to articulate precisely the distinguishing sound can cause confusion between two words. The confusion of the numbers *seven* and *eleven* in military orders has caused loss of life. Although listeners may eventually discover the right word from the context, poor articulation slows down communication and renders it inefficient.

A second criterion of satisfactory articulation is social acceptability. Articulation can be compared with diction in the matter of social acceptability; there are substandard, informal, and formal levels of articulation.

METHODS OF IMPROVING ARTICULATION

1 ***Study the organs of articulation.*** The organs of articulation are the jaw, lips, teeth, tongue, hard palate, soft palate, vocal folds, and breathing mechanisms. The muscles of the inner surfaces of the resonance cavities of the mouth and the pharynx also operate to determine the shape of the oral cavities, which modify tones to cause the distinctive quality of the vowel sounds. Chronic inflammation of these surfaces or deformities in them may seriously affect articulation. The vocal folds, moreover, are responsible for distinctions between the voiced and the voiceless sounds.

In a sense, the ear also serves as an organ of articulation. Unless you hear clearly the sounds you make, you may articulate poorly. Although our purpose here is not to present a detailed account of the structure and function of the articulatory organs, an explanation of the organic basis of articulation is presented to give you a better understanding of the classification of speech sounds.

2 ***Study the sounds of English speech.*** The sounds of speech vary considerably as different persons make them, and the purpose of this study is not to obtain absolute uniformity among all persons. Sounds exist in sound families called *phonemes,* and the student should learn to make each sound in such a way that it is clearly acceptable as a member of the phoneme to which it belongs.

Students usually associate sounds with the letters of the alphabet. It is helpful to think of the sounds themselves as the units of articulated speech. The sounds of the word *hurt,* for example, are *h-r-t* rather than *h-u-r-t.* Specialists in the study of language sounds have developed the science of phonetics, with a systematic set of phonetic symbols in which each sound family, or phoneme, has one symbol. These symbols are presented in Appendix A. The diacritical marks used in the dictionary, on the other hand, are an attempt to provide symbols for sounds by using marks over the letters of the alphabet. For the purposes of the average student, diacritical marks will be sufficient. The marks employed in the vowel classification presented in the next section are derived from Webster's *New International Dictionary.*

3 ***Distinguish among vowels, diphthongs, and consonants.*** The three main types of speech sounds are vowels, diphthongs, and consonants. Vowels consist of relatively unmodified voice (that is, vocal tone is resonated, but there is little interference with the outgoing air), whereas consonants consist of voice modified by some type of friction or stoppage which, in part, shapes the sound. One or more of the organs of articulation modify or interfere with the free exhalation of air to produce consonants. Diphthongs are combinations of vowel sounds produced as one sound, such as *i* in *ice*, a combination of *a* and *i.*

The differentiation of vowel sounds, initiated by the vibrations of the vocal cords, is in the resonators. These areas may be located on the accompanying vowel chart. Front vowels, in which the highest part of the tongue is toward the top of the mouth and ranging downward, are the *e* of *be*, the *i* of *bit*, the *e* of *bet*, and the *a* of *tan*. The *u* of *but* is a midvowel, as is the *a* of *about*, with the highest part of the tongue drawn back somewhat in the mouth. The back vowels range upward from the *o* in *operate* to the *oo* in *fool*, with the highest part of the tongue toward the back of the mouth.

VOWEL CHART

FRONT POSITION OF TONGUE	MEDIAL POSITION OF TONGUE	BACK POSITION OF TONGUE
ē	ȧ	o͞o
ĭ	ŭ	o͝o
ĕ		ō
ă		ô
		ä

The principal diphthongs are the *u* of *use*, the *o* of *hole*, the *ou* of *ouch*, the *a* of *day*, the *i* of *light*, and the *oi* of *oil*. Although some of these are considered single sounds, careful study will reveal them to be combinations of other sounds.

Consonants, as we have seen, are produced by interference with the free expiration of the voiced or unvoiced breath. All consonants may be classified as either voiced or voiceless, the voiced consonants being accompanied by a vibration of the vocal cords. Many consonants are matched or paired. The muscular adjustments that produce voiced and voiceless "twins" are alike except that the vocal cords are vibrated to produce the voiced sound. Examples are *g* and *k*, *d* and *t*, *b* and *p*, and *v* and *f*.

The nasal consonants *m*, *n*, and *ng* are resonated chiefly through the nasal passages. The stop plosives are formed, as the term implies, by blocking the airstream and then releasing the sounds explosively. Voiced stop plosives are *b*, *d*, and *g*. Voiceless stop plosives are *p*, *t*, and *k*.

4 ***Identify the sounds with which you have difficulty.*** Test yourself systematically to determine which sounds cause you difficulty. (Note the test in project 1 at the end of this chapter.) Vowels that are frequently misarticulated are *a* as in *bad*, *e* as in *get*, *i* as in *fish*, and *u* as in *just*. Do you say *git* for *get*, *jist* for *just*, *sich* for *such*, *feesh* for *fish*? The words are *penny* not *pinny*, former President *Kennedy* not *Kinnedy*, *lend* not *lind*, *send* not *sind*. *Feesh*, *deesh*, *weesh* are colloquial or substandard pronunciations. The same can be said for *peush* and *beush*. In a recent public broadcast the speaker was heard to substitute the *i* for the *e* sound regularly in such words as *benefit*, *attention*, and *attend*. The diphthong *ou* as in *down* is frequently perverted to an *au* sound. Consonants that commonly cause difficulty are the aspirate and fricative sounds such as *s*, *z*, *ch*, *j*, *sh*, *zh*, *f*, *th*, *v*, and *wh*, characterized by a rustling friction of the breath. The *n* sound is often substituted for *ng*, and *t* is often erroneously produced by a glottal stop rather than an explosion between the tongue and hard palate. The *t*, *d*, *p*, *b*, *k*, and *g* sounds are sometimes exploded when they should merely be stopped by the articulators. The *w* sound is sometimes substituted for *r* in such words as *bright*. These are some of the most common misarticulations. Make a systematic analysis of your articulatory habits to discover your personal variations in order to correct them.

5 ***Apply sufficient breath pressure as you sound consonants.*** Be sure you sound with sufficient accuracy and fullness such plosives as *p* in *pour*, *b* in *ban*, *d* in *dote*, *g* in *gill*, *t* in *talk*, *k* in *cap*, and *h* in *hill*. Be sure to articulate fully medial and final consonants such as *l* in *asleep*, *t* in *cut*, and the *s* sound in *trace*.

6 ***Mouth, jaw, lips, and tongue should be active in articulation.*** Make a tape recording of your voice and note your articulatory weaknesses and your progress. Read passages, including those listed at the end of this chapter, before a mirror and observe your vocal activity or lack of activity in articulation. Practice (see again the

projects at the end of this chapter) such words as *kept* versus *kep, ask* versus *ass,* and *exactly* versus *exackly.*

7 ***Avoid lip-laziness.*** Perhaps the most common difficulty in articulation is what is called *lip-laziness.* The difficulty, however, does not concern the lip alone; other articulatory organs are also involved. The result is mumbling or general oral inaccuracy. To overcome such a habit, you will need a sufficiently clear and vigorous tone to carry sound differences to your listeners and sufficient control of all the articulatory organs to use each of them as needed to modify the basic tone. Some persons, on the other hand, go to extremes in activating the articulatory organs and thus produce a kind of affected niceness of enunciation, particularly with certain words about which the speaker is self-conscious. This fault, however, is not so common as underarticulation.

8 ***Let the requirements of the situation govern your rate of articulation.*** When you are speaking in a large auditorium and when you are competing with noises, retard your rate of articulation to ensure the listener's comprehension. Slow articulation is also a means of stressing important ideas. These are characteristics of a formal level of articulation.

9 ***Analyze for articulatory excellence any of the speech recordings now available.*** For example, listen to the RCA Victor *Hamlet* as read by Laurence Olivier. Note especially Act 3, scene 2. (See project 3, item 2, Chapter 10, for this passage from *Hamlet.*)

METHODS OF IMPROVING PRONUNCIATION

Improving pronunciation is a matter of selecting the proper sounds, putting them together correctly into syllables and words, and uttering these combinations distinctly, giving each syllable the proper stress. Articulation, as we observed earlier in this chapter, forms the basis of pronunciation.

1 ***Use the pronunciations acceptable to the more careful speakers of this country.*** You are familiar with standard American, or with Eastern, Western, or Southern, standards of articulation and pronunciation. Good articulation and pronunciation for any one of these regions is not considered substandard in any other. There are, of course, a great many variations within each region. Extremes of regionalisms in articulation and pronunciation are atypical and sub-

ject to criticism by persons of exacting standards even within the region.

2 ***Reproduce speech sounds accurately.*** There are five common types of pronunciation errors: substitution, addition, omission, inversion, and misplaced accent. Although it is not always possible to place a mispronounced word exclusively in one rather than in another of these classes, the classification serves a practical purpose in understanding and improving pronunciation. Some examples of each class are listed below:

Substitutions

agin for *again*
fer for *for*
bak for *bag*
waz for *was*

Additions

l sound in *calm*
h sound in *forehead*
reminent for *remnant*
g sound in *pang*
acrost for *across*

Omissions

col for *cold*
reconize for *recognize*
dimond for *diamond*
eights for *eighths*
battry for *battery*

Inversions

occifer for *officer*
calvery for *cavalry*
interduce for *introduce*
pervent for *prevent*

Misplaced accent

ad′ult for a · dult′
re′search for *re · search′*
su · per · flu′ous for *su · per′flu · ous*
im · po′tent for *im′po · tent*
fu · tile′ for *fu′tile*

There are a number of reasons for mispronunciations. One is spelling. Words are not always pronounced as their spelling suggests; moreover, spelling provides no clue to accent. Some errors are caused by failure to note changes of pronunciation depending upon the particular linguistic function the word serves. Words are sometimes mispronounced because they are confused with similar words. Other words are mispronounced because of the misarticulation of sounds contained in them. But probably most mispronunciations occur because the words were originally heard mispronounced or because the first pronunciation was a bad guess which initiated the habit of mispronunciation. However, if most well-educated people "mispronounce" a word in a certain way, this pronunciation is almost certain to be accepted in a short time. The dictionaries attempt to follow rather than dictate cultured practice in pronunciation.

3 ***Pronounce each word according to its proper syllabication.*** Avoid omitting syllables. Children say *Ā'rab* for *Ăr'ab,* and some say *ho·mog'e·nous* when they mean *homo·ge'ne·ous.*

4 ***Obtain a good dictionary and check your pronunciation constantly.***

PROJECTS AND PROBLEMS

Project 1 A test of articulation

The following exercise in speech sounds should help you to identify any sounds with which you have difficulty. The sound to be identified and tested is indicated after each number by means of the markings used in Webster. The first word contains the sound in a prominent position. Some of the other words in the list contain the sound, and some do not. Pronounce the words aloud and underline those which contain the sound you are testing. Check the line to the left of the number for all sounds which need further work. Listen to the reading of others to note how they produce these sounds. For a short form of the test, do only the items marked by an asterisk.

___*	1.	ē	feet, fit, date, sat, me, egg, fill, seen
___*	2.	ĭ	dill, deal, it, pit, peat, pet, duck, dick
___*	3.	ĕ	get, git, dale, end, shall, yet, enter, out
___*	4.	ă	pat, pet, as, den, leg, rock, rack, dad
___	5.	ȧ	ago, up, lute, policy, fallen, bath, tuba, toot
___*	6.	ŭ	cud, cod, utter, just, shot, ruck, dude, put

___	7.	ä	far, fur, on, want, had, luck, caught, ah
___	8.	ô	caught, cut, doll, gun, tuck, owl, nod, gone
___	9.	ŏŏ	took, tuck, tune, could, crux, group, drew, wolf
___	10.	ōō	spoon, spew, ooze, whom, luck, shoe, beauty, put
___	11.	ū	few, hue, rue, food, fuel, feel, pew, full, fool
___	12.	ō	coal, cull, oboe, slow, mutton, brow, cod, opus
___*	13.	ou	cowed, kayoes, bough, ton, gun, rot, Crayola, out
___	14.	ā	pain, pen, pun, eight, tell, flay, Iowa, hail
___	15.	ī	like, lick, aisle, race, won, tiger, spy, ice
___	16.	oi	loin, line, bird, fine, toy, murder, voice, tall, oil
___	17.	m	mere, beer, ear, home, bill, robe, mop, summer
___	18.	n	new, drew, under, dole, pew, pan, pants, singing
___*	19.	ng	singing, sinning, rank, ran, rag, rang, ram, tinkle
___*	20.	p	pour, more, whip, paper, cap, bees, robin, slap
___	21.	b	ban, pan, robe, sober, baby, cob, ram
___*	22.	t	Ted, dead, cad, madder, cut, feed, biting, three
___*	23.	d	dote, tote, gad, mat, radio, fated, bat, tin
___	24.	k	cap, gap, bagging, tackle, brig, kill, crew
___	25.	g	gill, kill, rag, bucky, raking, core, fling, age
___*	26.	r	roar, wore, hear, weep, deride, very, bar, weed
___	27.	l	lay, pray, wake, little, camel, seal, sole, asleep
___	28.	f	fly, ply, safe, differs, divers, have, thigh, wife
___	29.	v	vain, bane, fat, proof, leave, unveiling, wail, live
___*	30.	th	thank, tank, they, zinc, swath, sin, anything, bass
___*	31.	~~th~~	thy, vie, thigh, loathe, fat, sign, mother, cloth
___*	32.	s	saw, thaw, miss, shaw, trace, recent, clash, graze
___*	33.	z	zoo, Sioux, boys, vice, lazy, noose, aphasia, place
___*	34.	sh	ship, sip, cheap, mash, explosion, suit, fishing, shoot
___	35.	zh	garage, garish, entourage, rajah, vision, mirage, ocean, cortege
___*	36.	wh	where, wear, vile, while, winter, wheat, witch, white
___*	37.	h	hill, gill, hinge, unhang, hurrah, who, rehash, wheel
___*	38.	w	way, whey, swine, whet, chair, fight, wise, quiet
___	39.	y	yam, lamb, jello, yellow, onion, jeer, set, young
___	40.	ch	cherry, sherry, Jerry, etching, leech, lush, ridge, chum
___	41.	j	gin, chin, just, badge, richer, soldier, magic, pitching

Project 2

Practice the following exercises on sound combinations and prepare to do them individually when called upon.

1. Peter Prangle, the prickly, prangly pear picker, picked three pecks of prickly, prangly pears from the prickly, prangly pear trees on the pleasant prairies.
2. Big black bugs brought buckets of black bear's blood.
3. Pillercatter, tappekiller, kitterpaller, patterkiller, caterpillar.
4. A big black bug bit a big black bear.
5. Better buy the bigger rubber baby buggy bumpers.
6. A tutor who tooted the flute,
   Tried to tutor two tooters to toot.
   Said the two to the tutor, "Is it harder to toot
   Or to tutor two tooters to toot?"
7. Betty Botta bought a bit of butter,
   "But," said she, "this butter's bitter.
   If I put it in my batter
   It will make my batter bitter;
   But a bit of better butter
   Will make my bitter batter better."
   So she bought a bit of butter,
   Better than the bitter butter,
   And it made her bitter batter better.
   So 'twas better Betty Botta
   Bought a bit of better butter.
8. Thomas A. Tattamus took two tees
   To tie two pups to two tall trees,
   To frighten the terrible Thomas A. Tattamus!
   Now do tell me how many tees that is.
9. He was a three-toed tree toad,
   But a two-toed toad was she.
   The three-toed tree toad tried to climb
   The two-toed tree toad's tree.
10. How much wood would a woodchuck chuck if a woodchuck would chuck wood?
11. Sister Susie went to sea to see the sea, you see.
    So the sea she saw, you see, was a saucy sea;
    The sea she saw was a saucy sea.
    A sort of saucy sea saw she.
12. Seven shell-shocked soldiers sawing six slick, slender, slippery, silver saplings.
13. A skunk sat on a stump. The stump said the skunk stunk, and the skunk said the stump stunk.
14. A biscuit, a box of biscuits, a box of mixed biscuits, and a biscuit mixer.

15. Theophilus Thistle, the successful thistle sifter in sifting a sieve full of unsifted thistles, sifted three thousand thistles through the thick of his thumb. See that thou, oh thou unsuccessful thistle sifter, sift not three thousand thistles through the thick of thy thumb.
16. Amidst the mists and musty frosts
    He thrusts his fists against the posts
    And still insists he sees the ghosts.
17. Let the little lean camel lead the lame lamb to the lake.
18. Nine nimble noblemen nibbling nonpareils.

Project 3

Find two to three pages of prose which develop an idea of interest to you. Go over the passage and underline all sounds with which you have difficulty. Practice reading until you can articulate all sounds clearly and acceptably. Read another similar passage to see if you can articulate all sounds effectively without further study of them. Listen to the typically difficult sounds as produced by others in doing this exercise.

Project 4

Turn to Appendix A and study the phonetic symbols until you know them. Your speech will be criticized at times with phonetic symbols; thus you should have a clear understanding of the sounds for which they stand.

REFERENCES

Black, John W., and Wilbur E. Moore: *Speech: Code, Meaning and Communication,* McGraw-Hill Book Company, New York, 1955.

Bronstein, Arthur I., and Beatrice F. Jacoby: *Your Speech and Voice,* Random House, Inc., New York, 1967.

Carrell, James A., and William R. Tiffany: *Phonetics: Theory and Application to Speech Improvement,* McGraw-Hill Book Company, New York, 1960.

Fairbanks, Grant: *Voice and Articulation Drillbook,* Harper and Row, Publishers, Incorporated, New York, 1960.

Grasham, John A., and Glenn G. Gooder: *Improving Your Speech,* Harcourt, Brace & World, Inc., New York, 1960.

Hanley, Theodore D., and Wayne L. Thurman: *Developing Vocal Skills,* Holt, Rinehart and Winston, Inc., New York, 1963.

Kantner, Claude E., and Robert West: *Phonetics*, Harper & Row, Publishers, Incorporated, New York, 1941.

Levy, Louis, Edward W. Mammen, and Robert Sonkin: *Voice and Diction Handbook*, Prentice-Hall, Inc., Englewood Cliffs, N.J., 1950.

Wijk, Axel: *Rules of Pronunciation for the English Language*, Oxford University Press, New York, 1966.

12 BODILY ACTION AS VISUAL COMMUNICATION

In Chapter 1 we stressed the idea that speech is a multisymbolic social process. The symbols of language as they function in speech were discussed in Chapter 9. Chapters 10 and 11 were devoted to the variables of vocal symbols. Our task here is to complete the analysis of the multisymbolic nature of speech by showing that the speaker's visual presence, together with his visible behavior and use of supplementary visual symbolic devices such as charts, diagrams, and models, should be made to contribute to the total representation of his message.

The speaker's physical presence, active or inactive, carries meaning. When he is active, he changes posture, moves his hands and arms, expresses his feelings about his message by his facial responses. He may smile, frown, show deep concern, etc. He may also show lack of confidence, fear, a pose of indignation, or other reactions which give away his innermost feelings. When he is not active, he may be judged as apprehensive, slow, insensitive, indifferent, haughty, or just plain bored. These negative postures and expressions may not be fair or typical, yet strangers may not be sensitive enough or kind enough to overlook these faults. Before a speaker or a stranger in a social situation opens his mouth, others will have been receiving first impressions.

Good speakers also make use of supplementary symbols for messages, which are often called *audio-visual aids.* Even such materials should be a fundamental part of the message system and not just an outside aid.

Signals of your intentions

Effective speaking demands sufficient control of the visual and tonal as well as of the linguistic symbols of your message to make them all suggest the same thing at the same time. Audiences can readily interpret visible expressions of the speaker's attitude.[1] In this respect, the eye appears truly to be quicker, or at least surer, than the ear. When there is a conflict between what is said in language and what is said by action, the action is more readily believed than the words. Consider the expression "Better smile when you say that."

The speaker who is unduly emotional in response does not obtain from his audience adequate consideration of the intellectual content of what he has to say. If your emotional reactions are not appropriate to the situation, you must learn to keep them under control. Physical expressions of dislike and distrust are likely to evoke a negative response from an audience or a vindictive response from a top sergeant or a shop foreman. On the other hand, your audience will respond positively to your expressions of emotional reactions to the socially approved content of your speech.[2]

Emphasizing your meaning

Recent experiments in immediate and delayed memory for facts and principles presented with and without visual aids indicate the superiority of instruction with visual aids.[3] Maps, charts, diagrams, and laboratory demonstrations have long been considered sound educational supplements to the informative lecture. It is not always

[1] Delwin Dusenbury and Franklin H. Knower, "Studies in the Symbolism of Voice and Action," *Quarterly Journal of Speech,* 24:424–436, 1938.

[2] Franklin H. Knower, "The Use of Behavioral and Tonal Symbols as Tests of Speaking Achievement," *Journal of Applied Psychology,* 29:229–235, 1945.

[3] Franklin H. Knower, David Phillips, and Fern Koeppel, "Studies in Listening to Informative Speaking," *Journal of Abnormal and Social Psychology,* 40: 82–88, 1945.

practical or possible to carry about actual pictures of the objects and events. As a substitute for pictures, develop the use of descriptive and suggestive action. Such action is especially helpful in suggesting size, shape, texture, distance, direction, location, movement, speed, weight, and force.

Getting attention

A significant characteristic of attention is that it does not remain focused on one subject for a very long time. The average person's span of attention is short, although it is possible to increase it. The speaker who makes adroit use of action enables his auditors to shift their attention and still follow his discourse. An extreme example of the use of action for controlling attention is provided by the magician. He directs our attention by the use of action in such a manner that other action necessary for performing his tricks goes unnoticed. More common examples of the use of action to direct attention are the salesman's use of paper and pencil, the habit of looking at an object to which we want to attract attention, and movement from one part of the patform to another to mark a transition in ideas. Try looking at your watch while you are speaking and note how many members of the audience do likewise.

Your visible action as a speaker will provide empathic release of the muscle tensions of your audience. The chairs in most halls where formal speeches are made are not designed for the comfort of the audience. For this reason, the members of a seated audience will become restless if the speaker sets a pattern of quiet and inactivity. If, on the other hand, the speaker accompanies his speech with appropriate visible action—especially if he delivers an energetic speech—he provides his audience with a release of tension through the suggestion of action and facilitates their comfort in listening. The same principle applies in some degree, as we have seen, to the speaker; if the speaker accompanies his speech with appropriate action, he releases his own tensions, which may otherwise find an outlet in distractive action. To keep your audience's attention, then, you should consciously develop habits of action which help you in speaking in order that your other habits of action may not handicap you.

CHARACTERISTICS OF EFFECTIVE ACTION

Let your action in speaking show that you are interested in communicating with your audience. Do not look at the ceiling, at the floor, or over the heads of your listeners. If you use a manuscript, read *to* the audience, not from your pages. Make your bodily action purposeful; avoid random activity such as squirming, fidgeting, pacing, fingering your ring, and rolling your handkerchief. Concentrate on your communicative goal and let your total bodily activity be controlled by this purpose. Deliver your speech with the physical liveliness that your theme demands.

Are you successful in using bodily activity in speech? Through study, you can improve in effective use of expressive action. Do not expect your action to be completely effective in the learning stages. The principal agencies of expression are the head and face, shoulders, arms, hands and fingers, torso, legs, and feet. Most expressive action involves a high degree of integration of parts of the body acting as a whole to produce positions, expressive lines, and patterns of movement.

Every character actor knows that the manner of standing or walking, the position of the shoulders, the placement and movements of the hands, the tilt of the head, and the expressive lines of the mouth and eyes suggest variations in physical conditions, moods, character, and personality types. Position and expressive lines are not so uniformly interpreted as are moving patterns of physical expression. This fact appears to indicate that the most effective form of physical expression is a pattern of action in which location, form, line, and movement are well coordinated in at least a brief, continuing series of actions.

Timing. An important aspect of adaptive action is timing. Effective action should precede by an instant the accompanying words and tone of voice expressing the idea. If the action either occurs at the same time or follows the verbal expression of the idea, the effect is ludicrous.

Audience adaptation. Consider the composition of your audience in connection with your visible action. If your listeners are primarily white-collar workers who lead a sedentary life, they will not be sympathetic to an overactive speaker. If they are persons who do and like physical work, the speech unaccompanied by energetic expression will not challenge them. Action in reading is less important than action in speaking; it should be suggestive only. Action used in informal speaking is more varied, more highly personalized, and less reserved than action appropriate to formal occasions. Action for large groups is ordinarily more formal than for small groups; it should be simple and slow but energetic.

Posture. Good posture allows the speaker to use freely his arms, hands, eyes, and other organs and muscles. In addition, posture itself conveys meaning.

We cannot formulate precise rules as to what posture is best. Your posture should express self-control, energy, and friendliness toward your audience. Effective bodily action and physical poise are the result of experience in speaking more than of special exercises or movements carefully rehearsed for a given speech. You will need the advice of your instructor and classmates on your individual case.

Purposefulness of movement. When you go to the front of the room or to the platform to address the group, walk with decision but without militancy. When you turn to face the group, do not make an awkward sweep; if you have a speaker's stand before you, do not fall upon it, entwining your legs wearily behind it. If, after you have talked for a few minutes, you wish to change your position, you may do so with such spontaneity that your listeners will not consciously observe it.

Immobility kills speech as surely as excessive movement. No set rules can be made concerning the amount and kind of movement, for both must be determined by the temperament and cultural habits of the speaker, by the character, size, and physical surroundings of the audience, by the subject, and by the occasion.

Appropriateness of gesture. Gesture usually refers to movements of hands, arms, shoulders, head, and eyes, as opposed to general bodily movements. The effective speaker keeps his arms relaxed and available to interpret his ideas. When the impulse comes, he will gesture appropriately. (See projects 1, 2, and 3 at the end of this chapter.)

Directness of eye contact. As we have observed, many speakers find it difficult to look directly at members of the audiences. Aside from the psychological value to your audience of direct eye contact, its principal value is that it enables you to observe and adjust to the responses of your listeners. Speaking involves reciprocal social stimulation. If you are to be an effective speaker, you must be sensitive and adjust to the feedback of your audience.

Developing effective habits of physical action is first of all a matter of recognizing the need for and the values of this aspect of speechmaking. Study the performances of other speakers and observe when their visible action is effective and when it is weak. Then follow this procedure:

1. Analyze your own performance to discover your problems. Study the principles and criteria of effective action.

2. Develop goals for your own achievement. With the help of your instructor and classmates, decide in what directions you should move to improve your physical activity in speechmaking. Give particular attention to this aspect of speech preparation.

3. Develop control over specific patterns of tension and relaxation in the muscles of the face, neck, hands, back, and legs. Learn to control and vary the release of energies. Practice characterization and the simulated expression of feelings and emotions.

4. Concentrate in speaking on putting across your full meaning through the use of all the agencies at your command. Develop conscious actions in study and practice in order to make action an unconscious habit when you speak.

5. Practice action particularly in those types of speech activity where action is easy to use—in demonstration or visual-aids speeches with sample objects, drawings, and maps; in routine patterns of action involved in the performance of some activity; in storytelling; and in speeches expressing strong conviction. Work on the types of action with which you as a person have most difficulty, as well as on those which you find relatively easy. Finally, be patient.

VISUAL AIDS

Our general remarks on the importance of visible action in speechmaking apply with equal force to visual aids. Here we can suggest only a few of the types of visual aids.

Types

Organization charts consist of labeled boxes or squares and connecting lines. Such charts are used to show the relationships of various parts of a company. They are also used to model the relationships of parts of complex ideas such as communication. Sketches or maps are useful where one must be exact in portraying detail. Diagrams and cartoons are useful where specific points must be exaggerated for emphasis. The bar graph serves for quantitative comparisons. If there are few comparisons, place the bars vertically; if there are many comparisons, place them horizontally. Scale comparisons accurately on the margin of the chart and space them evenly. Use a "pie" diagram for percentage comparisons, a line graph for trends. Label axes clearly in bar and line graphs, and draw line graphs on a graphed or squared surface. Use contrasting colors for comparison in bar and pie graphs and in line graphs when more than one line is used. The pictograph is sometimes more realistic in suggestive comparisons; it must be clearly labeled to reveal the quantities involved. Flash cards or charts from which the covering is quickly removed are useful for lists of words or phrases to be emphasized and for brief outlines of ideas.

Slides, filmstrips, and motion pictures are tools for showing visual aids. Phonograph records which serve as supplements to a speech have some of the characteristics of visual aids, although they are directed to the ear. Whenever you can do so, give preference to supplementary visual aids that appeal to more than one of the sense organs.

In selecting your visual aids, consider all the practical possibilities. Physical models should be small and easily handled. If you use descriptive action, it may be better to have another person demonstrate while you talk.

Making visual aids

It is not necessary to be an artist to make useful visual aids. Keep them simple and large enough to be easily seen by the audience. Experiment with various ways of representing the idea in visual form. If you are to draw diagrams during your talk, practice making them as you rehearse the speech. On a white background, use black or red for major comparisons; on a black background, use yellow or green. Use contrasting colors for emphasis; indicate relationships by lines and arrows. Number the steps to be observed in a diagram or the action pattern of a process in sequence. Keep points which are to be compared close together. Print titles and legends simply and clearly with block or capital letters and underline words which are to be emphasized. Avoid material and locations which will produce glare. Plan an appropriate setting and prepare an adequate place to show or hang cards, charts, or diagrams. Some objects may be distorted for emphasis if the visual aid is only suggestive, as in the cartoon. Sometimes humor can be used to advantage.

Using visual aids

When using visual aids for instruction, avoid staging a show. The materials should be kept as an aid to the speaker. The speaker still must do most of the communicating. Visual aids can be so overdone that they become obtrusive and call attention to themselves rather than the idea.

Stand behind or to one side of a chart. If you are left-handed, stand to the left; if you are right-handed, stand to the right. Use the nearest hand for a pointer. Watch the audience as much as possible. Cover or erase charts when not in use if they distract attention. Time their presentation in the speech as a whole. Use them for introduction, emphasis, or climax. Pass objects to the audience only when you have a sufficient number for all members to look simultaneously at the points to which you wish to call attention.

When visual aids constitute a large portion of a talk, they should be properly introduced. Prepare the audience for what they are to see. Describe points of emphasis carefully when the visual aid is shown. Draw inferences or conclusions and summarize. Permit questions from the audience in order to clear up any points of ambiguity. (See project 4 at the end of this chapter.)

PROJECTS AND PROBLEMS

Project 1

Make a collection of samples of visual communication and explain them. See how many types of charts, graphs, models, etc., you can collect for your demonstration and explanation.

Project 2 Expressing the mood of an experience

Briefly discuss three different experiences you have had in which you recall definite sensory or emotional reaction. Use such experiences as biting into a sour apple, observing the countryside in the fall, having the dentist fill a tooth, getting your first view of some natural wonder, observing the scene of a historical event, or viewing some feat or tragedy. Let your physical reactions to the idea be spontaneous and direct. Try to project them so that the audience may understand how you felt.

Project 3 A pantomimic characterization

Observe the actions of someone you might describe as a character type. Present a two-minute pantomime of the behavior of this person, working out as much specific action or "business" as you can. Have the class report their interpretation of the type of individual you have characterized and criticize the performance for adequacy and consistency.

Project 4 Studies in the use of visible action

Purposes of this assignment: (1) To develop a better understanding of standards and achievements in the use of action and (2) to develop skill in the use of expressive action.
Procedure: Select a subject and outline what you are to say. Anticipate and plan the general pattern of action you will use. Put yourself into the spirit of your ideas and respond as you concentrate on their expression.
Subjects for this speech:

1. An interesting character (in life or fiction)
2. Some examples of expressive action I have observed
3. This is the way it happened
4. This is how it is done
5. A circus barker or auctioneer's "spiel"
6. Formal and informal action adjustments

Project 5 The use of visual aids

Purposes of this assignment: (1) To learn to use visual aids in speaking, (2) to develop freedom of bodily action and responsiveness to material, and (3) to improve confidence in speaking.
Procedure: Select a topic and organize your information. If you are to draw a diagram, plan the essential features of the drawing. Complex and difficult diagrams should be prepared in advance.
Subjects for this speech:

1. Tracing the relationships of parts of a system
2. Performance of a play, game, or other act of skill
3. The construction of an object
4. The operation of a tool, instrument, or machine

REFERENCES

Brown, James W., Richard B. Lewis, and Fred F. Harcleroad: *A–V Instruction: Materials and Methods*, 2d ed., McGraw-Hill Book Company, New York, 1964.

DeCecco, John P.: *Educational Technology*, Holt, Rinehart and Winston, Inc., New York, 1964.

Institute for Communication Research: *New Teaching Aids for the American Classroom*, Stanford, Calif., 1960.

Harrell, John: *Teaching Is Communicating*, The Seabury Press, New York, 1965.

Kemp, Jerrold E.: *Planning and Producing Audio-visual Materials,* Chandler Publishing Co., San Francisco, 1963.

Kinder, James S.: *Using Audio-visual Materials in Education,* American Book Company, New York, 1965.

Turnbull, Arthur T., and Russell N. Baird: *The Graphics of Communication,* Holt, Rinehart and Winston, Inc., New York, 1964.

TYPES AND SITUATIONS

13 INFORMATIVE SPEAKING

Information is a unique commodity. Sharing it does not reduce the donor's supply as it does with apples, cigarettes, or sugar. Indeed the sharing of information increases the world's supply in proportion to the number of people with whom it is shared.

The world's information is growing at a tremendous rate today. This situation has led to a need for new concepts of information and new systems of analyzing, indexing, and storing of information. We need to know more today about the nature of information in order to cope with the old as well as the newer concepts of the field.

When we speak to inform we analyze and define and sometimes we illustrate, often using examples and analogies. We use various symbol systems such as a tape recording, chart, graph, diagram, or scale model to clarify some idea we want our listeners to understand. We may want to show that some event has a probable cause or that it is a cause which may produce some effect. We trace historical backgrounds, assemble facts for a report, or make critical interpretations so that others may gain clearer insights. If we are to speak effectively, we ought to learn as much as we can about informative speaking.

YOUR INFORMATIVE PURPOSE

Your obvious purpose is to help your listeners achieve a better or deeper understanding of a subject. To do this you must know that understanding is not usually an all-or-none matter. It typically exists in various levels. The simplest levels involve some brief experience, sketchy or poorly conceived explanation, or partial vocabulary of the subject. Somewhat greater understanding is shown by the achievement of a description or analysis of some of the subject's main features. The evaluation of a subject in terms not only of its parts but also of its processes, the understanding of what makes them work or fail to work, and of what effects may have been the result of what causes call for a still deeper explanatory level of insight. Perhaps the deepest of all levels of understanding is the level that enables one to be creative. To be creative one must not only know what is, but have some notions as to what might be. Thorndike has said that "the creative mind is the well informed mind." Each of these links has called for more and more bits of information. Deeper levels of information consist not only of more and more isolated facts and principles but also of more and more interrelations of facts, principles, and processes, in short, not only more information but more complex information.

In your informative speaking you will no doubt have occasion to perform at each of these levels. It is important that you learn to adjust the level of your informative speaking to the needs and expectations of your listeners. If you speak at too simple a level, you will bore your listeners with what they already know. If you make the assumption that they already know more than they do and try to go on from there, you will be talking over their heads. They may be polite, or not want to admit that they don't understand, but you will not add to their information if they cannot understand what you are saying to them.

You may get some cues about the nature of informative communication from learning theory and from education. How do we learn? Certainly there is no learning without motivation. Some of your listeners will probably be motivated or they would not come to hear you. But even with a captive audience, don't assume that everyone will be adequately motivated. To achieve much as a learner, one must want to learn. You may help some of your listeners by relating your subject not only to their understanding but also to their wants and needs. The stimulation of interests, organization of learning for active involvement in the process, dramatization for vividness, the rewarding of progress in the learning effort all tend to motivate the learning of information.

Effective learning of ideas as well as skills calls for a clear and precise wording of objectives. To state these objectives clearly involves definitions and analysis which breaks a larger set of ideas into smaller parts which can be learned piecemeal. Statements of principles and abstractions are explained by breaking them down into more and more specific and concrete levels until we reach the level of specificity which we can understand. Statements of abstractions and principles will enable your listeners to see relationships between details not manifest in the narrower wording. Restatement and the use of supplementary forms of statement such as aural and visual presentations increase the probability that ideas will be clearer.

The organization of the sequence of ideas has been shown in programmed instruction to be particularly important. Organization also achieves clarity and emphasis by appropriate simplification and amplification where needed. One way to simplify is to use examples, metaphors, and analogies. When we say that words as symbols are like money which has changing values depending on a variety of social and economic conditions, or indeed may be counterfeit and turn out to have no value whatsoever, we begin to get some understanding of the concepts of the symbol.

METHODS OF DEVELOPING THE INFORMATIVE SPEECH

The methods for effective informative speaking are those applicable to other types of communication. They are the supporting details amplified in Chapter 6. These specific modes of development are selected and incorporated in your speech not primarily to entertain, impress, convince, and persuade but to increase the knowledge of the audience. Some of these representative methods are commented on below.

The method of definition

Definition or explanation may comprise the entire speech—certainly at least those sections that deal with terms important for a clear understanding of what follows.

Excellent addresses have been given on such subjects as "What is a Republican in 1968?" "What is private enterprise?" "What is speech?" "What is a typical Bostonian?" "What is inflation?" In each case the aim is to make clear the term or terms; to increase the listener's knowledge rather than to stress argumentative or persuasive purposes and methods.[1]

[1] For further comment on development by definition, see Chap. 6.

The method of analysis and classification

In analytical speeches, the topic is divided into parts, to be treated as minor wholes or units. These units must be small enough to permit the listener to see them as separate parts of the whole. Since analysis is principally the process of dividing and classifying the material used in the development of a subject, the principles which apply to the methods of developing a subject discussed in Chapter 6 apply here to analysis. We analyze a subject to discover its elements. We classify these elements to make them easier to understand.

Principles for logical division and classification. Remember and follow these four principles for the logical division and classification of the data of your informative speech: (1) The units as a group should treat the subject comprehensively. Since it is obviously difficult in a short speech to cover the entire subject, your problem is to select the aspects for treatment most important to you and your audience. (2) The units should not overlap. (3) The units should be classified and developed on the basis of a single principle or point of view for all units. For example, it would be illogical to classify under "citizens of Middletown" such groups as Republicans, engineers, and husbands, because a different principle is illustrated by each of these three nonparallel categories. We might logically arrange the classifications as Republicans, Democrats, and Independents; or as engineers, doctors, and lawyers; or as husbands, bachelors, and widowers. (4) These classified items should be arranged in some suitable order for ready comprehension, such as size, sequence of events, cause and effect, functions of parts, or types; for example, the classification of music as vocal and instrumental; or of the instruments used in an orchestra as string, woodwind, brass, and percussion.

Note the classification of speech processes in Chapter 1. These processes are ideas, organization, language, voice, articulation, bodily activity, and the speaking personality. They cover the subject comprehensively, avoid undue overlapping, follow one principle for all units (that of a single view of communication), and arrange the units in a suitable order for consideration—in this case proceeding from ideas to organization, to formulation in language, to their expression through the communication act of voice, articulation, and bodily activity.

Other principles might apply in classifying the data of another topic, since topical classification of data is developed to fit the needs of the particular subject and speech purposes.

The method of illustration, example, and analogy

In informative speaking, examples serve many purposes. They clarify principles, general statements of conditions or trends, and types of classifications. Since ordinary conversation deals primarily with particulars, and few people develop the mental habits necessary for following abstract thinking, general and abstract statements should be illustrated abundantly. Examples serve to epitomize, crystallize, and concretize meaning. Specific examples have the dramatic and human-interest qualities of events, characters, and novelty. They arouse the curiosity of listeners; once listeners have heard the beginning, they are interested in following the speaker's story to its conclusion.

Many types of examples are used for informative purposes, such as general and specific illustrations. The speaker who is discussing cooperation, for example, may offer socialism as a general illustration of cooperation. If he goes on to say that publicly owned and operated utilities are socialistic, he is offering a general illustration of the operation of socialism. But if he discusses *the* publicly owned waterworks or *the* municipally owned light plant, in a particular town, he is providing not general illustrations but specific instances.

Hypothetical illustrations ordinarily begin with a phrase such as, "Suppose we had a case . . . ," or "Imagine a situation in which. . . ." Some real examples should be given fictitious elements to make them more typical, to disguise them, or to protect personalities.

Examples should fit the subject under discussion. When they are not to the point, they confuse rather than clarify. Examples should suit the audience in terms of its interest, experience, and the level of complexity of which it is capable. Examples from a common area of experience are ordinarily better than those selected from the experiences of the few. Well-known cases may be referred to briefly; unfamiliar ones should be elaborated. In one of Churchill's speeches, a brief reference to the Battle of Gettysburg was as effective as a detailed recounting of another battle would have been.

The more fitting the story, the less the speaker needs to say about its application to the subject. Elaborate pointing of the moral may spoil the story's effectiveness. Although the details of the example should be vivid, they should not be so spectacular that the story overshadows the point.

The method of tracing causal relationships

Often an informative speech will consist of tracing causes and effects. A significant event (or events) may be reported with an attempt to explain the background movements or facts that produce the situation. Or a past event may be described with careful citation of the chain of succeeding events. A lecture may deal with the causes of the Korean War or with an explanation of events prior to the international conferences of 1959. Speakers with such topics need to be doubly careful to keep within the informative pattern and to resist a tendency to establish decisive conclusions that reflect an argumentative or persuasive purpose.[2]

The use of visual aids

The use of television instruction has recently given renewed emphasis to techniques in informative speaking with visual aids. Not many of us will use television in our informative speaking, but all of us will have occasion to use objects, activities, and pictures in speaking. The materials for visual instruction are cartoons, maps, objects and working models, samples, demonstrative action by the speaker, and pictures, diagrams, and graphs drawn on cardboard or the blackboard or projected on a screen. Using such materials effectively lends clarity, attracts the attention of the audience, and maintains its interest. The materials also provide the speaker with an opportunity to use action in his speech.

TYPES OF INFORMATIVE SPEAKING

The representative types of informational speaking include the speech of operation, the report, the historical exposition, and the critical interpretation.

The informative speech of operation

The operations speech is designed to give precise directions on how to perform an action or carry out a process. Examples of this type of speech are directions for operating a computer, preparing a dish, cutting a linoleum block, or casting a fly. If your listeners are not familiar with the activity, it may be necessary to create interest in the process. Define any terms with which your listeners are not familiar. Describe objects to be used, explain their functions, and give directions for use. Compare and contrast objects and steps with similar materials and processes that are familiar.

Explain the steps in the order in which they are to be carried out.

[2] For further comment on the use of causal materials and reasoning, see Chap. 8, "Inference by Causation," and Chap. 15, "Argument from Causality."

Make the significance of each step clear as you proceed. Demonstrate as well as describe the action. Sometimes the listeners can carry out the action along with you—for example, the flip of the wrist in fly casting or the steps of a dance. Observe and correct the mistakes they make. Indicate acceptable variations in procedure. Anticipate difficulties and explain how they can be overcome. Present a clear picture or description of expected results.

The report speech

Classes, clubs, committees, community organizations, and business and professional groups often require reports. Furthermore, abbreviated reports of various kinds occur frequently in conversation, interviews, and other small-group, face-to-face situations, as well as in larger or more formal meetings. Consider the answers to such questions as: What did the speaker have to say? What is that book like? Did you have a good trip? What happened? These questions present occasions for report making, and the principles which apply to the formal report also apply to the answers to such questions.

Purpose. The primary aim of the report is to communicate information. Reports may or may not be supplemented by recommendations, although reports by experts or authorities may consist largely of recommendations. Even these reports, however, are based on information which should be presented if requested.

Types. Reports may be roughly classified into the experience report, the fact-finding report, the report of progress and achievement, and the summary report. Examples of reports are the radio news review, reports of committees to parent organizations reviewing their activities, and personal-experience reports.

In reporting on a personal experience, your first step is to orient the listeners. Describe the time, the place, and the situation. Focus attention on essential features of events as they occur in sequence, and interpret these events in terms of experiences meaningful to listeners. The explanation of personal reactions is as important in the experience report as the events themselves. The purpose for which the experience report is made determines what aspects of the report will be given major emphasis.

In presenting a book report, identify the book you are reviewing. Discuss the author and his apparent motivation for this particular work; reading the preface may be helpful. Classify the book as to specific type within its major classification. Describe the contents.

If it is a novel, give the time and setting of the story; discuss the characters, plot, events, points of highest interest, and what happens in the end. Works of nonfiction should be described in terms of the general subjects, the thesis or central idea, the main points (which may be sections and chapters), and the important details. The reviewer ordinarily reads extensively from a novel. Read exceptionally interesting passages for purposes of illustration. Evaluate the book as a whole and in terms of favorable and unfavorable features. Discuss its form if it has unusual features.

Fact-finding reports may be exploratory or systematic. The exploratory report is ordinarily made during the early period of fact-finding and is intended to determine the desirability of various methods and characteristics of the investigation. It is admittedly tentative. The facts may be sought by observation, experimentation, normative survey, or the study of documents. The form of fact-finding reports will be influenced by the method of securing data.

In presenting a fact-finding report that reviews and compares ideas (exploratory), enumerate the main ideas as they are presented, analyzing, defining, and exemplifying them. Interpretations should present qualifications, limitations, and conclusions. In the research report (systematic), state the immediate cause for the report—the persistence and importance of the problem, the points of view to be integrated, the new contribution to the subject. Sketch briefly the history and background of the topic and the general objective and the specific limitations of the study to be undertaken. Set forth specific objectives. Present the data under some well-considered plan of classification. Indicate the sources of data as you proceed. Summarize the data and evaluate the results of the study.

Reports of progress may be presented at various stages of their preparation. The preliminary report is largely confined to plans and limited data. A more complete progress report is concerned with broader data, tentative conclusions, and further plans. The achievement report is based on extensive data, comprehensive treatment, and interpretations or recommendations. There is some overlapping of major types of reports in the actual practice of presenting them; that is, many reports summarize available data, present new data uncovered by investigation, and are completed by critical evaluation and recommendations. They may become argumentative and so lose their character as informative presentation.

If an oral report is detailed and extensive, it is wise to provide a copy for each member of your audience. The most common practice in the oral presentation of reports is to point out features of special significance and to summarize orally the data presented in writing.

Principles. The materials of the report should be carefully organized. Main points should be clearly stated and summarized. Statistical data should be presented visually as well as orally. Use transitional statements to indicate definitely when you finish one idea and go on to the next one.

Do not make a fetish of completeness in reports, for it can lead to unnecessary detail, confusion, and waste of time. Include the most important materials which can be presented in the allotted time. If your listeners want more information on certain features of the report, they may request it.

The report should be adapted to the amount of knowledge the listeners already have on the subject. A report by one member of a profession to colleagues may be based on a presumption of certain knowledge which amateurs would not possess.

Critical interpretation of the material of the report is one of its most difficult features. Among the procedures which may be followed in interpretation are generalizing upon the data; stating the recognized limitations of the data; determining the values, implications, and applications of the data; making comparisons and contrasts with previously accepted facts; correlating findings with objectives; and finally, presenting the essential meaning and significance of the data. Remember that negative findings as well as positive findings are a legitimate outcome of research. If an investigation of telepathy, for instance, produced no evidence of the existence of this phenomenon, the investigator must so state this.

The speech of historical exposition

Our concept of history should be broad enough to include the story of the development of any subject worthy of our attention. Historical exposition is used primarily to throw light on the background of a subject. The method is well exemplified in the doctor's tracing the symptoms of his patient's illness. The account should be accurate and interesting, but it must also be brief, designed primarily to impart information rather than to entertain, and adapted to the purpose of a particular speaking situation. Some successful student speeches which included explanation by historical narrative concerned the development of jet aircraft, the history of hybrid corn, changes in the game of basketball, and the background of communism. This form of exposition has some of the characteristics of the extended example.

In preparing historical exposition, original sources are more reliable than secondary sources. Moreover, there should be sufficient data on consecutive events to provide a continuous narrative of significant changes or developments. The material should be arranged in sequence. As the exposition proceeds, sources should be identified by author, publication, and date. Questionable facts should be corroborated by two or more sources. The data should be summarized and the significance of the subject clarified.

Among the qualities to be achieved in methods of delivery are enthusiasm for and interest in the story, effective dramatization and projection, and a conversational tone.

The critical interpretation

This type of speech activity may appear to the reader to be argumentative rather than informative. Since criticism on an intellectual rather than an emotional level is the essence of teaching, however, it is considered here as a type of informative speaking. Criticism in this sense is the interpretation of a product or process in terms of acceptable standards of achievement. If the listener does not accept the standard or the interpretation, and if differences of opinion develop on the subject and its evaluation, then the exposition passes over into the field of argument. If both speaker and listener agree during the process of instruction on the purpose of the act performed, the standard to be applied, and the application of the standard to the act, then critical interpretation is identical with informative speaking.

The steps to be made in a critical interpretation include the accumulation of information on the production to be evaluated, the presentation of that information, and the application of appropriate standards in interpreting the data. A simple statement of like or dislike is criticism on an emotional rather than an intellectual basis. If the critic is not known to his listeners, he may well base his criticism upon an explanation of the amateur or professional capacity in which he serves.

Criticism should take into account the specific purpose of the activity. A piece of work performed for one purpose should not be criticized for failing to accomplish another. Adapt criticism of speech or writing to the personality and background of the performer. Remember that criticism should not be personal, smug, or malicious but objective in content and attitude. Do not elaborate the obvious or dwell upon minor slips or petty flaws. Exercise judgment in arriving at a fair interpretation of the work as a whole, remembering that the critic must accept responsibility for his criticism. Your status as a critic does not grant you license to be irresponsible.

Combinations of types and methods in informative speaking

As you study the types of informative speeches, remember that they can be combined in a variety of ways. It may have occurred to you that discussion is also a type of informative speaking. The techniques of sharing information in discussion are presented in Chapter 14.

PROJECTS AND PROBLEMS

Project 1 Analysis, classification, and definition

Purposes of this assignment: Occasionally we find it necessary to use words and ideas which are new or which may mean different things to different people. This assignment should help you explain your ideas through analysis, classification, and definition.
Procedure: Study the principles of informative speaking presented in this chapter. Select a topic for an instructional speech in which you can apply these principles. Prepare a five- to six-minute speech and deliver it to the class.
Subjects for this speech:

General de Gaulle
The nature of meaning
Automobile safety
The American image abroad
The Four Freedoms
Revolt in the colleges
The idea of human rights
Drug addiction
The city of tomorrow
The skyscraper
Conservation of natural resources
The world's major minerals
The new plastics
Milestones in the development of democracy

Project 2 Illustration, example, and analogy

Purposes of this assignment: Informative speaking often involves the consideration of general ideas, principles, and abstractions. We use examples and analogies to get the audience's attention, keep their interest, crystallize abstractions, demonstrate the working of principles, and facilitate memory for facts.
Procedure: Read the discussion on use of examples in speaking in this chapter. Select a topic which can be effectively developed by use of examples. Use general illustrations, specific examples, and analogies in developing the material. Outline the speech and prepare to present it to the class. Make it a point to present your material in an instructional rather than an argumentative mood.

Subjects for this speech:

- Government sensitivity to the needs of people
- Decentralization in a big industry
- A military holding operation
- Black power
- Changes in the television commercial

Project 3 Tracing causal relationships

Purposes of this assignment: Explanations often begin with the word *because*. This assignment should help you to improve your causal explanations.

Procedure: Read the discussion of informative speaking in this chapter. Select a subject appropriate for this assignment. Assemble and outline material and present it to the class.

Subjects for this speech:

- Communication satellites
- Automation
- Causes of juvenile delinquency
- The stock market today
- Subsidized air transportation
- Effects of the Versailles Treaty
- The values of education
- The significance of free enterprise in the United States
- The new Africa
- The effects of bureaucratic government
- Words are weapons
- Why we behave like human beings
- The failure of the League of Nations
- Self-determination of people

Project 4 Using visual aids

Purposes of this assignment: To develop skill in using visual aids in expository speaking.

Procedure: Read the discussion of informative speaking presented in the chapter. Select a topic and assemble materials for a five-minute speech. Be sure you have provided visual-aid materials.

Subjects for this speech:

- Regrouping of genes in cell division
- The operation of an oil-burning turbine
- Sighting a new rifle
- Newton's laws of motion
- The atomic structure of a chemical compound
- Communication satellites
- Climate and air circulation
- Jujitsu
- First-aid bandages
- The operation of a mechanical corn picker
- Landscape designing
- The city-manager plan of government

Project 5 Performance of a process

Purposes of this assignment: To improve your skill in making a speech that directs others in the specific operations required in carrying through some process.
Procedure: Read the section of this chapter entitled "The use of visual aids." Prepare a five-minute speech with visual aids and present it to your classmates.
Subjects for this speech:

Achieving communication
Preparing a speech
How to study
Making a steel casting
The peacetime uses of radar
Programming a computer
Artificial respiration
Making a blueprint
Using the library
Fly casting
A political convention
How to float on the water

Project 6 The informal report or review of ideas

Purposes of this assignment: Can you briefly review the early discussions of a group for a latecomer? This project is designed to improve your achievement in this kind of reporting.
Procedure: The members of the group sit informally in comfortable positions. The group chairman appoints a critic to evaluate performances when all have taken turns.
Subjects for this project:

Public-opinion polling
How glass is made
How a picture is painted
Communication models
The contents of an article I have recently read
My recollections of London

Project 7 The research or fact-finding report

Purposes of this assignment: This is the kind of formal report which anyone may be expected to make many times during his life. Experience with this project should help you in collecting, interpreting, and presenting the data of such reports.
Procedure: Read the discussion on reporting the research project in this chapter. Select a topic and specific purpose for making the report. Gather and organize material. Prepare and present the report to your associates.

Subjects for this project:

Corporate organization	Creativity
Cooperatives	The psychology of perception
Industrial morale	Buddhism
The manufacture of artificial rubber	Art as literature
The struggle for freedom of the press	Social security measures
	Leadership
	Sales taxes

Project 8 The historical exposition

Purposes of this assignment: The historical narrative informs and explains by presenting the background and development of a principle, institution, or object. Such subjects are appropriate for learning to use the historical narrative in informative speaking.
Procedure: Study the principles of the historical narrative in informative speaking. Select a topic for a historical narrative in which you can apply these principles. Prepare a ten-minute speech and deliver it to your associates. Have them rate your speech on a scale. Then conduct a discussion of the content and presentation of this speech.
Subjects for this assignment

The atomic submarine	The production of quinine
The fight against yellow fever	The electron microscope
Group medicine	The space telescope
The study of communication	The liberal arts college idea
Pop art	Mass media
The rise of Hitler	Democratic government
Hybrids in agriculture	The practice of dentistry

Project 9 Critical exposition and reviewing

Purposes of this assignment: To develop skill in critical exposition and to learn the nonargumentative methods of criticism. Whereas argument expresses a conviction for or against a point, criticism selects a standard and relates the point to it.
Procedure: Read the section of this chapter which discusses critical exposition. Select your subject and determine the standards you will use in the criticism. Formulate the judgment you will expound. Prepare and present the speech to meet the criteria of good criticism.

Subjects for this assignment:

- Pan-Americanism
- The agriculture of India
- The playing of bridge
- The food of Cairo
- The statuary of Italy
- The business practices of chain stores
- Academic freedom
- Communist countries
- The government in business
- The policies of Senator Fulbright
- The music of Cab Calloway
- A university play
- The turbine engine for automobiles
- Psycholinguistics

REFERENCES

Anderson, Richard C., and David P. Ausubel: *Readings in the Psychology of Cognition,* Holt, Rinehart and Winston, Inc., New York, 1966.

Bloom, Benjamin S. (ed.): *Taxonomy of Educational Objectives: Cognitive Domain,* Longmans, Green & Co., Inc., New York, 1956.

Braithwaite, R. B.: *Scientific Explanation;* Cambridge University Press, Cambridge, England, 1953.

Chisholm, Roderick: *Theory of Knowledge,* Prentice-Hall, Inc., Englewood Cliffs, N.J., 1966.

Creelman, Marjorie B.: *The Experimental Investigation of Meaning,* Springer Publishing Co., New York, 1966.

Deese, James: *The Structure of Association in Language and Thought,* The Johns Hopkins Press, Baltimore, 1965.

Galenter, Eugene (ed.): *Automatic Teaching,* John Wiley & Sons, Inc., New York, 1959.

Henry, Nelson B.: *The Measurement of Understanding, The Forty-fifth Yearbook of the National Society for the Study of Education,* The University of Chicago Press, Chicago, 1946, part I.

Lewis, C. I.: *An Analysis of Knowledge and Valuation,* Open Court, LaSalle, Ill., 1947.

Morris, Charles: *Signification and Significance,* The M. I. T. Press, Cambridge, Mass., 1964.

Smith, Donald K.: "Teaching Speech to Facilitate Understanding," *The Speech Teacher,* 11:91–100, 1962.

14
DISCUSSIONAL SPEAKING

WHAT IS DISCUSSION?

Discussion is not mere talking; rather it is directed interpersonal communication to solve problems relating to information, value judgments, or practical policy. Important as good conversation is in promoting good fellowship and exchanging ideas, it is usually not discussion. Nor is it debate or authoritative pronouncements. The arguer theoretically has his mind made up before he begins, and his aim is to persuade others to accept and to follow his beliefs.

Discussion, according to Horace Rahskopf, is an "orderly process of cooperative deliberation designed to exchange, evaluate, and/or integrate knowledge and opinion on a given subject or to work toward solution of a common problem." [1]

Though this explanation is complicated, it does suggest the chief characteristics of discussion. There are four inherent characteristics:

[1] Horace Rahskopf, *Basic Speech Improvement*, Harper & Row, Publishers, Incorporated, New York, 1965, p. 348.

1 The purpose of discussion is to deal with a problematic situation

As distinct from narration or other entertainment, discussion deals with questions that concern people and those issues about which they have not made up their minds. This perplexing situation may be that of fact, of value opinion, or of policy determination. A question of fact may be, "Does the surface of the moon permit the landing of earth-manned vehicles?" If sufficient evidence is assembled and evaluated, the problem may be decided for those who raise it. The aim is to supply knowledge.

A further problem for discussion has to do with value judgments. Here conclusions concern chiefly theoretical or even speculative positions. For example, the problem may be, "Is a policy of complete equality in housing in the United States desirable?"

A third type of topic deals with problems that lead to policy decisions. What specific program should deal with the disturbing situation? For example, "Should my city have more one-way streets?" "At my university should the undergraduate tuition be increased 50 dollars for the nine-month period?" "Should the United States cease bombing North Vietnam (a current problem in 1968)?"

Whatever the type of question, the procedure is the same. The discussants caucus to determine the problem, describe terms and issues, collect, examine, and evaluate the facts, analyze causes and tentative solutions, and arrive at some conclusion that reflects the group thinking and expression. Although added knowledge and learning are an important application of the process, the goal often aimed at is action.

2 Discussion is primarily a group activity

Discussion requires the association of several minds in thinking and acting. The assumption is that group judgments are superior to those of any one individual, because these decisions are enlightened by the thinking of several individuals, each with his experience. What discussion accomplishes as a unit rather than what some brilliant individual contributes is theoretically the measure of its success.[2]

[2] Robert L. Thorndike, "The Effect of Discussion upon the Correctness of Group Decisions When the Factor of Majority Influence Is Allowed For," *Journal of Social Psychology*, 9:343–362, August, 1938; see J. F. Dashiell, "The Effect of Group Discussion on the Individual's Work," in Carl Murchison (ed.), *A Handbook of Social Psychology*, Clark University Press, Worcester, Mass., 1935, pp. 1125–1140.

Obviously much depends on the size of the group and its homogeneity. If the numbers are large, less united individual and group thinking may result. If the composition of the participants represents widely different experiences, training, and cultures, the outcomes may be less satisfactory.

Research indicates that small groups rather than large are more productive (see footnote 2).

Those assembled may be drawn together by accident or by spontaneous attention to a common concern. Or the group may be homogeneous, under an aggressive leader—with organized goals and procedures. Or the group may be members of some professional organization—managers, clerks, or other units systematically dealing with their special problems. Or they may be a committee appointed by some governmental, or social, or other organization to report on a given issue. Still other groups may be learning units in adult education or in school or college classrooms.[9]

3 Discussion stresses reflective thinking rather than undirected emotional responses

The atmosphere of discussion encourages intellectual activity; it rules out disorganized and aimless mental give-and-take. The competent reflective thinker distinguishes mere opinion from facts, studies contexts and backgrounds, notes causes and effects, tests authority and testimony, generalizes carefully in view of the facts at hand, and checks his own and others' tendency to mistake assertions for proof and to substitute prejudices for well-reasoned conclusions. Reflective thinking as contrasted with *intentional reasoning* is characterized by a disciplined attitude and an orderly testing of evidence and argument.

4 Discussion is oral communication

It is group experience in socialization of thinking accomplished through the oral medium, as a rule. Although oral communication is cheaper and more expedient than written communication, it is sometimes less carefully thought out. Its advantages are nevertheless obvious for occasions where decisions should be made quickly.

See also for studies to indicate the influence of group interaction, A. Paul Hare, *Handbook of Small Group Research,* The Free Press of Glencoe, New York, 1962; A. Paul Hare, Edgar Borgatta, and Robert F. Vales, *Small Groups: Studies in Social Interaction,* Alfred A. Knopf, Inc., New York, 1965.

[9] Gerald M. Phillips, *Communication and the Small Group,* The Bobbs-Merrill Company, Inc., Indianapolis, 1966, chaps. 1, 2.

SMALL–GROUP AND PUBLIC DISCUSSION

As we have suggested above, many forms and varieties of discussion are practiced. These range all the way from the causal or incidental exchange by two people to the large gatherings of organized groups or to public lectures. Within these variations in group size, the format and purposes may range from enlightenment (information) to policy decision and action. The motives and sponsorship thus may be industrial, political, economic, or educational (as learning projects). Many of these formats and practices are discussion in name only and turn out to be series of public speeches, debates, or conventionalized persuasive occasions.

We summarize here representative types in which you may now or in your later career participate.

The small group

1 ***Small-group discussional conversation.*** Two or more may spontaneously engage in exchange of information and opinions concerning an imminent problem. Usually the talk moves on to other ideas or may result later in more optimistic treatment of the topic.

2 ***Round-table or informal discussion.*** A discussion in which perhaps five to ten people participate in a casual atmosphere, without a contributing audience, can be called a round table. Although there may be a chairman, he does not function formally. The participants should understand discussion techniques and the purpose of the specific discussion. Usually the aim is learning and expression of opinion.

3 ***Committee discussion.*** The purpose of committee discussions is to prepare a report to the larger organization. The discussion is conducted like a round-table discussion, but because of its purpose, it is under greater control by the chairman. He sees that the agenda is closely followed, that a secretary records the proceedings, and that the report itself is completed and accepted by the members of the committee. At times he calls for a group vote in order to determine group wishes. Committee discussions usually have specific purposes. Somewhat related is the public hearing, in which a congressional or other committee holds public meetings to gather information on some problem of public policy.

4 ***Panel discussion.*** A panel is made up of a chairman and a small group who carry on a discussion around a table. An audience, not

too large, is present and should be seated near the speakers. All present should be able to hear each member of the panel. After the discussion, the auditors should present questions and brief comments. At the end, the chairman summarizes. The success of the occasion will depend partly on the extent to which the audience participates in group thinking. At least half of the total time should be given to remarks from the floor. Each of these contributions, however, and the reply by a member of the panel should be brief.

5 ***Colloquy.*** This procedure may be limited to a discussion between two communicators. Informal conversation prevails yet with well-organized analysis and synthesis. The audience participates. An alternative pattern is to have an audience panel supplemented by experts who serve as resource agents to contribute needed facts and opinions.

6 ***The symposium.*** The symposium consists of three or four speakers, each of whom is assigned a specific phase of the problem to be discussed and given at least five minutes in which to deliver a prepared speech. Each speaker must adjust his prepared remarks to the preceding contributions. The purpose of the individual contributors is chiefly to provide information and to analyze the issues. At the conclusion of this standardized part of the program, the chairman and discussion leader will direct the meeting so that the audience dominates the thinking and discussion.

Large-group discussions

1 ***Public forums and large-group participation.*** The panel and the symposium are conducted with small audiences, preferably not more than one hundred. The public forum may have an audience of as many as two or three thousand. This occasion is discussion in name only. The speaker must be an energetic and experienced public speaker, who lectures for perhaps thirty minutes, creates an atmosphere of open inquiry, and then invites (although the chairman may offer the actual invitation) audience comments on the issues on which he has lectured. The speaker must create an atmosphere of discussion; if he is a rabid protagonist for a cause or if he propagandizes his audience, the discussion will probably not be very fruitful.

2 ***Radio and television discussion.*** Discussions over the air are not distinct in form or content from the types of discussion we have described; they may take the form of the round-table discussion,

the symposium, or the panel. Even the forum can be televised to show the audience in action. However, broadcasting techniques impose limitations that modify the spirit of the discussion. Time allotments, the selection (on some programs) of audience participants, and preliminary rehearsals tend to remove the element of spontaneity. The radio-television talks, such as "Meet the Press," "Face the Nation," and "Issues and Answers" are usually cross-examination challenges and replies that seldom reflect the method or spirit of true discussion, even though often labeled as such.

RATIONALE OF DISCUSSION

Discussion is a form of intellectual inquiry. Discussion requires the application of sound argument, analysis, marshaling of logic and evidence, clear statement. This discussional scene breeds intellectual activity and an atmosphere of free inquiry—a basic goal of college education.

Assignments in discussion have been incorporated in many required first courses in speech. As Donald Dedmon recommended, "I would include from the Fundamentals of Speech approach to the required first course, practice in discussion as an important part of the course." He justifies in detail such inclusion.[4]

Discussion provides constructive training in group association and adaptation. The aim is effective group interaction. Discussion calls for open-mindedness toward the ideas; a sensitivity to the group interests, attitudes, and personalities; and a sense of personal responsibility in the promotion of group thinking and atmosphere, a sincerity in the speaker's effort to achieve such cooperation and individual-group identification. Research studies to support such discussion values and aims are given by Laura Crowell in "Maintaining Effective Attitudes in the Group."[5]

Discussion contributes importantly to freedom of speech. It is not too much to conclude that conservation and growth of American democracy depend on the practice of free public and informal discussion. Axiomatically successful free government rests on well-

[4] Donald Dedmon, "The Required First Course in Speech as Oral Communication," *The Central States Speech Journal,* 16:120–125, May, 1965.

[5] Laura Crowell, *Discussion: Method of Democracy,* Scott, Foresman and Company, Chicago, 1963, pp. 169–219; see Corwin Cartwright and Alvin Zander, *Group Dynamics: Research and Theory,* Row, Peterson & Company, Evanston, Ill., 1960.

informed and mature public opinion. Among the more important agencies for the clarification of issues and the resulting policy determinations is discussion. Faith in free and full discussion will enable our civilization to adjust to the constantly recurring problems and to the new and more complex political and other demands and thus will best ensure our national stability and progress.

"Democracy is at the bottom an agreement to hold civilized discussion of issues that count, and those that cherish it must find and cultivate the techniques of reason." [6]

AGENDA FOR DISCUSSION PROCEDURE

Careful planning can make the difference between a profitable discussion and a pointless waste of time. The following suggestions will serve as a guide for planning a discussion.

1 Select and define the problem

Subjects for discussion should be of concern to all who participate. Since the object of the occasion is to reach a group decision or to further group thinking, the subject should concern a problem about which each participant should eventually reach a decision.

Be sure there are at least two defensible points of view connected with the problem. There is no point in selecting subjects on which no real difference of opinion exists. Avoid also those topics about which debaters have already made up their minds.

Subjects that deal with policy decisions probably have more appeal to school and college students than do problems of fact. Issues that call for extended definition and analysis with little prospect of specific settlement seem to encourage more individual speculative talk without results than do those that focus on direct action.

2 Limit the question

Many discussions are futile because the issue is too broad or is vaguely stated. Take account of the time limits and the reality of the facts and issues involved. Can data be gathered on the issue?

[6] Charles Rossiter, "The Democratic Process," in *Goals for Americans*, report of the President's Commission on National Goals, administered by the American Assembly, Columbia University, Prentice-Hall, Inc., Englewood Cliffs, N.J., 1960, p. 72; Crowell, *op. cit.*, chap. 14; Waldo Braden and Earnest Brandenburg, *Oral Decision Making: Principles of Discussion and Debate*, Harper & Row, Publishers, Incorporated, New York, 1955, pp. 13–20.

Can the problem be based on observable facts? Can the relevant questions be so phrased and limited as to make probable discussionable progress?

A problem such as, "How, if at all, shall we reorganize the liberal arts program of the university?" should be limited to some specific aspects of its content, such as, "Shall courses in plane and solid geometry and college algebra be required of students in the liberal arts college who have not completed satisfactorily such courses elsewhere?" Narrowed subjects require more specific information, but they produce better results in discussion.

3 The structure of discussion

The typical discussion follows a definite organizational pattern. We assume that those involved have common interest in the problem, whether they are present through appointment by some professional organization or through assignment by the classroom instructor. Definite steps in the analysis and solution should be adhered to.

If the aim is to deal with action, the problem-solving pattern proposed by John Dewey has been successfully followed. Though experimentation during the past thirty or more years has modified somewhat the Dewey procedure, the same general process has been justified. The Dewey steps include: (*a*) analysis or recognition of the "felt difficulty," (*b*) analysis of its specific area and definition, (*c*) the goals and aims to be considered in any solution, (*d*) application of reasoning to the causes and results, and the weighing of each proposed solution, (*e*) diagnosis and verification of the solution preferred by the group, and (*f*) if a problem of action, the framing and justification of a program to implement the conclusions arrived at.[7]

The various steps deal with the following standard questions:

1. What are the character and scope of the problem?
2. What is the meaning of the concepts and terms involved?
3. What are the tentative issues?
4. What are the facts and how are they tested for validity?
5. What are representative causes of the problem?
6. What goals and solutions are proposed?
7. What are the advantages and disadvantages of each solution?

[7] John Dewey, *How We Think* (rev. ed.), D. C. Heath and Company, Boston, 1933, pp. 107–118.

8. What is the preferred solution? (Synthesis of the conclusions arrived at after examination of each solution, and justification of the preferred outcome.)

9. What program is to be followed for putting the preferred solution into action?

For a question of fact or value step 9 above is obviously not applicable.

The solution agreed upon needs later reexamination to further test its success or failure. If the decision of this group later seems unwise, it should be modified or replaced. Time and later circumstances continually affect the judgments of a given hour and place.[8]

OUTLINING THE DISCUSSION

The following skeleton outline for a discussion illustrates how this pattern of organization can be applied to a problem of policy.

The question is:

I. What explanations are needed?
   A. What is meant by . . . ?
   B. What is meant by . . . ?
   C. What is meant by . . . ?

II. Does this question constitute a major economic, social, and political problem that calls for solution?
   A. What are the chief facts or events that created the problem?
   B. What are the chief causes of these disturbing facts or events?
      1. What are the alleged economic causes?
      2. What are the alleged political causes?
      3. What are the alleged social causes?
   C. What are the alleged economic, political, social results of the problem?

III. What are the proposed solutions?
   A. What is solution A?
   B. What is solution B?
   C. What is solution C?

IV. Are the suggested solutions for dealing with this problem satisfactory?
   A. What are the alleged advantages and disadvantages of solution A?

[8] See Phillips, *op. cit.*, chap. 4, "The Method of Problem Evaluation and Review Technique," pp. 88ff.

1. What are the alleged advantages?
2. What are the alleged disadvantages?

B. What are the alleged advantages and disadvantages of solution B?

1. What are the alleged advantages?
2. What are the alleged disadvantages?

C. What are the alleged advantages and disadvantages of solution C?

1. What are the alleged advantages?
2. What are the alleged disadvantages?

V. In view of the discussion above, what solution is, on the whole, preferable?

A. What are the advantages of this solution that indicate its superiority over others?

B. Does the operation of this preferred solution justify its selection on grounds of practicability?

VI. What program for putting the proposed solution into operation should be set up?

Naturally these steps need not be followed slavishly. You may pass over entirely any step on which all agree, and you may thoroughly investigate any one if it represents a significant aspect of your problem.

In your preparation, draw up an individual outline for your private help, dealing with each of the questions in some detail. This organized preview of the ground that may be covered in the discussion itself will give you added insight into what takes place in the group. But your outline should never replace the method and thinking of the group.

LEADERSHIP IN DISCUSSION

Discussion develops from the participation on an equal footing of the individuals who make up the group. There are no official titles of distinction, no priority in seating arrangements, no set order of speaking, no timing of speeches. Because discussion often requires administration, many groups choose or appoint a leader or chairman.

The function of the chairman is to guarantee genuine discussion and to prevent anyone from impeding the free flow of ideas. Actually, every member should be qualified to act as moderator. Special qualifications are required of the chairman such as the following:

1 Know the subject

The discussion chairman must be much more than a figurehead. He should know whether the facts are accurately reported and should be able to evaluate ideas.

2 Know discussion techniques

Under the chairman's guidance, the discussants must function as a unit, focusing in turn on each step of the analysis and demonstrating the values of group thinking. It is the chairman's duty to discourage wordy or belligerent questions and replies, to draw out nontalkers and contributors worth hearing, and to keep both the speakers and the audience active throughout the discussion.[9] He will often be called upon for impromptu remarks. He will be required to introduce speakers and deal with unexpected questions, and he must be able to repeat accurately the queries addressed to a speaker and amplify both question and answer. He should be able to summarize completely and accurately.

3 Know the audience

Whether a chairman is dealing with an audience of ten, a hundred, or a thousand, he should (in theory at least) learn as much as he can about their ages, sex, occupational interests, education, affiliation with social or professional organizations, probable attitudes toward the subject, fixed beliefs and motives, and training in discussion. This information will help him to gauge more effectively what is happening during the talking and to bridge the gap between speakers who are specialists and an audience of laymen.

4 Cultivate personal qualities of leadership

At the outset the chairman may lead merely because some authority has committed the group to his charge. Ultimately, however, he will remain the leader only if the group has confidence in him; artificial efforts to govern quickly collapse. The group must be able to respect the chairman's knowledge of the subject and his demonstrated ability to run the meeting. Perhaps even more important is his genuine interest in and understanding of group interests.

[9] For a detailed discussion of these techniques, consult, for example, A. Craig Baird, *Argumentation, Discussion and Debate,* McGraw-Hill Book Company, New York, 1950, chaps. 20–23.

If the group is small, the chairman should learn the name of each person present and put him at ease. This spokesman should introduce the members of the group but avoid behaving like a monitor. In addition to being tactful, he should be open-minded. He need not be a yes-man but must give each one opportunity to state his point of view. The chairman should review in advance the various opinions on the subject and be prepared to be tolerant of each position.

The chairman should be genial and pleasant, but should not descend to wisecracking or joking. Cooperation will thrive in a genial atmosphere.

5 Create a favorable climate for the discussion

Provide favorable physical conditions; arrange the lighting and furniture so that the group will be comfortable and in close association with one another.

6 Properly introduce the subject

Show the importance and immediate interest of the topic. Relate a case history or use visual aids to stimulate interest and discussion.

7 Help develop the discussion structure

Limit the problem. See that terms are defined, that the problem is fully analyzed, that goals are clear, that representative solutions are clearly stated and analyzed, that differences of opinions are aired, and that group synthesis is achieved at the end or at least intelligently attempted.

Ask questions relating to the sources of information, and questions that deal with the overassertive, overtalkative, or unduly timid member.

8 Use frequent summaries and transitions

Keep your eye on the clock and make the best use of the time at your disposal. Keep the talkers on the subject and use judgment in the amount of time given to each phase of discussion.[10]

[10] Dean C. Barnlund, "Experiments in Leadership Training for Decision-making Discussion Groups," *Speech Monographs,* 22:6, March, 1955.

RANK AND FILE PARTICIPANTS IN DISCUSSION

In small-group discussions little or no distinction needs to be made between the leader and the others of the group. All are leaders, as we have stated above, or really the occasion is largely leaderless. However, if an audience is seated apart from the nucleus of speakers, then the duties and importance of the leader-chairman become apparent. He is to direct a panel, or introduce a symposium, or relate to a large audience, especially if radio or television is involved.

As a participant in an informal round-table discussion or as a less conspicuous questioner from the floor in a large forum, your participating behavior and technique are the same. You will follow the principles of discussion outlined in this chapter and as suggested above for the leader.

Follow through, as best you can, the orderly evolution of the discussion structure. Apply the open-minded, tolerant, and cooperative traits of your own personality. Your experience here is that of a group member. You are not to assert yourself as an uncompromising authority or as a vigorous advocate. Inquiry is your method throughout, but not inquiry devoid of reflective thinking and utterance. Your cooperation is not to be that of a shallow yes-man.

If competition dominates, then discussion should terminate—at least for the time—and debate ensue. Listen carefully and show your awareness of the discussion trends and the significance of what others may say. Hold back on your precipitate judgments, encourage your own creative thinking and that of the others.

Knowledge of the problem under discussion, understanding of your role as an inquirer after truth and as a cooperative thinker with your colleagues, ability to handle facts skillfully and to reason soundly, and adjustment of your delivery and speaking personality to discussion rather than to strong persuasion or debate will make you a highly satisfactory participant or leader in this type of basic speech.

PROJECTS AND PROBLEMS

Project 1 A review of the theory and practice of discussion

Purposes of this assignment: To encourage the systematic understanding of the nature, types, and methods of discussion.

Procedure: The members of the group will each present a three- to five-minute informal report on one of the following topics. It is desirable that the topics be assigned to the group so that the entire range is treated. Each will present a one-page summary of his talk, with the source or sources specifically indicated.

Subjects for this speech:

1. A working definition of discussion
2. Discussion as impracticable in an important decision-making situation
3. Debating as preferable to discussion for getting at a problem
4. Relation of discussion to democracy
5. Justification of . . . (a given subject) as selected and framed by this group
6. Necessary steps for successful discussion
7. The problem of a group organization of an outline
8. Functions of the leader
9. Factors of personality that help or hinder a discussant
10. How to organize and conduct a forum

Project 2 The practice of group discussion

Purposes of this assignment: To provide for a series of group discussions by the class.

Procedure: Four or five members of each group will give an informal discussion to demonstrate the principles of group discussion as dealing with an issue of fact. The discussants will frame a group outline before the class session and will individually or otherwise collect evidence and ideas.

The following topics are suggested:

1. Does the complete freedom of the classroom teacher to say and write his political and other opinions constitute a menace to the purposes and aims of higher education?
2. Are college students of today unduly rebellious against academic administrations?
3. Do we have effective leadership in American foreign policy?
4. What is the problem of controlling insecticides?
5. What is the place of the Black Muslim in American political-social life?
6. Do the chief features of the urban renewal plan promise its success?
7. What is the relation of the present Common Market to the agricultural prices of the United States in the world market?

8. Is the present economic foreign aid program of the United States adequate?
9. What is the problem of unethical advertising over radio and television?
10. Shall we endorse the suppression of books that society regards as ethically and culturally highly objectionable?

Each group will select its leader. Limit each discussion to approximately half the class hour. The class will comment on the demonstration. This project will obviously take more than one class period.

Project 3 The practice of informal group discussion on a problem of fact and policy

Purpose of this assignment: To provide further experience in group discussion for each member. The class will select and word a currently significant problem and prepare to discuss it. The six or seven members of each group will select a chairman. The group will prepare a tentative outline and otherwise prepare for the class program. At least two periods will be used. Limit the discussion of the first session to a consideration of definitions and analysis of the problem. After group A has given its discussion for twenty minutes, group B will comment on the performance. Then the process will be reversed, with group B as discussants and group A as critics. To give each group its participation, the project may use several class periods. The entire procedure may then be repeated at a later meeting or meetings with each group concentrating entirely on solutions. If the groups can discuss simultaneously in more than one room with at least one competent critic present in each case, the execution of this project can be simplified.
Suggested topics:

1. Shall my state prohibit automobile driving more than 60 miles per hour?
2. Should my state prohibit the death penalty?
3. Should my college require for graduation at least two years of two foreign languages?
4. Should the United States, Great Britain, Russia, and France adopt a program to prevent the spread of nuclear weapons?
5. Should the United States recognize Red China?
6. Should the federal government adopt policies that prohibit further increase of the national debt?
7. Should my state adopt measures to permit lotteries?

Project 4 The continued practice of discussion

Purpose of this assignment: To provide additional experiences in the practice of discussion.
Procedure: The group will concentrate on one of the following procedures:

1. The class will organize a forum. Two members will present the problem briefly (five minutes each). An experienced moderator, the instructor, if necessary, will receive and direct remarks and questions from the floor. Observe the techniques and procedures of a community forum.
2. The class will listen to and observe a filmed discussion or lecture (fifteen minutes in length) and will follow with a discussion of the problem.

REFERENCES

Barnlund, Dean C.: "Experiments in Leadership Training for Decision-making Discussion Groups," *Speech Monographs,* 22:6, March, 1955.

——— and Franklin S. Haiman: *Discussion,* Houghton Mifflin Company, Boston, 1960.

Bass, Bernard M.: *Leadership, Psychology, and Organizational Behavior,* Harper & Row, Publishers, Incorporated, New York, 1960.

Berlo, David K.: *The Process of Communication: An Introduction to Theory and Practice,* Holt, Rinehart and Winston, Inc., New York, 1960.

Bonner, Hubert: *Group Dynamics: Principles and Application,* The Ronald Press Company, New York, 1959.

Brandenburg, Earnest, and Waldo Braden: *Oral Decision-making,* Harper & Row, Publishers, Incorporated, New York, 1955, pp. 191–192.

Cartwright, Dorwin, and Alvin Zander: *Group Dynamics Research and Theory,* Harper & Row, Publishers, Incorporated, New York, 1960.

Crowell, Laura: *Discussion: Method of Democracy,* Scott, Foresman and Company, Chicago, 1963.

Dashiell, C. F.: "The Effect of Group Discussion on the Individual's Work," in Carl Murchison (ed.), *A Handbook of Social Psychology,* Clark University Press, Worcester, Mass., 1955, pp. 1125–1140.

Dedmon, Donald: "The Required First Course in Speech as Oral Communication," *The Central States Speech Journal,* 16:120–125, May, 1965.

Dewey, John: *How to Think* (rev. ed.), D. C. Heath and Company, Boston, 1933.

Gulley, H. E.: *Discussion, Conference and Group Process,* Holt, Rinehart and Winston, Inc., New York, 1960.

Haiman, Franklyn S.: *Group Leadership and Democratic Action,* Houghton Mifflin Company, Boston, 1951.

Hare, A. Paul: *Handbook of Small Group Research,* Free Press of Glencoe, New York, 1962.

———, Edgar F. Bogatta, and Robert F. Bales: *Small Groups: Studies in Social Interaction,* Alfred A. Knopf, Inc., New York, 1965.

Harnack, Victor, and Thorrel B. Fest: *Group Discussion: Theory and Technique,* Appleton-Century-Crofts, Inc., New York, 1964.

Maier, Norman R. F.: *Problem-solving Discussions and Conferences: Leadership Methods and Skills,* McGraw-Hill Book Company, New York, 1963.

Nilsen, Thomas: "Interpersonal Communication: A Conceptual Framework," *Central States Speech Journal,* 15:31–35, February, 1964.

Olmstead, Michael: *The Small Group,* Random House, Inc., New York, 1959.

Phillips, Gerald M.: *Communication and the Small Group,* The Bobbs-Merrill Company, Inc., Indianapolis, 1966, chaps. 1, 2.

Rahskopf, Horace: *Basic Speech Improvement,* Harper & Row, Publishers, Incorporated, New York, 1965, p. 348.

Rossiter, Charles: "The Democratic Process," in *Goals for Americans,* report of the President's Commission on National Goals; administered by the American Assembly, Columbia University, Prentice-Hall, Englewood Cliffs, N. J., 1960.

Sheidel, Thomas, and Laura Crowell: "Feedback in Small Group Communication," *Quarterly Journal of Speech,* 52:273–278, October, 1966.

Tannenbaum, Robert, Irving R. Weschler, and Fred Massarik: *Leadership and Organization: A Behavioral Science Approach,* McGraw-Hill Book Company, New York, 1961.

Thorndike, Robert L.: "The Effect of Discussion upon the Correctness of Group Decisions When the Factor of Majority Influence Is Allowed For," *Journal of Social Psychology,* 9:343–362, August, 1938.

Utterback, William E.: "Radio Panel vs. Group Discussion," *Quarterly Journal of Speech,* 50:374–377, December, 1964.

Wiseman, Gordon, and Larry Barker: *Speech: Interpersonal Communication,* Science Research Association, Inc., Chicago, 1967.

15
PERSUASIVE SPEAKING: LOGICAL TECHNIQUES

Persuasive speaking goes on endlessly. In classrooms, among friends, acquaintances, or even intermittent strangers, we all join in with these controversial challenges and replies. Our arguments, pro or con, concern the nucleus of such trivial or important subjects as whether this summer is unseasonably hot; whether White College for professional training is superior to Courant College; whether Professor Styles is the best lecturer on our campus; whether we should picket for more student freedom; whether we should try to join the Air Force; whether we should condemn draft-card burners; whether our President should be reelected; whether more national football leagues should be established; or whether our Vietnam policy is a failure.

"What is persuasive speaking? Persuasion is the conscious attempt to modify thought and action by manipulating the motives of men toward predetermined ends." [1]

We may act on a newly explained proposal because we have been motivated and await only a decision about what is to be done. We may have strong beliefs favoring action but remain inactive be-

[1] W. L. Brembeck and W. S. Howell, *Persuasion*, Prentice-Hall, Inc., Englewood, Cliffs, N.J., 1952, p. 24.

cause we also have conflicting beliefs which inhibit our action. Information and impelling evidence or reason can then be persuasive, but in many cases these factual and logical approaches are not effective. Men act because their motives are stimulated in a manner calling for action. Persuasion then includes but goes beyond the cold facts of information and argument.

The persuasive aim is to influence hearers to think and act in a specific way through spoken (and sometimes written) discourse. If a speech succeeds, the resulting beliefs and behavior of the hearers conform to the purpose of the speaker or speakers.

The speaker has basic ways of influencing the listeners through his oral presentation. He may affect their beliefs and conduct mainly through his reliance on logical techniques (facts, inferences, examples, analogy, causality, testimony and authority, deductive patterns).

Or he may also influence their beliefs and behavior through psychological forms of communication (appeals to drives, motives, habits, attitudes, sentiments, stereotypes, personal character).

In this chapter we concentrate on persuasion that chiefly relies on reasoned discourse, including debating. In the following chapter we will discuss the nature and application of psychological techniques in persuasion.

How does persuasive speaking differ from the purely informational type? The latter should add to the knowledge held by the audience. Persuasion, however, uses such informational materials to change opinions, beliefs, and conduct of the hearers.

What is the relation of persuasion to argumentative speaking? Sound reasoning and dependable evidence, Aristotle said, must be buttressed by ethical and pathetic proofs. Ethical proofs demonstrate the goodwill, wisdom, and character of the speaker; we might relate this type of proof to the speaker's candor in presenting the truth as he sees it. Pathetic proofs involve the relationship of the subject to the attitudes and emotions of the listeners; that is, the "truth" can only be presented in terms comprehensible and palatable to the listeners.

It is a mistake to assume that logical and emotional elements are mutually exclusive in any given speech. Both are necessary. In speechmaking, as in our daily lives, we must establish a balance between the two. John Dewey has given us an excellent description of the place of emotion in our lives.

> *The conclusion is not that the emotional passionate phase of action can be or should be eliminated in behalf of a bloodless reason. More "passions," not fewer, is the answer. To check the influence of*

> *hate, there must be sympathy, while to rationalize sympathy there are needed emotions of curiosity, caution, respect for the freedom of others—dispositions to which evoke objects which balance those called up by sympathy, and prevent its degeneration into maudlin sentiment and meddling interference. Rationality, once more, is not a force to evoke against impulse and habit. It is the attainment of a working harmony among diverse desires.*[2]

Some of the highest achievements of man have their foundations not in coldly and closely reasoned logic but in attitudes, loyalties, sentiments, and aspirations. Many roads lead to the good and the true. They are exemplified in the persuasion of drama, poetry, painting, and religion. Persuasion provides a means of ordering motives, a means not opened to the narrowly logical mind.

Most of us are aware of the value in our lives of emotion and of openness to persuasion. But how do we function psychologically and physiologically in response to emotional appeals? The words *emotion* and *motivation* come from the same root as the word *motion.* An emotionally stimulated response is an energized response, at least for all the emotions associated with approach to or withdrawal from the stimulus object. When the organism responds emotionally, the energy suddenly provided by the body prepares the individual for action. It is therefore no mere accident that the persuasive speaker has found the appeal to the emotions a practical device for stirring the listener to action. It is only when the listener's emotions have been conditioned by logic that the logical appeal results in action. Thus even the use of logic to produce action is dependent ultimately upon the emotions.[3]

Argumentative discourse begins with a clear-cut proposition to be defended or condemned, an analysis of the problem as selected, the mustering of facts and inferences, the inclusion of motivational appeals, and conclusions derived from logical elements.

One type of argument, regulated by time limits and other par-

[2] John Dewey, *Human Nature and Conduct,* Holt, Rinehart and Winston, Inc., New York, 1922, pp. 195–196.

[3] John Dewey, *How We Think,* new ed., D. C. Heath and Company, Boston, 1933, p. 71. For points of view about the aims of persuasive speaking by argument and debate, see for example: A. Craig Baird, "Responsibilities of Free Communication," *Vital Speeches,* 18:699–701, Sept. 1, 1952; Maurice Natanson, "Rhetoric and Philosophical Argumentation," *Quarterly Journal of Speech,* 48: 24–30, 1962; Glen E. Mills, "Argumentation in General Education," *Southern Speech Journal,* 26:313–317, Summer, 1951; Halbert E. Gulley, *Essentials of Discussion and Debate,* Henry Holt and Company, Inc., New York, 1955, chap. 1; James G. McBurney and Kenneth G. Hance, *Discussion in Human Affairs,* Harper & Row, Publishers, Incorporated, New York, 1950, chap. 1.

liamentary or forensic rules, is debate. Proceedings on the floor of the United States Senate, like courtroom procedures, are debated in that they are circumscribed by rules and by the gavel of the presiding officer, the symbol of the deliberative body. School and college debate is simply argumentative speaking in which each side is usually represented by two speakers who speak in a specified order, with rebuttals, and for a specified and equal amount of time for each debater. Although in this chapter we will explain these procedures in some detail under "Conducting a debate," most of our discussion will apply to both persuasion by individual argument and by debate.

SELECT AND FRAME THE PROPOSITION

Persuasion by argumentative speaking is based upon propositions. A proposition is a problem formally stated: *Resolved,* That Congress should establish a system of universal military training. The same statement may be put in the form of an impartial question: Should Congress establish a system of universal military training? The resolution type of statement is to be preferred unless the speaking situation is extremely informal. Exact statement, however, should be the aim, whatever the sentence type.

Limit the scope of your proposition. If the speaking time is five minutes, weigh your subject carefully and limit your proposition to only one phase, for example, *Resolved,* That railroad X is facing bankruptcy.

Phrase the proposition in a simple rather than compound sentence. See that it is free from ambiguous, vague, or question-begging terms. If the problem is proposed for a school or college debate, construct it so as to give the affirmative the burden of proof. Borrowed from courtroom parlance, the term *burden of proof* simply means that the resolution should advocate a change from the existing order, or a continuation of the existing order in the rare cases in which it is clear that the overwhelming sentiment of the audience is opposed to the status quo. This wording means that speakers opposed to the proposition normally have a majority of the audience on their side before the argument starts. Word the statement, then, so that it proposes a change or proposes a policy counter to audience opinion.

Propositions are of three kinds. *A proposition of fact* asserts the truth or falsity of a given view or idea. It calls for mental agreement or belief rather than for action. Some typical propositions of fact are:

Resolved, That in the United States the standards for graduation from public high schools have declined during the past fifty years.

Resolved, That Lee Harvey Oswald assassinated President Kennedy.

A *proposition of value* is one that argues for or against the quality of a person, event, situation, or idea, according to which it is thought of as being more or less desirable, useful, estimable, important, worthy. The aim is to evaluate or appraise rather than merely to inform or to call for action. Note these examples:

Resolved, That the concept of county government in the United States is undesirable.

Resolved, That a liberal arts training is desirable for all professional students.

A *proposition of policy* places the emphasis on action rather than on acceptable information or evaluation. The differences between the types of propositions can be illustrated by restating the subjects. Note how mere assent to the facts is changed to a call for action in those propositions.

Resolved, That the standards for graduation from the public high schools in the United States should be more rigid.

Resolved, That the public should vote the Republican ticket (or the Democratic ticket) in the November elections.

ANALYZE THE PROPOSITION

Analysis is the process of dividing the problem into its main and subordinate divisions. To analyze a proposition, (1) define clearly the terms in the statement and any other terms that become prominent as the argument unfolds; (2) outline the conflicting arguments for and against the resolution; (3) discover and state the issues themselves—the controversial points the answers to which will make up the pattern of the argument. Issues should be stated as impartial questions. Thus on the subject of universal military training, the chief issues might be: Is the present military power procurement system (the draft) adequate? Would universal military training fill the need? Would it be more satisfactory than other proposals? Would it be practicable?

In the analysis of a proposition of policy, the central questions usually arise from a cause-and-effect analysis of the problem. Inquire into the alleged causes of the resolution. What will be the alleged results of its establishment or application? These questions involve several apparent subissues: (1) What factors call for a change or for action? (2) Will the establishment of the proposal produce satisfactory results? Will the difficulties be removed? Will positive benefits result? (3) Is the proposal practicable? Can the organization or machinery necessary for its success be established? Has it demonstrated its successful operation in other places or areas? Is it to be preferred to other proposed solutions?

These questions, representing stock issues, are familiar to most students of argumentation. These inquiries are mechanical, we admit; they are to be applied as a means of helping the student to focus on the outstanding lines of investigation. Other pertinent questions can be added to this list, for example (4) Is the proposal fair to the groups that have a stake in the problem?

To illustrate the process, consider the problem, "Shall we start a new political party in the United States?" Following the pattern above will reveal these issues: (1) Are there important problems that the political parties should deal with and attempt to settle? If so, do the major political parties face these problems squarely? (The affirmative answers *no,* the negative, *yes*). (2) Would the creation of a new major political party facilitate the settlement of such important problems? (3) Would the establishment of a new major political party be practicable? Stock issues are therefore helpful in the formulation of specific inquiries.

Stock issues are also useful in the analysis of a proposition of fact. Methods of discovering the issues involved in such propositions include analysis of the forms of proof (evidence, authority, causal relations, comparisons, instances); analysis of historical periods; analysis of the parties involved (students, faculty, the college in general); and the classificational method such as division according to social, political, economic, and moral factors. This method is perhaps the most convenient approach to analysis of propositions of fact.

ORGANIZE AND OUTLINE THE PROPOSITION

The persuasive speech that stresses argumentation should provide answers, with reasons or evidence to support those answers, to the questions or issues raised in the analysis of the problem. These decisions enable the speaker to state the points he intends to develop in support of or in denial of the proposition. Note the following issues:

> *Resolved,* That Congress should pass legislation providing for a family allowance. (A family allowance means that all parents with dependent children should be paid a flat sum each month to supplement the family income.)
>
> I. Does the economic-social condition of many families in the United States call for such a federal program?
>   - *A.* Do present programs dealing with unemployment provide sufficiently for family needs?
>   - *B.* Do present programs providing for retraining for industrial jobs deal sufficiently with family needs?
>   - *C.* Does the lack of adequate family incomes contribute directly to increased juvenile delinquency, crime, and general lawlessness?
>
> II. Would such a program for providing for each family whose income is below a sustenance level minimize strongly the present economic-social evils?
>   - *A.* Would the family's economic status be directly improved?
>   - *B.* Would the problem of raising economic standards of such families be largely solved?
>   - *C.* Would this program largely alleviate the problem of raising educational standards?
>   - *D.* Would this program minimize to a large extent the problem of broken homes among this group?
>
> III. Is the proposed program practicable?
>   - *A.* Would the ultimate cost (for example, 9 billion dollars the first year) be comparatively little?
>   - *B.* Would the added family income be largely spent on necessities rather than on "junk"?
>   - *C.* Does the experience of some sixty nations that adopted this program twenty years ago justify it?
>   - *D.* Would the flat sum distributed each month to qualified families be properly administered?
>   - *E.* Do economic-social authorities and organizations advocate such a program?

The argumentative speech which presents these issues and contentions should have an introduction, a main body or argument proper, and a conclusion. Although these three divisions are flexible and should not be rigidly adhered to at the risk of boring the audience, this standard pattern is of advantage to both the speaker and the listener.

Usually, the introduction should (1) state the reasons for the discussion and the immediate cause of the controversy (in the case of the resolution above, a revenue bill may recently have been introduced in the House of Representatives); (2) explain briefly the terms (in this case, explain a *family allowance*); (3) state the issues; (4) enumerate the points or contentions to be established.

The main body or argument proper should be a comprehensive treatment of each contention or proposition. Think of each argument as a speech in itself, with its introduction, main body, and conclusion. If you are arguing a proposition of policy, be sure to discuss (1) the necessity (or lack of necessity) for the proposal, (2) its benefits (or evils), and (3) its practicality (or impracticality). In arguing a proposition of fact, each phase of your classification will be a heading in your main body.

The purpose of the conclusion is to summarize and enforce your points and to appeal for cooperation or action. You may insert a series of persuasive questions or refer again to the occasion.

This entire procedure above suggests a speech of considerable length. Select and limit the introduction, main body, and conclusion, according to time at your disposal.

Your argument should be outlined in an *argumentative brief.* Drafting your outline will clarify your thinking, test the logical consistency and factual completeness of your ideas, and increase the clarity and persuasiveness with which you present your case. From this outline you may draft speaker's notes to be used as you talk. Do not keep your written outline before you as you talk, for you may be tempted to adhere to it mechanically and slavishly. Outlining is, however, a significant though laborious step between investigation and delivery. Review in Chapter 7 the principles and methods of outlining.

FOLLOW A LOGICAL PATTERN OF DEVELOPMENT

Your speaking purpose in persuasion by argumentative development means that you will rely primarily on the materials of reason and supporting fact. The set of your talk is that of reflective thinking and avoidance of random emotional utterance. The pattern is that suggested by John Dewey when he outlined the process of reflective procedure as involving these steps: (1) the recognition of a felt difficulty; (2) description or diagnosis of the problem; (3) description of the representative hypotheses on solutions of the problem; (4) rational elaboration of these suggestions and the testing of each; (5) further verification leading to the acceptance or rejection of the preferred solution.[4]

The details of this reflective process consist of facts, the inferences from these facts, and the conclusions. Reason and inference occur when we mentally explore and take a position in relation to the facts and related details. Inference, in a sense, is guessing, but it is also a methodical, cautious, and critical examination of the facts and connections. It is based on a critical survey of the probabilities and hazards that accompany the conclusion that represents a new stand. We leap the gap from facts to conclusions and assume that our leap is well justified.

When you infer or reason you do so in one or more of several well-defined ways. You may view details that have similarities, then generalize concerning the whole array (inference from specific facts); you may limit your description and inference to a comparison between specific objects or relationship (inference from analogy); you may focus on two or more particular events that seem to have an invisible but definite connection (inference from causality); you may view the statements of others that speak with surety and experience on an event or theory (inference from authority); you may draw specific conclusions from general statements (inference by deduction).

These typical modes of logical techniques we consider below. They are the practical substance of your talk. They are not rigid forms to be followed in sequence, but are to be flexibly introduced at points that call for their application. These logical forms, we should add, are a unit, but are usually described separately by logicians and students of communication for purposes of detailed explanation and application.

The logical method is to set up the facts or data; to state and explain the inferences that bridge the gap between these data and conclusions; to defend these inferences by refutation, if necessary, from those who disagree with the reasonings; and finally to frame the conclusions that summarize the specific proposition presumably accepted by the listeners.[5]

[4] John Dewey, *How We Think*, pp. 71–78, 91–101.

[5] See A. Craig Baird, *Argumentation, Discussion and Debate,* McGraw-Hill Book Company, New York, 1950, pp. 38–51; Stephen Toulmin, *The Uses of Argument*, Cambridge University Press, London, 1958, chap. 3; Wayne Brockriede and Douglas Ehninger, "Toulmin on Argument: An Interpretation and Application," *Quarterly Journal of Speech*, 46:44–53, February, 1960.

1 Evidence (facts)

To convince the listener to think and act as you wish, you must appeal to him through facts. What are facts (or evidence)? They are historical events, statistics, other concrete details, and the citation of authorities. President Franklin D. Roosevelt, in his address to Congress, calling for war against Japan, cited a considerable number of facts to prove beyond a doubt that the United States was "suddenly and deliberately attacked by the forces of the Empire of Japan."

In addition to the major fact of the Japanese attack on Pearl Harbor, the President also cited that "last night the Japanese forces attacked Hong Kong. Last night the Japanese forces attacked Guam." And other instances were cited.[6]

Be sure that your facts are verified. Your confidence in them will make your delivery more persuasive. Test your supporting materials by asking yourself these questions: Are the facts in my argument stated clearly and concisely? Have I included enough facts? Do acceptable authorities subscribe to them? Are the sources of these facts or the authorities cited specifically identified? Are these authorities unprejudiced, intellectually honest, competent to testify? Do they have special knowledge? Are the facts from a primary source? Is the source corroborated by other sources? Are the facts acceptable to the audience? Are the facts reasonable according to the tests of causation? [7]

Your argument can be strengthened by incorporating all the representative types of inference—specific instances, analogy, causation, authority, and general propositions.

2 Inference from specific instances

In using argument from specific instances you will reason from specific instances to a general conclusion. Suppose you talk for five minutes on the topic "The representative South American nations are unprepared for a major international war." Your evidence unfolds somewhat as follows: Brazil is unprepared for a major war (in equipment, finances, etc.); so is Argentina; so is Chile; so is Colom-

[6] F. D. Roosevelt, "For a Declaration of War against Japan," in A. Craig Baird (ed.), *American Public Addresses: 1740–1952,* McGraw-Hill Book Company, New York, 1956, pp. 265–267.

[7] Gerald Miller, "Questions of Fact and Value: Another Look," *Southern Speech Journal,* 28:116–122, Winter, 1962.

bia. Therefore you generalize: "The representative South American nations are unprepared for a major international war." After examining a number of cases or instances, you draw up a statement that covers the entire field of the topic, including those cases that you may not have had opportunity to inspect.

How can you check your own thinking and that of others as you thus generalize from instances? You will see that the cases are sufficient in number. You will note also whether the cases are representative or typical. If you wish to prove that the leaders of the Republican party are on the whole conservatives, you will in all fairness not limit your instances to the "old guard," or to those over seventy; you will include the obviously younger Republican governors and congressmen and study a cross section of the party leadership. Furthermore, you will look closely to the sources of your facts—to yourself as observer and collector, or to official or unofficial sources in print from which you quote them. You will check the character, authority, reliability, and corroborative value of your sources. Avoid hasty generalization.

3 Inference from analogy

A second type of inference is that from analogy (inference by comparison). The isolated facts, cases, objects, or relationships between such objects are compared with other similar facts, objects, cases, or relationships about which our information is relatively hazy. From such matching and contrast you may draw conclusions concerning these relatively unknown situations, facts, objects, or relationships. By analogy we Americans compare the democratic ways of the American with the Englishman, about whose democratic ways we are less sure, and we conclude that the Britisher is also a supporter of these democratic principles which we support.

The worth of your analogies or comparison will obviously depend on the accuracy with which the factors of similarity are carried out. We ask: Do the objects or relationships under comparison actually have a considerable number of items in common? If so, have these items significance or importance with respect to the conclusion we would draw? Do important differences exist? Are the alleged facts on which the comparisons are based fully established and clearly stated? Can the alleged comparison or conclusion be in turn verified by argument from generalization, by causal reasoning, by testimony of experts? Avoid false analogy.

4 Inference from causality

A basic form of inference is that of reasoning from causation. We conclude that assumed facts effect alleged results (cause-to-effect reasoning). Or we focus our attention on these same instances or cases and attempt to describe other factors, cases, or situations that may have produced them (effect-to-cause reasoning). Like analogy, such inference attempts to establish relationships between particulars.

What are the tests of such reasoning? Almost every argument will contain inferences from the causal relations—either specific arguments within a section or large arguments encompassing the entire proposition. How shall we analyze their validity? We may ask four principal questions: (*a*) Does a genuine connection appear between the antecedent (prior fact, event, situation) and the consequent (subsequent fact, event, situation)? (*b*) If so, is the alleged cause adequate to produce the alleged effect, or is the alleged effect determined by the alleged cause? (*c*) Even if an alleged cause is sufficient to determine the character of an allegedly related event or situation, are not intervening factors at work to cancel or minimize the controlling influence of the connection or relationship? (*d*) Have the alleged facts in this case been properly verified? Avoid false reasoning.

5 Inference from authority

Still another method of inference is to cite authorities or expert sources for verification of your idea. The gist of such inference is that "so-and-so is true, because Mr. X so states." Here you identify an authority with an alleged conclusion. The reasoning really amounts to the assumption that whatever Mr. X has to say on this subject is sound. You may test every assumption by means of these questions: Is the source accurately quoted? Are the facts (if facts are given) properly reported? Is the source especially qualified on this subject? Is he unbiased? Is the testimony offered contrary to the interests of the authority? Does reasoning from causal relation, analogy, generalization, and specific instance confirm this conclusion or assumption? Avoid illogical reasoning by authority.

6 Inference from general propositions and assumptions

Effective arguments are based partly on general propositions or statements. This is argument from deduction. The speaker here uses a general statement to apply to a concrete example or case. He may begin with either the general statement or the case to which it applies. These general statements, whether uttered or not, are assumptions, or hypotheses, or principles. Practically every speech relates to or implies such basic concepts that give logical solidity to what is said. Many students of American political and economic policy, for example, assume in their remarks that the American system is one primarily of private enterprise. Under such principle, if accepted by the listeners, any program of governmental economic activity is to be vigorously questioned. Similarly, assumptions are often taken for granted that America is a nation of racial freedom and equality; that the state and church are to be rigidly separated; that all wealth should be equitably distributed; that the government owes every man a job; that speech should be free; that honesty is the best policy. Each assumption is to be analyzed in detail by those who question it.

To the logician deductions are often framed as syllogisms, in which the first proposition is labeled the major premise; the related or more specific propositions, the minor premise; and the connecting proposition, the conclusion.[8]

The following statement with its three propositions is a typical categorical syllogism:

I. Major premise: Cigarette smoking produces lung cancer.
II. Minor premise: Harold Howswer smokes cigarettes.
III. Conclusion: Harold Howswer has or will have lung cancer.

Such inferences, framed to include three propositions, are of two general types—categorical and conditional. The conditional type, again, is subdivided into the disjunctive and hypothetical forms.

The categorical syllogism assumes or states an unqualified affirmation as illustrated above. In the disjunctive syllogism, the assumption states choices or alternatives. Thus:

I. Either we cease smoking or we have lung cancer.
II. We cease smoking.
III. We will not have lung cancer.

In the hypothetical type, the major premise or assumption is a condition. To illustrate:

[8] Walter R. Fisher, "The Uses of the Enthymeme," *Speech Teacher*, 13:197–203, September, 1964; Samuel L. Becker, "Research in Emotional and Logical Proofs," *Southern Speech Journal*, 28:208–218, Spring, 1963.

I. If America puts sufficient money and research into outer space, we will land on the moon by 1970.
II. America will put sufficient money and research into outer space exploration.
III. America will land on the moon by 1970.

Note the logical testing to be applied to such general propositions:

a. Rarely are speeches framed as full-fledged syllogisms. You piece out the major premises to examine your own thinking and that of other speakers.

b. These major premises, whether stated or implied, are to be carefully proved rather than assumed. The major premise of the categorical illustration above, for example, calls for further scientific establishment. Cigarette smoking needs definition. Is it a package a week, or three packages a day? And are the cigarettes equipped with fiber tips? And does the smoker inhale? Thus, we need to qualify the major proposition in terms of *sometimes* and *some people* and so on to harmonize with whatever research justifies. Howard Howswer may be an exception.

c. All general statements are probabilities rather than certainties. Use *some* or an equivalent qualifying term in the so-called categorical statements. Avoid *allness* or other unqualified assertions like those applied above to cigarette smoking. Avoid sweeping statements such as "Americans are democratic." The implication here that *all* Americans are believers in democracy is obviously invalid. At least some oppose democracy.

d. Thorough testing of the premises and conclusions of the hypothetical and disjunctive examples above also reveals obvious statements that need full proof and much revision. Use evidence and arguments from causation, analogy, and generalization from specific cases to verify each proposition.

e. All facts need to be verified and all terms definitely explained and defined.

f. Rigid syllogistic reasoning has little place or practicality in persuasion-by-argumentation speaking.

DEVELOP REFUTATION

All argumentative speaking is both constructive and refutatory. Refutation is the process of producing arguments and evidence and of defending your own statements. If you are the sole speaker, you are to understand such possible undeclared arguments and to remove the inhibitions that an audience may have to your ideas and conclusions. Or, you may in a question period reply to arguments you have heard. Here are a few suggestions for your refutatory methods:

1. Before you begin your argument or your reply to another's, arm yourself on the subject.
2. In your own speech or in your reply to another's begin by a clear statement of the opposing argument. Represent fairly and fully what the rival position and argument has been—or would be if expressed.
3. Express your refutational materials clearly and fairly without pugnacity or dogmatism.
4. Match evidence with evidence.
5. Test a rival argument, whether expressed or not, by examination of its underlying assumptions, its hasty generalizations, its weak analogies, its false causal relations.
6. Show the inconsistency of the opposing arguments, or their irrelevancies to the question at hand.
7. Also, see suggestions under debating for rebuttal.[9]

CONDUCTING A DEBATE

To ensure that both sides of an argumentative speech are given, a debate is presented. One speaker (or two or three) on each side speaks. Debating is thus persuasion by argument conducted under strict parliamentary rules, as is done in legislative, courtroom, or other situations conforming to law. The rules in theory at least ensure equal treatment of both sides of an issue. This is the procedure of democratic government.

Discussion and debate, as we explained in a previous chapter, are complementary. Discussion implies analysis and disinterested review of arguments and evidence. Debate emerges when special arguments at any stage indicate the temporary abandonment of cooperative reflection. Discussion is not to be dismissed as impracticable. We use it as far as we can. Debate, moreover, is justified. When well-grounded convictions prevail, democratic action requires that the various positions be argued with votes and action to follow. But the minority vote is not trampled on. Debate, properly handled, contains the elements of good discussion.

[9] Robert H. Thouless, *Straight and Crooked Thinking,* Simon and Schuster, Inc., New York, 1932.

What is the relation of debate to argumentative speaking? In debate (1) time limits are observed, (2) the argument is under parliamentary rules, (3) each side has an equal number of speakers and an equal amount of time, (4) the subject is framed in resolution form, (5) an equal amount of time is given to each side for rebuttal, (6) a vote is taken at the end on the merits of the question.[10]

Let us assume that you are to take part in a debate—to argue according to specific rules. What are the rules and regulations of formal debates?

Note the time limits. Intercollegiate debates, for example, usually last one hour. During this time, according to the conventional plan, each of the four speakers speaks twice. Each speaker makes a constructive speech ten minutes long, and each is allowed five minutes for rebuttal to ensure review of the arguments presented. Thus the distribution of debating time is usually as follows:

Constructive Speeches	
First affirmative	10 minutes
First negative	10 minutes
Second affirmative	10 minutes
Second negative	10 minutes
Rebuttal Speeches	
First negative	5 minutes
First affirmative	5 minutes
Second negative	5 minutes
Second affirmative	5 minutes

For classroom debates the number of speakers and time limits may obviously be shortened. Four speakers may each have seven and three minutes. If two speakers only make up the debate, each may have a total of fifteen, ten and five minutes. The parliamentary rules guarantee to the two sides equal protection and opportunity. The affirmative opens and closes the debate, and the negative speaks first in rebuttal, even though in a two-speaker program, he has just completed his first speech.

The purpose of debating is to arrive at and record a decision. In student debates, engaged in for learning purposes, the critic judge

[10] A. Craig Baird, "Discussion and Debate in the Space Age," *Central States Speech Journal,* 50:48–52, Spring, 1959; Douglas Ehninger, "Decision by Debate: A Re-examination," *Quarterly Journal of Speech,* 45:282–287, October, 1959.

decides in favor of the team that does the most effective debating.

In intercollegiate debate in the early twentieth century, three critic judges were often used.

Preparation and Presentation

As a student of speech, you will work under the close supervision of your speech instructor. With your fellow speakers, select a topic that is of interest to you and word it carefully. Prepare or secure a list of references on your topic, and take careful notes on the material you read. Develop your argument with constant reference to the logical techniques outlined above. Draw up a tentative brief and submit it to your instructor or adviser for criticism. Revise this brief repeatedly as your command of your material develops.

In preliminary occasions with your teammates (unless you are the sole speaker for your side) report to one another on your readings, analyze the problems, and frame the issues. Decide upon your team case—the series of propositions that you want the judges and the audiences to accept in your argument. For example, the case for an affirmative proposition of policy might follow closely the stock issue propositions.

First Affirmative

I. The present situation is unsatisfactory.
II. Defects are inherent in the present system. (These two contentions prove the contention of the second affirmative that the proposition is necessary.)

Second Affirmative

I. The proposal will remedy these defects.
II. It is a practicable proposal.
III. It is preferable to other remedies. (These three contentions prove the advantages and practicality of the proposal.)

For the negative, the case might be exactly the reverse:

CASE A

First Negative

I. The present situation is satisfactory.
II. The alleged defects can be corrected without destroying the present policy.

Second Negative

III. The proposal will be detrimental.
IV. The proposal is impracticable.

The negative may vary these *cases* by some such plan as the following:

CASE B

First Negative

I. The proposal is impracticable.
II. The proposal is detrimental.

Second Negative

III. The proposal is not needed.

CASE C

First Negative

I. The plan is unworkable.
II. The plan is detrimental.

Second Negative

III. A better plan is proposed.

Other choices of case are also open to the negative. The case for a proposition of fact resolves itself into a series of statements that usually reflect (1) causes and results or (2) classification of the arguments or evidence.

Write your debate speech as a means of achieving effective condensation, clarity, and persuasiveness. But leave your written speech at home. Good debating must be extempore.

Practice rebuttal

You can improve your techniques in rebuttal by studying both sides and by collecting and classifying rebuttal cards in advance. In order to refute your opponents' ideas, listen attentively and take down the substance of his arguments. State clearly the idea to be refuted. Refute the central ideas, and avoid replying to points not made. Refute your opponents' ideas by attacking the accuracy of the facts, the weakness of his authorities, and the weakness of his arguments based on generalization, false analogy, and false causation. Then summarize your own case to indicate its superiority to that of your opponent.

When you are preparing to debate, practice delivery each day, even if a vacant chair is the only audience available. Your delivery in debate should be direct and conversational, free from bombast and insincerity. Finally, observe the conventions of debating courtesy. Remember to recognize the chairman at the beginning of each speech. In the debate itself, invariably be courteous to those of the other side. Let your attitude at every stage be friendly. While others are speaking, listen closely. Accept your responsibilities for genuine sportsmanship. Above all, argue in public (including radio debating) only on the side that reflects your convictions.[11]

Judging Debate

How good or bad is a given debate? What standards shall we apply? One method of judging is to get audience response. If most of the hearers vote for you, either by show of hands or by ballot, you have succeeded. But what should be the basis for judgment beyond merely "I like you" or "I like your argument and delivery."

The critic judge and you as an audience listener-observer usually follow some such basis of evaluation as the following: (1) skill in defining and analyzing the subject (selecting the proper issues), (2) skill in the use of evidence, (3) skill in the use of inference, (4) excellence in organization, (5) skill in audience adaptation, including the use of persuasive techniques (see also next chapter), (6) skill in refutation (to be noted especially in the second or rebuttal speech), (7) effective language, (8) effective delivery, and (9) general effectiveness. These items overlap; they do not have equal weight, and not all are to be strongly noted in each given speech. But they cover quite thoroughly the field of criticism.

Critic judges use them, or some similar criteria, for their decisions in the learning situations, "on the merits of the debate."

To measure a debate according to a life situation, audience votes on the merits of the question itself are provided. These votes with a shift-of-opinion ballot follow a listing of audience attitudes on the question before the debate begins and a second vote afterward to note whether a shift takes place from favorable to neutral or opposed, or in the reverse direction.[12]

[11] For further treatment of the subject consult A. Craig Baird, *Argumentation, Discussion and Debate*, McGraw-Hill Book Company, New York, 1950, especially chaps. 24–27; Richard Murphy, "The Ethics of Debating Both Sides," *Speech Teacher*, 12:242–237, September, 1963.

[12] See Waldo Braden and Earnest Brandenburg, *Oral Decision-making*, Harper & Row, Publishers, Incorporated, New York, 1955, chap. 24, "Evaluating Debate."

PROJECTS AND PROBLEMS

Project 1 Effectiveness in argumentative speaking

Purpose of this assignment: To demonstrate effective use of analysis, organization, evidence, argument, refutation, and delivery in a five-minute speech.
Procedure: Each member will select and limit his topic for a five-minute argumentative speech. Prepare and present to the instructor a brief to accompany your oral argument. In the presentation, define terms and state the issues (make this introduction not more than one minute long); develop a point or two with accompanying evidence and inference; conclude with a summary and a brief appeal for audience acceptance of your thesis or proposition.

Project 2 Class debate

Purpose of this assignment: To give the members some information about the conduct of a debate and to provide experiences in this type of speech.
Procedure: The class will select and word an important local or regional topic for debate. Assign to each member the presentation of the affirmative or negative side. Attempt to give each his choice of sides. Divide the time equally; for example, allow the affirmative seven minutes each for the constructive speech, the negative each ten minutes, and the affirmative three minutes for the rebuttal. If more convenient for the instructor and class, a two-speaker team can be organized for each side. Each debater should prepare and present to the instructor a brief of his constructive argument. The class and instructor will comment briefly on each debater.

The following are possible topics for debate for project 1 or 2 above. Each may be rephrased by the group.

1. Farm price supports should be discontinued.
2. The United States should withdraw all military forces from the European continent, including West Germany.
3. Dissemination of birth control information should be legalized.
4. Student protest demonstrations at my university should be condemned.
5. The United States and Russia should adopt a joint program for prohibiting the worldwide proliferation of hydrogen bombs.
6. College and university grades should be abolished—except Pass and Fail.

7. The Federal government should regulate all rates of interstate trucking.
8. The phrase "God is dead" is meaningless.
9. The United States should drastically reduce all foreign aid.
10. Congress should prohibit strikes in all major industries.
11. The United States should abandon its program of sending men to the moon.
12. Class attendance in all colleges should be optional.
13. The Central Intelligence Agency (CIA) should be abolished.

REFERENCES

Baird, A. Craig: *Argumentation, Discussion and Debate,* McGraw-Hill Book Company, New York, 1950.

Bauer, Otto F.: *Fundamentals of Debate: Theory and Practice,* Scott, Foresman and Company, Chicago, 1966.

Capp, Glen R., and Thelma R. Capp: *Principles of Argumentation and Debate,* Prentice-Hall, Inc., Englewood Cliffs, N. J., 1965.

Ehninger, Douglas, and Wayne Brockriede: *Decision by Debate,* Dodd, Mead & Company, Inc., New York, 1963.

Freeley, Austin J.: *Argumentation and Debate: Rational Decision Making,* 2d ed., Wadsworth Publishing Co., Inc., Belmont, Calif., 1966.

Haney, T. K.: *An Introduction to Debate,* Ginn and Company, Boston, 1965 (paperbound).

Huber, Robert B.: *Influencing Through Argument,* David McKay Company, Inc., New York, 1963.

Kruger, Arthur N.: *Modern Debate: Its Logic and Strategy,* McGraw-Hill Book Company, New York, 1960.

McBath, James H. (ed.): *Argumentation and Debate,* rev. ed., Holt, Rinehart and Winston, Inc., New York, 1963.

McBurney, James H., and Glen E. Mills: *Argumentation and Debate,* 2d ed., The Macmillan Company, New York, 1964.

Miller, Gerald R., and Thomas R. Nilsen (eds.): *Perspectives on Argumentation,* Scott, Foresman and Company, Chicago, 1966.

Windes, Russel R., and Arthur Hastings: *Argumentation and Advocacy,* Random House, Inc., New York, 1965.

16 PERSUASIVE SPEAKING: PSYCHOLOGICAL CONSIDERATIONS

In the last chapter we dealt with the logical basis of persuasion; in this chapter we shall be concerned with persuasion as a psychological phenomenon. The change could be described as a change from a philosophical to a scientific approach to the subject. Although we shall employ a different language for a different set of concepts, we shall have the same goal, a better understanding of communication as used to develop and modify attitudes and other human behavior in a socially acceptable manner. We do not believe that the scientific study of persuasion is any less worthy, honorable, or useful than is its philosophical study. Indeed the scientist may claim that his methods are more exact, and in this very exactness he may get closer to the "truth" than the speculative philosopher.

The purpose of rhetoric is the discovery within any subject of the available means of persuasion. The goal of the communication behavioral scientist might be paraphrased as the discovery within people, subjects, and situations of the available means of communication. People as well as subjects make a difference in persuasion. Inherent features of human nature are the affective and motor, as well as the cognitive, systems. These are all subsystems of the total organism, and this organism strives to maintain a working consistency and harmony of these subsystems. It is true, however, that these subsystems do frequently get out of tune or consonance with each other. When the cognitive system perceives this inconsistency, the system is said to be in a state of cognitive dissonance or conflict. Although we do not consider the cognitive dissonance theory of persuasion to be a complete persuasion theory, it has in recent years generated a substantial amount of research on communication.

We do not consider the affective or emotive system as inherently inconsistent with the logical or cognitive system. Logical behavior is not necessarily unemotional. These systems are not opposite ends of a single continuum but rather independent continua which may cross each other at any place between the two extremes on each of the continua. Although the demagogue and the charlatan will abuse the use of emotive appeals, they will as blithely violate the simple test of validity of fact and inference. One may suspect that the narrow defender of the unimplemented logical appeal may be guilty of the fallacy suggested by the line of argument which says the charlatan employs an emotional appeal, the charlatan is a socially undesirable exploiter, and therefore anyone who uses emotional appeal is a socially undesirable exploiter. There can be no place in persuasion for either logical fallacy or bogus appeals. Psychological considerations in persuasion have their value in their use for worthy and socially desirable modifications of the way people feel and what they believe or do.

Some who object to the use of appeals which are personal and emotional do so because they consider their emotional behavior primitive or immature and are embarrassed by evidence of its personal arousal. These people are often high-order intellectuals or at least perceive themselves in this way. In self-fulfillment they devote themselves to the development of cognitive skills. Even such people, however, become emotionally upset when their source of security in intellectual behavior is challenged.

Another objection to some thinking about emotions is the conflicts among scholars as to the nature, functions, and conceptual value of drives, emotions, and motivation. The difficulty of classifying patterns of biologically adequate emotional responses has led to a variety of classifications. This situation has led some psychologists to the omission altogether of such words as emotion and motivation. Young has said, "Views concerning the nature of motivation diverge widely and differ among themselves. The different views, however, are compatible to a high degree and are supplementary. Not all of them are mutually exclusive."[1] And in another place he says, "It is possible to avoid concepts like *drive* and *emotion;* but these concepts are often found to be useful. Skinner's position has been described as a 'psychology of the empty organism' to contrast it with physiological psychology."[2]

The concept of the emotional appeal as we have said earlier has been useful.[3] It is one of the oldest aspects of persuasive theory we know. It has been maintained because it works. It works because the affective system involved in these appeals is the energizing system. As Young says, "Affective processes have activating (energizing, driving) functions in that they provoke action. They lead the organism to do something."[4] We refer here not to nervous energy as such but to the muscular and kinetic energy released by nerve impulses.

Since much of our research in motivation is evaluated by the use of attitude scales, they call for at least a brief description. The attitude scale is a device for the measurement of the interest, set, attitude, belief, and opinion syndrome. These words are used to designate much the same state of readiness and direction in the employment of the energies of the organization. An attitude is not a qualitative all-or-none matter. It represents degrees along a continuum revealed by scaled words or sentences to which the subject reacts. The reaction to the scale is validated against the behavior of people toward the stimulus object, represented by word and sentence symbols. Since the stimuli are quantitatively scaled, attitudes are revealed by measures of central tendency, internal variability and change.[5] Since beliefs are complex generalized reactions, they tend to consist of a large number of subbeliefs as a part of each belief system. A collection of subbeliefs therefore provides a better index of attitudes than does either the generalized conception in itself or any one of the subsystem beliefs.

EVALUATION OF PERSUASIVE APPEALS

We have already pointed out that evaluating persuasive appeals is important to intelligent speaking as well as listening. There are

[1] Paul Thomas Young, *Motivation and Emotion,* John Wiley & Sons, Inc., New York, 1961, p. 23.

[2] *Ibid.,* p. 20.

[3] See Chap. 15.

[4] Young, *op. cit.,* p. 201.

[5] See Marie Jahoda and Neil Warren, *Attitudes,* Penguin Books, Inc., Baltimore, 1960.

basically three types of persuasive appeals to action: valid, marginal, and bogus.

Valid appeals. Valid appeals are directed toward worthy motives which have a reasonable prospect of satisfaction through the action proposed. Few satisfactions are absolutely certain, but only those which are free from reasonable doubt may properly be considered valid. An example of such an appeal was the request for a declaration of war on Japan in 1941 on the basis of the belief that only by going to war could we survive as a nation.

Marginal appeals. Marginal appeals are proposals in which the satisfactions suggested may be real but are of minor or incidental value. These short-term appeals to action may be accepted as appropriate for particular needs, but they can scarcely be approved for use in connection with the satisfaction of more permanent and important ones; for example, "Join my club and you will meet the right people."

Bogus appeals. These are appeals which foment hasty and ill-considered action or which offer false and improbable claims of satisfaction through the action proposed. They include appeals which frustrate the higher codes of society by arousing the baser emotions. Most of the abuses of persuasion belong to this class. Some patent-medicine advertisements provide examples: for instance, "Restore your health with a bottle of Zixolon." [6]

TECHNIQUES OF PERSUASION

Genuine persuasion depends upon focusing the attention and interest of the audience on your ideas, winning the goodwill of your audience, and stimulating an active response. Note how each of these techniques is applied.

Getting attention and sustaining interest

William James's theory of persuasion is that what holds attention determines action.[7] If this theory is true, your ability to hold the audience's attention will determine your success as a persuasive

[6] Review Chap. 5, "Listening," for more detailed discussion of propaganda and emotional appeals to guard against the fake and the unworthy.

[7] See William James, *Psychology: Briefer Course,* Henry Holt and Company, Inc., New York, 1900, p. 448.

speaker. The audience must remain focused upon the job to be done. However, man's attention span is limited because tension is involved, which must be relaxed occasionally. If the speaker does not give his audience opportunities to relax, it may cease to follow him. The speaker must make it easy for his audience to be attentive.

1 ***Show the significance of the proposal.*** Presenting an idea as something vital to the listener is the most important way of attaining credibility. The listener must be well motivated to be attentive. Your proposal must appeal to important wants, desires, and needs. By focusing your audience's attention upon the benefits to be derived from your proposal, you can arouse responses of anticipation, acceptance, and approach—responses which are only a short step from action.

2 ***Use reasoned discourse.*** Without supercharging your speech with dull facts, you should include valid evidence and inferences that will convince hearers of your logical soundness. Most people want the truth. Therefore, they resort to reason and expect that their speakers will do so. We have indicated above the necessity for logic as well as emotion. Your use of generalizations, authorities, analogies, causal reasoning, and deductive patterns becomes the basis and an intrinsic part of your psychological effectiveness.

3 ***Make use of conflict concerning your proposal.*** When our goals are threatened, our energies are renewed. To direct this energy through your persuasive speech, show the dangers which threaten the audience's ideals and standards if they do not accept your proposal. The dissonant responses of your listener open the door to the understanding of your message. If your audience feels that their cherished ideals are threatened and your proposal will protect them, they will identify themselves with you as a person and endorse your proposal.

4 ***Sometimes shock the listener.*** If the listener accepts his goals as a matter of course, he may need to be jolted out of his complacency. Pearl Harbor was a shock which awakened many Americans to the need for fighting to preserve our way of life. Many drivers are more careful after witnessing an automobile wreck. The introduction of surprise has in it elements of the shock response. Use this technique carefully in order to avoid creating resentment, which will damage rather than help your cause.

5 ***Arouse curiosity.*** Tell a story which has a conclusion that is pertinent to your cause. Expound causes whose effects will arouse the audience's curiosity. An unexpected pause attracts attention. When you use these techniques, be sure to show their significance for your speech.

6 ***Make your speech easy to follow.*** Any proposal which puts a strain on attention will be dull. Make attention easy for your readers by appealing to the various senses—visual, auditory, kinetic, olfactory, gustatory, and others. Organize your proposal so that main points are arranged in a natural and easy-to-remember sequence. Repeat and restate your ideas so that there can be no chance of confusion. Provide adequate transition from point to point.

7 ***Use variety.*** A speech in which the new is balanced with the familiar is more interesting than a speech in which all the materials are completely new or familiar. Methods of achieving variety, which we have discussed in earlier chapters, are movement which appeals to the eye; variations in rate, loudness, pitch, and quality of voice which appeal to the ear; and changes in words and sentence length and form.

Attention is contagious and cumulative in an audience, and it can be increased by the deliberate use of the methods we have suggested. But beware of attention-getting devices which call attention to themselves; "ham" acting is not good speaking. To acquire skill in the use of attention-getting techniques requires practice.

Creating goodwill

The goodwill of the speaker toward the audience is essential in persuasive speaking. But it is not sufficient that the speaker simply be a person of goodwill; he must communicate his attitude to his audience. He must aim at that quality of expression that makes him seem credible.[8]

1 ***Know your audience and respond quickly to their reactions.*** Recognition of the right to disagree must be the basis of any attempt at persuasion, for the persuaded person must be won, not pushed, to agreement. Recognition of this right is part of respect for one's audience and their ability to make a wise decision. Even though you will disagree with your audience on major issues—if you did not, you would not be making a persuasive speech—you will yield

[8] Carl I. Hovland, Irving L. Janis, and Harold H. Kelley, *Communication and Persuasion,* Yale University Press, New Haven, 1953, chap. 2.

to their views in some respects in order to win their acceptance of your views in other respects. Sometimes you can do this by praising what the listener approves or condemning what he hates. But if you cannot do these things honestly, you should not resort to them.

2 ***Demonstrate your mastery of the subject.*** Evidence of your knowledge of and ability to handle the materials of your subject—to interpret soundly and organize well—will influence your audience strongly. If you can demonstrate your ability to resolve problems and conflicts through unusual insight, you will win their respect and admiration. Avoid dogmatism, often a defensive attitude suggesting weakness. Evidence that your experience has contributed successfully to others' needs in like situations is very persuasive.

3 ***Give evidence that you are a worthy leader.*** The record of your achievements, if it is well presented, will add to your prestige. It is difficult tactfully to prove your ability to your audience, but if you solicit the support of others, you must indicate to them that you are a good leader. Courage to fight for one's convictions, the ability to meet tests, and evidence of past successes demonstrate to your audience your capacity for future successes. Learn to use your record without a vulgar parade of egotism and conceit.

4 ***Your character will influence your audience.*** Character, to your audience, means a record of conformity with the virtues they recognize. As a persuasive speaker, you must identify your character with the just, the virtuous, the magnanimous. The good guys win in persuasion as well as on television. Where character is in doubt, other qualities of personality are useless.

Certain personality traits can be depended upon to contribute to persuasive speaking. Modesty and restraint are preferable to egotism, lack of control, and exaggeration. Develop the ability to adapt your moods to listeners—to be earnest, good-humored, amusing, and forgiving on minor matters but uncompromising concerning major matters and ideals.[9]

Goodwill toward your subject may be created by showing its altruistic nature, the benefits it would provide to your listeners, and its practical advantages. Although objections must be taken into account and duly eliminated, they should not be heavily stressed. Keep the true strength of the proposal in focus by emphasis on its benefits. Lead the audience to the desired conclusion by placing the necessary information in their hands and encouraging them to make their own decisions.

[9] *Ibid.*, chap. 6.

Stimulating a favorable response

1 ***Appeal to dominant motives.*** Good persuasion is in effect the successful appeal to motives. An appeal consists of showing by statement or implication the relationship between the motives of the listener and the goals you believe to be the worthy purpose of your discourse. This appeal, to work, must achieve a close harmony between the proposal and the dominant motives of the listener. Motives are usually complex and variable. Behavior is organized through an arrangement of the motives of the moment in a hierarchy of values; motives dominant at one time may play a subordinate role in influencing behavior at a later time. Different persons do the same thing for different reasons.

Effective persuasion succeeds by creating such cognitive dissonance [10] in the subject that he acts to escape from his unhappy awareness of the problem. Cognitive dissonance is that type of motivated state which causes the listener to want to act. If he is in this state he is most apt to be ready for the action you suggest. To create this readiness for action by the listener, the speaker should know something of the drives which motivate men.

The four different types of drives, which overlap in some degree, are (*a*) the biological, (*b*) the ego, (*c*) the social, and (*d*) the habitual.[11] Many other attempts have been made to catalog human motives, and the various classifications differ greatly with regard to the nature and value of the motives. We do not maintain that our classification is complete. The student may add to this list as his knowledge and experience warrant.

Many of the *biological* drives may be called hungers. They are cyclical in nature, and their force depends upon the state of the organism. They are among the strongest of the drives. The desire for food and shelter, for example, is basic to life; our efforts to acquire and retain these necessities consume much of our energy. However, the particular forms in which we satisfy biological drives are largely matters of personal or cultural habit. The desire to avoid danger may also be considered a biological drive. Depending upon the person, the sex drive may be related to the desire to care for and rear children. The desire for freedom from restraints on action appears, to some extent, to be of biological origin; the newborn babe struggles when held too tightly. Derived from this may be the adult's seeking of personal freedom of belief and action. Also bio-

[10] Leon Festinger, *A Theory of Cognitive Dissonance,* Row, Peterson & Company, Evanston, Ill., 1957.

[11] Hovland, Janis, and Kelley, *op. cit.*, chaps. 3 and 4.

logical in origin are the drives to release emotional tension—often in the exercise of pleasant sensations and emotions—and to avoid unsatisfying sensations and emotions. The biological drives are stronger and more primitive than most others. They are commonly considered the basic motives to action.

Desires for self-respect, pride, and dignity can be classified as *ego* drives. These drives have been called the desire for a feeling of personal worth. Men commonly seek to excel, to gain power, to control, to create, to meet the challenges to their abilities. The acquisition of property is one of the ways in which this drive finds expression. Care of one's appearance is, no doubt, a function of the desire for self-respect. The attainment of self-images and ideals is also a manifestation of an ego drive. These drives are subject to modification by experience and learning.

The *social* drives are to a great extent the product of experience, and may be largely habitual. They appear in the desire for conformity, favorable attention, and status. We like to be approved by our associates; as a result, we are stimulated by praise and reproof, by social sanctions and taboos. The self may be sublimated to serve the social virtues of trust, integrity, loyalty, precedent, fair play, good sportsmanship, and justice. Social drives are altruistic and unselfish as contrasted with the more immediately selfish desires, and for this reason they are sometimes called the higher motives. They offer longterm appeals to enlightened selfishness.

The drives of *habit* include intellectual work, and emotional activities, and the maintenance of tastes, interests, and preferences. They also may involve the search for new experience, adventure, and growth as well as the preferences for the traditional, the familiar, and the maintenance of the status quo. We often retain for years habits that have ceased to serve their original purpose.

2 ***Remove inhibitions.*** Persuasion cannot be expected to work where action is inhibited by conflicting drives. The causes of objection to action may be met by strengthening favorable drives and reducing the strength of competing ones. Competing motives can be eliminated by showing that they do not apply to the proposal or that they may be satisfied in other ways. If the drives that inhibit action are successfully removed, a proposal for action which stimulates a dominant motive develops and releases the energy necessary for action.

3 ***Aim at action.*** The persuasive speech derives much of its force from the presentation of a practical plan of action. The plan may

be the deciding element in persuasion when powerful motives and drives are closely associated with the proposal in the mind of the audience but lack direction and organization. Emphasis on the benefits to be derived from carrying out the plan serves to strengthen the relationship between desire and method.

Conciliation and restraint of action

Conciliation as a type of persuasion differs from others in that, instead of stimulating interest, conviction, or action, it seeks to stop action, create doubt, and reconcile opposing groups. To do these things it is necessary to counteract the intensity of motivation; thus many of the principles we have discussed will apply in reverse to conciliation.

As a conciliatory speaker, you must create goodwill. An objective and impersonal manner provides little opportunity for positive emotional response. Keep the attention of the listener pleasantly distracted and focused on inaction. Delay action by appealing to motives that conflict with those which are aroused. Pit motive against motive. Concede on some issues as an appeal to pride and tolerance and emphasize pertinent grounds of agreement. Show better ways of satisfying the motives for action, and appeal to the higher and more critical motives.

We have considered persuasion as the use of motivation added to the evidence and logic of argumentation in appeals to action. The persuasive speaker should carefully consider the motives to which he is directing his persuasion to assure himself of their validity. The techniques of persuasion involve such processes as creating goodwill, getting attention and maintaining interest, and showing the relationship of the proposal to the dominant motives of listeners. Although most persuasion is designed to release the energies in action, occasionally inhibition or cessation of action is called for.

PROJECTS AND PROBLEMS

Project 1 The study of slanting in persuasion

Read one of the speeches employing persuasive technique in Baird's *Representative American Speeches* [12] and make a report to the class on

[12] A. Craig Baird, *Representative American Speeches,* H. W. Wilson Company, New York, annual; see also Lester Thonssen, editor of this series after 1959.

(1) attention-getting devices, (2) slanting, and (3) the quality of emotional appeals.

Project 2 Development of interest in the subject

Purposes of this assignment: (1) To develop knowledge of the techniques of making speeches interesting, (2) to develop in arousing interest.
Procedure: Select a topic for a persuasive speech, and outline two or three main points to support the central idea. Develop your main points by using material which applies one or more of the principles for making material interesting.

Project 3 The persuasive appeal to action

Purposes of this assignment: The persuasive appeal to action adds the use of emotional appeal to evidence and logic. Carefully select a few persuasive techniques adapted to particular listeners or readers as a better method of persuasion than attempting to use a large number of such devices in a particular argument.
Subjects for this speech:

- Buy government bonds
- Join a hobby club
- Sign this petition
- Have an annual health examination
- Learn to swim
- Drive carefully
- Become a church member
- Buy a school paper
- Keep a budget
- Buy Christmas seals
- Keep to the campus walks
- Write your letters with scripture ink
- Form new study habits
- Take a course in psychology
- Make government service a lifework
- Contribute to the Red Cross
- Read this book

Project 4 The speech to restrain action

Purposes of this project: The speech designed to inhibit or restrain action operates on principles which are quite dissimilar to those which arouse action. It is essentially the refutation of the emotional appeal. Work on these techniques in a three-minute speech.
Subjects for this speech:

- Break the smoking habit
- Learn to control your temper
- Don't spend money foolishly
- Don't speed
- Stop drifting
- Some "don'ts" of human relationships
- Don't take advantage of the little fellow
- Don't walk on the grass

Project 5 The speech of conciliation

Purposes of this project: To reach the antagonistic listener or reader or the person who has a closed mind on the subject. In the development of the idea and its support, conciliation techniques function not as a substitute for evidence and reasoning but as a method of handling evidence for a particular purpose.
Subjects for this speech:

1. Southerners are responsible for the plight of the Negro in the South.
2. Racial prejudice against minority groups is to be deplored.
3. Compulsory teacher oaths will not produce better democracy.
4. The rights of labor must be preserved.
5. Modern society demands some governmental control of business.
6. Civil liberties do not excuse citizens from social responsibilities.
7. Conscientious objectors are not necessarily cowards.
8. American democracy can be improved.
9. Religious freedom does not include the right to prevent compulsory vaccination of children.
10. War crimes cannot be punished as ordinary crimes in a nation are punished.
11. Progressive education is not a panacea.
12. New ideas and practices do not always mean progress.
13. The various Christian denominations have much to learn from one another.
14. Someone in a position of authority over you has emphatically denied a request. You do not consider the case closed. How would you get a hearing?
15. A friend takes offense because of some imagined insult. Straighten out the misunderstanding.
16. You are accused unfairly and maliciously of an act you did not commit. How will you square yourself?
17. As a committee chairman, you are to present a request to a group in which there is tension and irritation toward the proposal.

REFERENCES

Brehm, Jack W., and Arthur R. Cohen: *Explorations in Cognitive Dissonance,* John Wiley & Sons, Inc., New York, 1962.

Brown, J. A. C.: *Techniques of Persuasion,* Penguin Books, Inc., Baltimore, 1963.

Cattell, Raymond B.: *The Scientific Analysis of Personality,* Penguin Books, Inc., Baltimore, 1965.

Festinger, Leon: *A Theory of Cognitive Dissonance,* Row, Peterson & Company, Evanston, Ill., 1957.

Fotheringham, Wallace C.: *Perspectives on Persuasion,* Allyn and Bacon, Inc., Boston, 1966.

Hovland, Carl I.: *The Order of Presentation in Persuasion,* Yale University Press, New Haven, Conn., 1957.

, Irving L. Janis, and Harold H. Kelley: *Communication and Persuasion,* Yale University Press, New Haven, Conn., 1953.

Jahoda, Marie: *Attitudes,* Penguin Books, Inc., Baltimore, 1966.

Janis, Irving L., et al.: *Personality and Persuasibility,* Yale University Press, New Haven, Conn., 1959.

Johannesen, Richard L.: *Ethics and Persuasion,* Random House, Inc., New York, 1967.

Katz, Elihu, and Paul F. Lazarsfeld: *Personal Influence,* The Free Press of Glencoe, New York, 1955.

Minnick, Wayne C.: *The Art of Persuasion,* Houghton Mifflin Company, Boston, 1957.

Rosenberg, M. J., et al.: *Attitude Organization and Change,* Yale University Press, New Haven, Conn., 1960.

Scheidel, Thomas M.: *Persuasive Speaking,* Scott, Foresman and Company, Chicago, 1967.

Sherif, Muzafer, and Carl I. Hovland: *Social Judgment,* Yale University Press, New Haven, Conn., 1961.

——— and Carolyn W. Sherif: *Reference Group,* Harper & Row, Publishers, Incorporated, New York, 1964.

———, ———, and R. C. Nebergall: *Attitudes and Attitude Change,* W. B. Saunders Company, Philadelphia, 1965.

Young, Paul Thomas: *Motivation and Emotion,* John Wiley & Sons, Inc., New York, 1961.

17 ORAL READING

The preceding chapters are devoted to processes and types of communication activity in which the speaker chooses what he is to say and how he is to say it. We can call this chapter the study of original or creative speech. Here we are concerned with reading to others what someone else has said. This we call oral reading or interpretative speech. The speech skills used in these two types of communication are similar. They differ as types of activity. College students often read aloud less skillfully than they speak. Perhaps this is to be expected because they do less of it. On the other hand typical college graduates will do a great deal of oral reading. Since they will be expected to read aloud, they should know how to do it reasonably well.

We are not concerned about the reading of specialized forms of literature characteristic of the radio actor or the teacher of literature. The person who is to do this should take a course devoted to interpretation. We are concerned about comparatively simple problems in reading as suggested by the following examples. Part of religious services, including the congregational responses, is oral reading. Secretaries of organizations read the minutes. Educational and other leaders often read their detailed reports to professional colleagues. Teachers read much to their classes. In family gatherings reading aloud is still widely practiced.

Much of this oral performance is poor. The ideas are poorly digested; words and phrases are stumbled over. Listeners are bored, confused, or bewildered. The interpreter himself is lifeless or uncertain in the reading.

The problem is how to convey the words that you or others have composed, with skillful reflection of ideas, purposes, and language nuances and constructive use of tonal and visual symbols. Many literary works come alive only when they are read aloud. Great speeches, too, regain something of their power when properly interpreted.

Effective oral reading depends upon many of the same factors that produce effective speech. Articulation, voice control, self-confidence, physical expression, and directness play their parts in both activities. The crucial difference between the two appears to center around the speaker's ability to communicate ideas from another source.

The source of the ideas you express in extempore speaking is recollection and the creative imagination. The source of the ideas you express in reading is the interpretation of the printed page. Some persons find it easier to express their own ideas. Others, freed from the responsibility of determining what ideas to express and how to express them, do better in interpreting ideas already expressed by others. Effective communication requires skills of both the creative and the interpretative types.

Oral reading must be judged by the meaning it communicates; it cannot be evaluated merely as expression. It is not just a show or an exhibition. The reader may be very proud of his techniques, or think he is a good reader because he has studied some of the devices of reading. But if he is mature, he will realize that he is just an instrument or channel for projecting the author's message to others. If the author's intent and meaning are not sought and emphasized, then the reading has failed. Some beginning readers are so fearful that their audience will consider them exhibitionistic that they hold back. This may detract seriously from the meaning received by the audience. Anything which is worth reading is worth reading well. This means that a reader must neither make of his interpretation an exhibition, nor be content with being so inadequate a channel that the meaning is lost or distorted. Faults of the latter type are frequent among today's college-student readers.

PRINCIPLES OF ORAL READING

1 ***Understand the reasons for success in developing skill in oral reading.*** Many of our difficulties in reading aloud are traceable to the faulty methods by which we were taught to read. The flash-card method often results in word-by-word reading: Words are printed on cards, and the student learns what the word looks like on each card; when the word is exposed, he says it aloud. Soon the cards are placed together to form a sentence, and the student reads the sentence by naming the word on each card.

Other difficulties have their origin in the failure to distinguish between the processes of silent and oral reading. Silent reading often involves skimming a paragraph or page to get the meaning of a passage as a whole. If the meaning of a word or phrase is not readily apparent, the reader may hurry over it with the hope of understanding it from the context. Moreover, much of our silent reading concerns light material, which can be grasped at a faster rate than more serious instructional material. Although these habits may be appropriate to silent reading, depending upon the reader's purpose, they are destructive to good oral application when they appear as mumbling. Since the listener does not have the benefit of punctuation marks, the oral reader must use techniques of phrasing and inflection to take their place. Rapid or slow oral reading is often monotonous and fails completely to convey the intended meaning. However, oral reading usually requires a slower rate for comprehension than the silent process. The reader must adjust his speed to the distractions and responses of his listeners. In silent reading, if we do not immediately undertand a word or passage, we can go back and study it; in oral reading, if the material is not instantly intelligible to listeners, the meaning is lost. Their interest wanes and reading ceases to be communication.

2 ***Study the meaning of the material you are to read.*** Before you can share ideas, you must understand them. The first step is learning unfamiliar words. Words often have several meanings; you must therefore determine the appropriate one on the basis of context. Read with a provisional interpretation until the exact meaning is clarified.

Find the central idea of the passage and keep it in mind as you read. Analyze the purpose for which the material was written. Purpose, when it is not clarified by exact statement, is frequently revealed by the mood of the material; even simple informative prose reveals a great variety of attitudes on the part of the writer. The reader must understand and express these meanings clearly if he is to interpret them.

Analyze and evaluate the ideas presented and judge for yourself the soundness of the causal relationships involved. Ask yourself if the generalizations fit the evidence. Relate the ideas to your own experience in order to interpret their meaning. Preparation for oral reading should do justice to the importance of the material.

Sometimes we find it necessary to read with minimum preparation or at sight. The techniques of analysis which we have discussed apply even to reading on short notice. A brief glance may orient the reader to the more significant aspects of the material. The beginner cannot expect to read well, however, without devoting considerable time to preparation.

3 ***Develop an appropriate and flexible rate of reading.*** The rate of oral reading must be slow enough for clear comprehension but fast enough so that the listener's attention does not lag. According to one study, the average oral-reading rate for simple informative prose is about 165 words a minute.[1] Experience in observing untrained readers warrants the conclusion that more of them read too fast than too slowly. Reading rates should vary with the reading situation: Light or simple material may be read faster than heavy or complex material; but if the reader's purpose is to give the audience a thorough or exact understanding of the content, the rate should be slower than that of reading for amusement. For a large or formal audience, the rate should be slower than for a small informal one. This timing should be adapted to the style, the mood revealed by the material, and the importance of the idea expressed.

4 ***Phrase words intelligently within sentences.*** Phrasing is usually accomplished by means of pauses, but other vocal processes such as variations in rate, pitch, quality, and loudness are also useful in setting off phrases for purposes of making meaning clear. The phrasal pause cannot be clearly differentiated from the emphatic pause, since both are used to clarify meaning; but length of the phrasal pause should be adjusted to suggest variations in meaning as revealed by differences in punctuation. Consider the length of various phrasal pauses in the following sentence:

> *He spoke sharply, but with consideration, to the prisoner; quietly, but with feeling, to his mother; and confidently, but with deference, to the captain.*

[1] Frederic L. Darley, "A Normative Study of Oral-reading Rate," unpublished master's thesis, State University of Iowa, Iowa City, 1940.

Rules for phrasing cannot be based precisely on punctuation, although the careful study of punctuation will suggest the proper phrasing of many sentences. Overphrasing, or the mechanical breaking up of the sentence into minor units, will only confuse the meaning. Underphrasing is, however, a more common fault than overphrasing.

There are three important reasons for careful phrasing of the material you read aloud. First, units of meaning in oral communication are ordinarily derived from phrases rather than from words or sentences. Study each sentence to find the methods of phrasing which make the meaning clear. Phrasing or word grouping within the sentence is often—but not always—revealed by punctuation. Consider the differences in meaning of the two ways of punctuating or phrasing the following sentence:

The Captain said the mate was drunk today.
"The Captain," said the mate, "was drunk today."

A second reason for careful phrasing is that the shortness of the listener's span of attention may permit him to keep in mind only a limited number of words at one time. If the phrases are long, he may lose track of the sequence of ideas. Thirdly, phrasing helps the oral reader maintain effective control of his breathing for vocalization. Although the first of these reasons is the most important one, the others are also significant.

5 ***Emphasize and subordinate ideas effectively.*** In spite of the fact that the ideas in any reading passage vary in importance, one of the most common faults of oral reading is monotony—of rate, force, or pitch. Whereas the hypnotist, through monotony, may put his subject into a trance, the oral speaker may only succeed in putting his audience to sleep. The chief purpose of vocal variation, however, is not to catch attention but to clarify meaning. Rhythmical variations in voice which produce a singsong pattern may be as monotonous as a completely even delivery, and arbitrary variations for the sake of arousing attention are confusing. The student of oral reading should make a careful study of vocal variation as presented in Chapter 10.

Use vocal emphasis to make transitions clear. Climax is achieved by using minor vocal variations in the introduction and more radical variations near the point of greatest emphasis. Descending cadences, moderation of tempo, and softening of intensity are difficult but important techniques for indicating that the conclusion is near. Beware of overemphasis; shouting only irritates and tires the listener. Remember that the repetition of a phrase or sentence in oral reading, as elsewhere, is a good technique for emphasis.

6 ***Read loudly enough to be heard easily.*** The level of intensity of a bedtime story is not adequate for group reading. Concert pianos are tuned to a higher pitch than chamber pianos to increase the effectiveness of projection. Some sounds in the English language are difficult to hear unless the reader uses sufficient force to project them clearly and sharply. Such unvoiced sounds as *f*, *t*, *p*, and initial *th* are especially difficult.

7 ***Read fluently and precisely, pronouncing words clearly.*** Stumbling over words, reading hesitantly, and repeating of words or phrases at random confuse the listener. Learn to anticipate meaning and the inflectional changes necessary to communicate it. Focus words sharply so that you do not fall into the habit of making wrong and confusing guesses at their importance and their meaning. Learn to follow the lines of type even as you look up at your listeners. It is better to pause briefly to scan a line than to guess wildly and therefore to find it necessary to repeat and correct the inflections or phrasing.

8 ***Read factual and emotional material with the expression appropriate to each.*** Anyone who has listened to an inexperienced person read from a script in responding to the questions of a radio interviewer should have a good idea of the purpose of this principle. Read informative materials sympathetically but objectively. Conversational reading is difficult, but it is a skill which can be developed with practice. Variations in rate, pitch, and loudness contribute to a conversational tone. One phrase may be slowed down and uttered in a light, soft voice; the next may be speeded up, with a marked change in pitch and tonal vigor. All changes must reflect the meaning and mood of the ideas involved.

It is possible to read emotionally toned materials in a manner which reveals the mood without suggesting that you share the emotion. You will not seem sincere, however, unless you respond to the mood. For example, a formal ritual would not be effective if read as the routine of a radio comedian. Much of our discussion in this chapter has had to do with principles for reading relatively simple prose. In the reading of the story, a play, or poetry, the meanings may be more connotative than denotative. This writing may be considered a more creative work of art. The art reflects some life value, conflict, or interest. To sense the true affective as well as the logical meaning of the piece and to communicate this meaning without distortion to listeners is a challenge to any reader.

The principle of first importance is to keep your mind clearly focused on the meaning to be communicated. Work to respond actively to the ideas you are reading.

9 ***Adjust to the situation.*** Learn to hold the reading material up so that you can see it clearly and can avoid constriction in your jaw and throat. Do not hold a paper or book in such a way that your face is hidden from your listeners. Be sure that you have adequate light. Practice reading with and without a reading stand. But do not become so engrossed in your materials that you act them out. Respond with facial expression and bodily action to ideas, but avoid distracting mannerisms. Learn to respond effectively to humor without conspicuously laughing at your own jokes.

10 ***Adjust to your listeners.*** The ultimate objective of oral reading is to affect your listeners. Good reading is not exhibitionistic or elocutionary. Keep the social purpose of your reading in mind, and develop the techniques which will achieve it. Think of your work as projection to *listeners* rather than merely reading *from a manuscript.* If your material needs introduction, orient your listeners before you start; do not plunge in and expect them to catch up with you. On the other hand, if some factor in the situation has operated as an introduction and your listeners are ready to hear what you are to read, you do not need a further introduction.

PROJECTS AND PROBLEMS

Project 1 The basic skills in reading aloud

Purposes of this assignment: (1) To obtain a better understanding of the standards of effective reading; (2) to work on the development of skill in reading aloud; (3) to provide practice in working on voice problems. Procedure: Study the material suggested for this assignment until you understand clearly the meaning of the selection as a whole. Look up the meaning and pronunciation of any unfamiliar words. If you have difficulty with phrasing,/ mark off the words/ that are to be grouped together,/ as you find them in this sentence. Decide which *words* in each *sentence* should receive emphasis; draw a *heavy* line under words which are to receive *strong emphasis* and a *dashed line* under words to be stressed lightly, as has been *done* in this *sentence.* Practice reading the selection with a full resonant voice, clear articulation, and a rate which makes it easy to understand the meaning of the passage. When you read in class, concentrate on the meaning to be communicated.

Select 1½ to 2 pages of simple informative prose. It should express an idea you think worth sharing with others. You may select a passage from one of the speeches in the Appendix.

Project 2 Projection

Purposes of this assignment: (1) To gain further skill in applying the elementary principles of oral reading; (2) to learn to correct points of criticism in your first reading performance; (3) to work specifically on effective projection to the audience.

Procedure: Select a passage of informative prose of moderate difficulty which you have not read aloud before. Be prepared to read about one page. Study the passage carefully so that you understand clearly just what it means. Look up unfamiliar words for pronunciation and meaning. Read the passage aloud to work on phrasing, emphasis, and inflection of the sentence, and concentrate on the meaning of the passage as you read. Practice on long words and words or phrases of difficult sound combinations until you can say them clearly and forcefully. If you have a special reading problem, practice to improve in that particular factor. Apply the methods of effective projection to your audience.

Project 3 The oral reading of literature with connotative meanings

Purposes of this project: (1) To learn to interpret the emotional and connotative, as well as the intellectual and denotative, meaning of a piece of literature; (2) to develop a relatively high standard of skill in the oral interpretation of literature.

Procedure: Select a poem, essay, play, editorial, or part of a speech which expresses a deep feeling or emotional attitude. Carefully analyze your rating on earlier readings, and practice to eliminate any weaknesses indicated on those reports in your preparation of this project. Study carefully the meaning and pronunciation of all words and the implication of references. Analyze the dominant motive of the author in this piece of writing and work to interpret it precisely and fully. In interpreting emotional literature, the voice should be made to respond in force, quality, pitch, and time. An effective interpretation of emotional literature ordinarily requires a response in bodily action which is suggestive of the mood to be interpreted. It will be necessary to use basic skills of fluency, phrasing, timing, and intensity in careful coordination.

Fine oral interpretation requires the reader to maintain his own identity as a reader and to avoid exaggeration in his suggestive use of voice and action. The best reading will ordinarily be done when the reader has assimilated the meaning to be interpreted and has a moving desire with the author to share the moods of the piece with his audience. Introduce your reading to the audience with a few comments selected for the purpose of orienting them toward what is to be read.

Project 4 Exercise in reading with effective oral punctuation

Practice reading the following sentences as a study in adapting oral reading to punctuation marks. Your material may not always be well written or punctuated. You must determine the intended meaning, and punctuate it orally, when reading aloud.

1. The doe was seen four nights running in the woods.
2. The teacher, said Earl, taught the class skillfully.
3. The teacher said Earl taught the class skillfully.
4. Can you pull, Tim?
5. Can you pull Tim?
6. The pilot without his life jacket is poorly equipped.
7. The pilot, without his life jacket, is poorly equipped.
8. The firing continued, as the tank plunged across the ditch, to hit the mark.
9. Normal speech requires two or more persons; writing, but one.
10. Those courses which are not well prepared should be eliminated.
11. Do your best; it is all we expect of any man.
12. I will take the duffel—blanket, mattresses, food, and fishing tackle—in the canoe.
13. You call it propaganda! Better say deceit, exploitation, murder!
14. He was a tactful (!) man in his thievery.

REFERENCES

Bacon, Wallace A., and Robert S. Breen: *Literature as Experience*, McGraw-Hill Book Company, New York, 1959.

Brooks, Keith: *The Communicative Arts and Sciences of Speech,* Charles E. Merrill Books, Inc., Columbus, Ohio, 1967, pp. 270–349.

Geiger, Don: *The Sound, Sense, and Performance of Literature*, Scott, Foresman and Company, Chicago, 1963.

Grimes, Wilma H., and Alathea Smith Mattingly: *Interpretation,* Wadsworth Publishing Company, Inc., Belmont, Calif., 1961.

Lee, Charlotte I.: *Oral Interpretation,* 3d ed. Houghton Mifflin Company, Boston, 1965.

APPENDIX A

MAIN SYMBOLS OF THE PHONETIC ALPHABET, FOR ENGLISH

PHONETIC SYMBOL	DICTIONARY SYMBOL	EXAMPLE	PHONETIC SYMBOL	DICTIONARY SYMBOL	EXAMPLE
i	ē	be	t	t	lit
ɪ	ĭ	hit	d	d	lid
ɛ	ĕ	bed	k	k	wick
æ	ă	tan	g	g	wig
ə	ȧ	about	r	r	rice
ʌ	ŭ	but	l	l	lice
a	ä	far	f	f	fine
ɔ	ô	law	v	v	vine
ʊ	o͝o	foot	θ	th	both
u	o͞o	fool	ð	t̶h̶	bathe
e	ā	ape	s	s	lace
iu	ū	mute	z	z	lazy
ou	ou	coal	ʃ	sh	rush
au	ou	ouch	ʒ	zh	rouge
aɪ	ī	light	h	h	hit
ɔɪ	oi	oil	ʍ	hw	whine
m	m	men	w	w	wine
n	n	new	j	y	yes
ŋ	ng	sing	tʃ	ch	char
p	p	pin	dʒ	j	jar
b	b	bin			

APPENDIX B

'THE ONLY SIN—SILENCE'

by Jerome Lawrence [1]

A funny thing happened—to all of us—on the way to the Stadium this morning! When I heard that thunder early this morning, I thought the New York drama critics were in town.

Frankly, I'm a little disappointed that this is not at the Stadium because I never played football on that famous field. I was never a member of the Marching Band. I wasn't a cheerleader. I wasn't even a water boy. And when I received my BA—it was in March, not this March—our exercises were held over in University Hall, that great shrine to modern architecture. So this was to be my premiere performance at Ohio State's Stadium. If you will all come over after we're through here and it stops raining, I just may kick a field goal.

Playwrights and football players have a great deal in common. We both love long runs. But I don't want you to worry. My run here is scheduled to close in 18 minutes.

Last night, I couldn't sleep and I wandered around campus in a mood of nostalgia. And there was University Hall, for which I have a kind of terrible affection. Annetta Lu Cornell was one of my classmates. (Her father, incidentally, wrote "Carmen Ohio.") Annetta and I used to smoke

[1] Playwright Jerome Lawrence (co-author of *Inherit the Wind* and *Auntie Mame*), recipient of an honorary Doctor of Humane Letters degree at the June, 1963, Commencement, had this advice for the 2,500 graduates of the Ohio State University. The speech appears here with his kind permission.

between classes, and I have a confession to make after all these years. Annetta and I used to drop matches down the stairwell, hoping to burn down the building. We never succeeded. Future generations, I apologize. I remember one other thing happened when Annetta and I were smoking between classes. A spinsterish-type female instructor came up to her when Annetta was puffing away at a cigaret, and with a stony look said, "Young lady, I would just as soon be caught in a compromising situation with a strange man as to be caught smoking in public."

And without missing a puff, Annetta looked her right in the teeth and said, "So would I, but we only have ten minutes."

Memories, memories. . .

Fellow graduates, what a world we live in, what a fabulous age! What a time for beginning! What a decade to be young, to be starting! You are going out into a world where there is a Christopher Columbus named John Glenn, where Magellan is a guy from Oklahoma named Gordon Cooper, where Vasco de Gama and Amerigo Vespucci are called Titov and Gargarin. And just think, they are our contemporaries.

My young friends, the Universe is your onion. Remember, the human mind is capable of traveling farther than any space ship. The human spirit goes beyond missiles and projectiles. Inside each of us is unused rocket fuel. Unassisted, we can soar to the stars.

Horace Greeley said, "Go West." Well, I've been West and it isn't far enough any more. The farthest reaches of the human mind are still unexplored, waiting to be discovered. Reaching other worlds of the mind takes courage, as much as blasting off at Canaveral. But even a kid with a space toy will tell you that nobody ever goes into orbit by standing still.

We write plays. No play is worth anything unless it has structure. What does that mean? That the characters change, grow, develop. If they didn't you'd be bored; you'd walk out; you'd demand your money back.

I say walk out on the pattern of your own life, if you do not change and develop every day of it. Particularly develop your powers of imagination. (Sometimes I wish I could take some of my friends and some of my relatives out of town and rewrite them.)

I want to read you an appropriate short speech from a play my partner, Dr. Robert E. Lee, and I have just completed writing for motion pictures. Here is the first performance anywhere of one speech from "The New Yorkers" without stars or wide screen, though I hope I'm in living color:

It is 1939 in this scene, and a writer with a frivolous hit on Broadway meets on the street a very wise man who had once been his producer of a more significant play. Remember, it is 1939, before America's entry into the War. And the producer says to the writer:

"Well, you've got a hit. I've got nothing against hits, I love 'em. I like comic strips, too. But I don't mind at all if a newspaper prints something besides 'Gasoline Alley.'

"I'm a funny fellow, Johnny. I think that what happens in a theater ought to mean something, too. You're a craftsman in the theater, Johnny; what the newspaper boys call a working stiff. I don't know any higher compliment. But you can't stop with Act I.

"Let me explain what I mean. I've got a piece of a play on my desk, only the first act, by F. Scott Fitzgerald. He's been promising me the rest of it for months. I talked to him long distance this morning in Hollywood at a place called the Garden of Allah, for God's sake. And he was a little drunk, but he made a kind of Socrates sense. Not just about himself but about this whole sleeping continent. Scott said, 'Maybe Act I is as far as we ever go, Louie. There are no second acts in American lives.'

"Now, Johnny, I think Fitzgerald's wrong. I think America is giving up the worship of adolescence. Act II is the best part. It can be, it should be. That's when you take responsibility and start looking at who we really are. In Act I, everybody's still got their baby fat—mostly between the ears. Act II is when you get slimmed down and go to work.

"Besides, that's the only way you get to Act III."

End of scene.

Fellow graduates, welcome to Act II.

Some people think you must stick to the same point of view all of your life. I say it is as necessary to change your mind as it is to change your underwear. I sat in Derby Hall (that was before Denney Hall was built) and read the two most valuable lines I know: "A foolish consistency is the hobgoblin of little minds"—Emerson; and Walt Whitman, "Do I contradict myself? Very well, I contradict myself. I am large; I contain multitudes."

Do you know the brief colloquy between Drummond and Brady in our play, "Inherit the Wind"? Drummond, leaning against the lamp post in the twilight, sees Brady, once a giant of a man, three-times candidate for the presidency, coming toward him. And Brady says to Drummond: "We were good friends once. I was always glad of your support. What happened between us? There used to be a mutuality of understanding and admiration. Why is it, my old friend, that you have moved so far away from me?"

And Drummond stares at this man and says: "All motion is relative. Perhaps it is *you* who have moved away by standing still." [2]

My friends, you don't need Faith 7 to get you moving, to put you into intellectual orbit. Do it every day. How? Talk back to your TV sets. Challenge your newspapers and magazines and your congressmen. Use your franchise as a human being, as an individual human mind.

Don't let them turn us into a nation of transparent stomachs and little

[2] From *Inherit the Wind*, by Jerome Lawrence and Robert Edwin Lee. Copyright © 1955 by Jerome Lawrence and Robert Edwin Lee. Reprinted by permission of Random House, Inc.

hammers hitting into our subliminals. And when they start to think for you, speak up. Say "*Please*, Mr. Opinion Maker, I'd rather do it myself."

Know the value of anger, constructive anger. Be vocal. Write letters. (I write letters all the time; but *approving* letters as well as disapproving letters.)

Perhaps the only sin is silence. The major crime against the democratic process is the inability to be heard, the lack of opportunity to listen.

I have faith in the American public, particularly in the American student. Open every door to him and he will choose wisely and well. Close doors to him and you are in danger of becoming the very thing you are fighting.

Let me use the yardstick of the theater again. Why is Laurence Olivier a great actor? Why do we all consider him a fine actor? Because he is suspicious. Remember that word—*suspicious*. Of what? The commonplace, the habit in himself. He will never repeat anything he has done previously.

We all have the tendency to say, "This has worked, I will repeat it"; to say, "I know how to do that; I will let it harden into a mold, a habit; I will play it safe." My dear young friends, nothing has ever been accomplished in this world by playing it safe. Safety is for crossing streets and driving a car and climbing into a bathtub. The imagination is never set loose by the careful man or by the cliché expert. Be intellectually daring, be suspicious of habit, particularly habits of thought.

I know playwrights who have written the same play 15 times. They have different titles, the characters have different names, but it's the same play. I promise you that our next play may not be successful, but it will be *different*. Because I hope I can continue to be suspicious, analytical of our failures, and doubly suspicious of our successes.

I would like to read you one more speech from "Inherit the Wind," a short one. Drummond, speaking to his client just before the jury comes in, tells him about Golden Dancer. It's one of my favorite speeches.

"Golden Dancer," he says, "that was the name of my first long-shot. She was in the big side window of the general store in Wakeman, Ohio. I used to stand out in the street and say to myself, 'If I had Golden Dancer, I'd have everything in the world that I wanted.' I was seven years old and a very fine judge of rocking horses. Golden Dancer had a bright red mane, blue eyes, and she was gold all over with purple spots. When the sun hit her stirrups, she was a dazzling sight to see. But she was a week's wages for my father, so Golden Dancer and I always had a plate glass window between us. Let's see, it wasn't Christmas, it must have been my birthday. I woke up in the morning and there was Golden Dancer at the foot of my bed. Ma had skimped on groceries, Pa had worked nights for a month. I jumped in the saddle and started to rock. And it broke! It split in two. The wood was rotten. The whole thing was put together with spit and sealing wax. All shine and no substance." And, turning to his client, he says, "Bert, whenever you see something bright, shining, perfect-seeming, all gold with purple spots, look behind the paint; and if it's a lie, show it up for what it really is!" [3]

You, too, "look behind the paint." Look behind the sure thing.

When my partner and I direct, we always tell the actors one thing. Care—one word—*care*. Now you are all about to enact your roles as mature citizens, responsible human beings, not leaving the university, but taking the university to the world. And I give you this one direction: Care! Give a damn!

Remember the John Donne ethic—you are involved in mankind. Disinvolve yourself and you are dead. You are cut off from the greatest bloodstream of all—humanity. I challenge you all to stay in intellectual orbit, to be a lifelong student, each of you; counting every day wasted if you do not explore something new.

Live the life of the mind for the rest of your life, if you do not want to become a vegetable. And do not ever diminish or underrate the power of *one* vote, *one* angry or disapproving voice, *one* conviction, *one* passion, *one* man standing up to be counted.

Do you all know the story about the fantastic new computing machine, the size of an office building? The scientists felt they had to put a very profound question into it for the first time. They put their heads together and they came up with this question, "Is there a God?" They fed it into the machine, and all the bulbs and tubes flashed on and off, and the tapes spun around. And out came this answer: "There is . . . *now*."

My young friends, let us not believe in the divinity of IBM. The giant computers may be able to deal with numbers so astronomical as to be staggering, but I can tell you *there is no number larger than one*—one human being, you today, each of you, going out as an individual, thinking citizen of the universe.

The men who taught me here at Ohio State walk beside me, sit beside me all the days of my life. I learned a love of Shakespeare from Professors Walley and Wilson. My typewriter is disciplined because Professors Pollard and Getzloe helped me to write a clean and clear sentence and gave me a journalist's fierce respect for the unvarnished fact. I wish all of you had known Herman Miller, Robert Newdick, and Harlan Hatcher, who is now president of Michigan. All of them kicked me in the literary pants and helped to strip me of artsy-crafty affectation. The men in the history department—one of our fellow graduates today is Dr. Wittke—taught me that there is no better way to interpret today than to study yesterday. In the words of Santayana, "Those who do not remember the past are condemned to re-live it." Professor Titchener doesn't know it, but that fine

[3] *Ibid.*

classical scholar goes with me on every trip to Greece. Rabbi Harry Kaplan, never by sermonizing but by the glowing example of himself, showed me that you are an incomplete person if you neglect your spiritual side. Beanie Drake, whose door was always open at the Ohio Union, taught me there is no replacement for a great human being.

Accept no substitutes. And, oh fellow graduates, accept no substitutes in yourself. Cultivate individuality. Cultivate the courageous mind.

Why do we admire Benjamin Franklin? Why are we writing a play about him, to be called "Ben," and to be presented first, we hope, here at Ohio State? Because everybody said to him, "You're internationally famous, Ben, the Leonardo of the new world. Don't waste your time with these revolutionaries, these crackpots." Even his own son said to him, "Don't stick your neck out, Papa. Play it safe."

But Franklin knew, didn't he—as we know—that if you don't stick your neck out, you're a turtle; not a man with a God-given mind.

Do not be a carbon copy of anybody, particularly not yourself of last week, or last year, or even ten minutes ago. Don't call breathing living. Don't call sitting back living. Be part of the tide of life. Be part of the motivating force of it.

President Fawcett, look at those 2,494 intelligent faces. Under those mortar boards, in those heads, I think our group has forty per cent fewer cavities.

I've written something especially for today—it's very short—for your graduation and for mine. I'd like to close by reading it to you. It's called, with apologies to the medical students,

A HIPPOCRATIC OATH FOR A DOCTOR OF HUMANE LETTERS

I am not today the same man I was yesterday, and I shall strive to be a changing, different, and still-growing man tomorrow. For yesterday's answers may not be true today and perhaps even the questions will be different tomorrow.

I shall be angry, passionate, enthusiastic—like a child with wonder, and I shall not be afraid of being foolish.

I shall be a disturber of the peace and a disturber of the war. With the fusing of words and the detonation of laughter, I shall set off dynamite charges under complacency, conformity, censorship, carbon-copy living.

I am and shall try to continue to be a belligerent optimist, to wake up each day and say: "Good morning, God!" instead of "Good God! Morning!"

This is the age of the dialogue. But I shall listen as intensely as I speak.

I do not believe the chronological age of a man has anything to do with the youngness in his heart, the newness of his conceptions. I shall never retire from the arena of thought, believing absolutely in the immortality of ideas.

I believe in the dignity of the individual, in every man's right to speak, to teach, to write, to doubt, to challenge, to dissent.

I shall stick pins in the fat balloons of pomposity and pretension, particularly in myself.

And from the original Oath of Hippocrates, I affirm that I will look upon him who taught me, even as one of my own parents.

All these things I swear, by those other honorary Doctors of Humane Letters: SOCRATES, *the questioner,* VOLTAIRE, *defender of the anomaly,* FRANKLIN, *citizen of the universe.*

"TELSTAR" [1]

On July 10, 1962, at 4:45 a.m., a Delta rocket blazed off pad 17 at Cape Canaveral carrying the Bell System's Telstar Satellite. It was a "shot heard around the world!"

The launch of the experimental satellite by the National Aeronautics and Space Administration opens up an entirely new approach to global communications. Stated in somewhat technical terms, Telstar is now in orbit testing the actual use and reliability of "active" satellites for the transmission of broadband microwave radio signals. But the implication of that mouthful of words could touch the lives of all of us in many wonderful ways. The concept of space communications is nothing short of fantastic even in this fast-moving world where yesterday's science fiction is today's fact. Telstar gives us a chance to test the use of space for international business and personal telephone calls. It heralds the advent of "live" overseas telecasts from the cultural and entertainment centers of Europe. It might be interesting, for example, to watch the changing of the guard at Buckingham Palace. Or, the Olympic games in Tokyo. Even perhaps a fashion show direct from Paris.

Telstar comes in a small package like so many other amazing devices in our miniaturized wonder world of electronics. This little sphere of aluminum and magnesium is 34½ inches in diameter—only slightly larger than a beach ball. But it's worth more than its weight in gold. Four hundred Bell Telephone Laboratories scientists, engineers and technicians worked on the development of Telstar and associated microwave experiments. More than 15,000 components had to be put together, inspected and tested before it could be boosted into the blue. The electronic equipment is sealed in a 20-inch aluminum canister which is suspended inside

[1] Reprinted by permission of Office of Public Relations, American Telephone and Telegraph Company, New York.

the housing with nylon cord lacings. This helped absorb blast-off shock and space vibrations.

Let's take a close look for a moment at Telstar now orbiting the earth at an altitude varying from about 590 to 3,500 miles. At the top is a spiral antenna which sends out tracking signals and information about the satellite's performance. It also receives the command to turn Telstar "on" or "off" from the command tracker on the ground. In the dark squares are some of the 3,600 solar cells that are mounted on the exterior of the satellite. They are protected by coverings of clear, man-made sapphire. These solar cells charge 19 small batteries that provide Telstar's power. One of the things we are most interested in knowing is the effect of space radiation on the solar cells. Their four specially prepared silicon diodes are giving us that information. Around the middle of the satellite, in the small squares, are the receiving and transmitting antennas. In all, Telstar relays to earth 115 different measurements and data on operating conditions every minute. Now, why are satellites going to be so necessary in modern communication?

During 1962, the existing 700 overseas circuits, terminating in all parts of the world, handled over 5,000,000 calls. Reliable estimates say that by 1980, overseas requirements will approach 100 million calls and the kind of volume will take 10,000 circuits. This tremendous increase is due to the expansion of our international trade which means more foreign voice communications and much more information in the form of data will have to be transmitted. In fact, within a few years, we expect that this business of data machines in our country talking to similar machines in foreign lands may make up at least half of the total overseas traffic.

An interesting possibility was brought up recently by a group of prominent medical men. They want to establish a world-wide communications diagnostic center. This would allow for almost instant diagnosis of even the rarest diseases anywhere in the world. It could also mean that your medical history, including such things as television pictures of electrocardiograms, could be transmitted instantly to Rome, Cairo or wherever you happened to require treatment by specialists. Benefits such as these certainly point up the need for forging ahead rapidly with satellite communications. Not only that, but our government's defense needs are constantly expanding, even into the remote corners of the world.

Another important consideration is that satellite communications can make it possible for you to see on television, "live," the great news events of the world, when they happen, regardless of where they happen. Present underseas telephone cables do not have the ability to carry television programs. The last point I would make here is the extreme importance of having alternate facilities, so that if one system is put out of operations for any reason, there is another one available that can still do the job.

We do this now on land, supplementing underground cables with microwave radio routes, and by building alternate systems around large cities so communications could continue uninterrupted even if large cities were destroyed in the event of war. You are no doubt aware of the fact, that calls travel by these microwave radio routes, as well as by long distance cable. Let me mention something here about how microwave sends telephone calls—because this is actually the transmission technique used by the Telstar Satellite.

The Bell System built the first transcontinental microwave system early in the 1950's—a system of more than 100 towers, spaced at approximately 30-mile intervals across the United States. Since that time, we have been able to satisfy our customers' needs for additional telephone circuits as well as for cross-country or network television. Microwave has one disadvantage, however, which shows up when we come to the ocean. That is, the waves won't bend! Instead of following the curvature of the earth, they continue right out into space. Obviously then, we would either have to float microwave towers at 30-mile intervals across the ocean or face the equally impractical task of building one tower in the middle of the ocean high enough so that it would capture the signal for reamplification.

If we built such a "tower," it would have to be about 475 miles high. The answer then is to build our "towers in the sky" to supplement our present and future cables and to allow for diversification. And this is exactly what communication satellites are.

There are at least two altitudes in which satellites might be placed. One is a medium range (3,000 to 7,000 miles) system of encircling the earth with a number of satellites in random orbit. We would then relay our signal as necessary with at least one being always in view from any place on earth. The other possibility is to place three satellites, which would obviously have to be more powerful, in a fixed orbit about 22,000 miles up. At this altitude they would rotate at the same speed as the earth, always seeming to hang in the same position in the sky. A big problem here is getting a powerful enough launch vehicle to put the satellite in the precise orbit required at such a height. At this time, no one knows just how many communications satellites will be needed. Both systems have advantages and disadvantages and the final finished product may well be a combination of the two.

I'd like to mention here the Transistor and Bell Solar Battery, which are two of the key elements in Telstar. Without these two inventions and some others developed by the scientists at the Bell Telephone Laboratories, these things we are doing in space would almost certainly not have been possible. The transistor was invented at the Labs in 1948 and since that time has come to be known as the "Mighty Midget." Practically overnight, the transistor made miniaturization possible. Its other chief properties are its light weight, its low-power requirements and its reliability. The solar cells, held in the right hand, came along a few short years later, also a result of Bell Labs scientists' efforts, and are the first practical devices for converting the sun's energy into useful amounts of electricity.

There are several other scientific break-throughs important to space communications, and the combined story makes as exciting a talk as the satellite itself. An interesting thing is that most of these developments came about with no specific thought of satellite communications. There is, for example, the MASER. MASER stands for "microwave amplification by stimulated emission of radiation." It is an amplifier which reduces by one hundred times the noise inherent in the very best receiving amplifiers of only a few years ago. The central element in the MASER is a man-made ruby crystal, cooled by liquid helium to 456 degrees below zero Fahrenheit. This is only two degrees above absolute zero.

Working right along with the MASER is the traveling wave tube . . . , which can boost a satellite's signal strength 10,000 times. This was produced back in 1943. If you have any doubt that these things are necessary, let me point out that the power received from the satellite is only one billionth of a watt. It gets pretty weak after traveling several thousand miles through space.

Another stepping stone in the path that led to Telstar was in August of 1960 when the Project Echo *balloon* satellite was successfully launched. It was used for telephone experiments by Bell System scientists in New Jersey. Echo was simply a highly reflective mirror in the sky. It had no equipment aboard, as Telstar does, but its shiny surface permitted us to bounce voice signals back to earth, just as light reflected from a mirror. Echo looks simple now, but it was quite a step toward practical space communications. It was an immediate success. And it caught the public's fancy. Millions of people watched nightly for it to pass over at the times predicted in the newspapers or on news broadcasts and they still do! Echo is still up there, perhaps a little worse for wear but scientists are still conducting communications tests with it. To make communicating by satellite practical, however, we had to do more than just bounce the signal off a passive satellite like the Echo balloon. *This* we have achieved . . . with Telstar . . . which is capable of receiving, amplifying and retransmitting huge amounts of information over an extremely broad band of frequencies. We have been talking up to now primarily about the satellite itself. Of course we need more than a satellite to have satellite communications. There are other considerations.

The main one is the very complex ground stations needed to track and connect the space-relayed information to the nation's existing communications network where it can do its work. Ground stations have been built in the U. S. and in Great Britain and France. Italy and West Germany have theirs under construction. The Bell System's principal ground station is located on a 1,100-acre tract of land near Andover, Maine. Some of the considerations that led us to select this location were these: first, it is protected by a ring of hills and is away from concentrations of radio sources that might interfere. Also it is near good highways and is readily accessible to the Bell System telephone network. Lastly, it is almost the nearest site to Europe available and this is important since we're testing overseas communication by satellite.

We in the Bell System are glad to have played a part in the development of present domestic and international communications. We are also pleased with the contribution of the transistor, solar battery, traveling wave tube and the MASER in Communications Technology. But we are happiest of all because the dramatic accomplishments of Telstar have moved the world closer to the realization of world-wide satellite communications. On the evening of July 10, 1962, Telstar marked up these firsts in communications history:

One, it handled the first telephone calls by active satellite.

Two, it received and transmitted the first television picture of the American flag waving against the background of the Andover radome. This television transmission was also received in France and England, thereby accomplishing the first overseas telecast. If you were at your own television sets that night, you saw some of this yourself.

Three, press association news stories were sent by way of the satellite, using the dataspeed device, a Bell System development which sends and receives 1,000 words a minute.

And four, representatives from the press used Telstar to transmit the news photo of the day—a telephoto of the satellite itself.

No question about it, July 10th was a spectacular day in the history of communications. And leaders all over the Free World spoke of the scientific achievement and the possibilities it brought for greater international understanding.

NEED FOR UNIVERSAL MILITARY TRAINING [1]

Dwight D. Eisenhower

During the years in which I served as Chief of Staff of the Army, I tried hard but unsuccessfully to persuade Congress to establish a sound system of Universal Military Training in this country. I felt that UMT

[1] "This Country Needs Universal Military Training," *Reader's Digest*, September, 1966. Copyright © 1966 by Dwight D. Eisenhower. Reprinted by permission of Doubleday & Company, Inc.

was desirable not only from the standpoint of military preparedness, but for reasons of fitness and discipline among our youth. I also believed that it would provide the fairest approach to the always thorny problem of manpower procurement.

War, of course, is always unfair to youth. Some young men have to fight and others do not, and I see no complete cure for that until the blessed day arrives when men have learned to live in peace, and there will no longer be need for military force. That day is not here, however, and it cannot come so long as an implacable enemy of human freedom strives to enslave the world. Today more than ever, therefore, I think that this country should adopt, as the cornerstone of its defense establishment, a workable plan of universal training—and I mean *universal,* with a minimum of really essential exemptions.

Dissent from the draft. First, let's take a look at what our present manpower-procurement system is doing to this country.

During the past year, I have watched with dismay the rising tide of rancor engendered by our draft system. Yet it is not hard to understand why this clamorous dissent should exist. At one end of the manpower spectrum we have had the college students, who until recently were deferred almost automatically. At the other end, we have had the young men whom the military authorities deemed unfit because of physical, mental, educational or moral deficiencies. Thus, as regards military exemption, we have had two large, privileged classes.

It is from the middle of the spectrum that Selective Service has drawn the bulk of its manpower in recent years. These are the boys who are physically fit and possess sufficient education to make good soldiers, but who for various reasons have not gone on from high school to college. With harsh irony, they refer to themselves as the "sitting ducks." They feel, and justly, that they are a highly important segment of the nation's work force and are entitled to the same consideration as our future scientists and engineers, doctors and lawyers, professors and industrial managers.

Now, I believe implicitly in the necessity of higher education for great numbers of our young people. Yet I also look back to World War II and the postwar years, and I remember vividly what happened to that generation of students. Before that conflict ended, we necessarily were taking nearly all of our able-bodied young men for military service; hundreds of thousands of college careers were delayed or interrupted. Yet when peace came, the boys who really wanted an education returned to college and in most cases finished their courses of study with a determination and a maturity that were heartening to behold. Education and military service certainly are not mutually exclusive.

There have been other inequities in the draft. For several years young married men were deferred, and when our growing commitment in Vietnam necessitated increased quotas we had for a time the spectacle of many youths rushing into marriage—before they were ready to undertake the establishment of a home—in order to avoid military service. That rule is now changed. Others, by their own admission, have started fathering children as quickly as possible after marriage. This, I am told, is called "babying out."

Many graduate schools have experienced substantial recent increases in enrollment—considerably beyond natural year-to-year growth—because some young men preferred to prolong their education rather than do their stint for their country. Deferments have also been given for so-called critical occupations, and this unquestionably has influenced some boys in the choice of careers.

Duty vs. loopholes. All of this has resulted not only in unfairness to those young men who *are* called, but also in a state of mind which I think is very bad for America. We still have in this country, thank the Lord, a great majority of young people who do have a strong sense of patriotism, who understand and believe in the United States' effort to contain communism before it engulfs the world. But we also have a minority who use every legal loophole to avoid their obligations, who seem willing to accept the splendid opportunities that this country offers without lifting a hand to preserve our way of life. And on the outer fringe we have a few who even use deceit and other illegal means to avoid the draft. The latter should be dealt with sternly and with dispatch.

It is my hope that out of this frustrating and humiliating experience will come a better way of providing the military manpower that we must have—a system which will help revive among *all* our young people a deep sense of "duty, honor, country." It is surely one of the fundamentals of our democratic system that every young person should love and believe in his country and feel a conscientious obligation to *do something* for his country—in peace and in war. Patriotism is not only a noble emotion but an emotion that is necessary to national survival. It is also an emotion which can be diluted by bitterness engendered by a system that is deemed unfair by so many.

The ends in view. In hammering out any new system of manpower procurement and training, therefore, we must keep certain objectives firmly in mind:

1. It must be a system which will provide the men we must have for our worldwide commitments.

2. It must have sufficient flexibility to permit us, in times of emergency, to bring additional men into our armed forces quickly and in substantial numbers.

3. It must, as far as possible, eliminate present unfairness.

4. It should bring to every young man an understanding of his obligation to his country and a sense of participation in its affairs.

5. It should be a builder of physical fitness, self-discipline and decent personal habits.

6. It should include the vast numbers of boys who are now exempted because of educational deficiencies or moderate physical disabilities such as trick knees, overweight problems and a host of other minor and often correctable infirmities.

I realize that to accomplish these objectives will take a lot of doing. But, looking back at the miracles that were achieved in World War II, I am convinced that it can be done—once we understand the need and go about the task with determination.

Other proposals. In the studies of this problem now being made by Congress, the special Presidential panel and other agencies, various solutions have been suggested.

One, of course, is to retain our present system of Selective Service, but to tighten up on student and occupational deferments, broaden the base of military standards to permit the induction of some who are now ruled unfit, and make other changes in the interest of fairness. Some of these things we have been doing during the past year. In my opinion, such procedures can never be more than a palliative. They leave untouched several essential objectives. They are not a long-term solution.

Another plan is to eliminate citizen service entirely and build a completely professional military establishment. Such a force would have the advantage of better training and higher combat efficiency, and some of our top military men would prefer it for that reason. Also, in eliminating the draft, we would, of course, eliminate the unfairnesses which cause so much controversy.

One weakness of such a plan is that it would not provide the flexibility that we need in times of emergency. It is difficult to expand a wholly professional force quickly, and in the absence of any functioning draft machinery it would take many months to re-create even an *untrained* citizen army. In the event of another world conflict, I doubt that we would be permitted months.

Such a system would also be costly. To get the needed volunteers, without the pressure of the draft, pay scales all along the line would have to be raised substantially. As an old soldier, I am a firm believer in adequate pay for our career officers and men, but we might find the cost prohibitive. I have seen estimates ranging all the way from four to ten billion dollars a year, above present costs, for a wholly volunteer establishment of three million men.

The greater objection, however, is that the above plan would not achieve the broader objectives that I have mentioned. It would do nothing to create the sense of obligation to country that I feel is so essential in a democracy. And for the vast majority of our boys it would not promote more disciplined minds and habits or build better bodies.

Still another suggestion is that we return to the lottery system—the drawing of numbers—to select our draftees, as we did in World War I and the early part of World War II. I agree that this method—the turn of the wheel, blind chance—would be fairer to the individual than our present system. But, as with the other plans reviewed above, it would not fulfill some of our more important aims.

It has also been suggested that the lottery be used in conjunction with other plans. For example, we might increase pay so as to recruit a largely professional military force but fill in the gaps through selection by lottery. As a matter of fact, lottery selection has a place in the basic plan that I should like to see adopted.

The framework of UMT. Under the system that I envision, every young male American, no matter what his status in life or his plans for the future, would spend 49 weeks—one year minus three weeks' vacation—in military training. Only the barest minimum of exemptions would be permitted: obvious mental incompetents, those with some drastic physical defect, perhaps a few extreme-hardship cases.

Basically, I have always felt that 19 is about the right age to begin military service. Boys of 19 are young enough to be flexible, and in most cases they are more mature than those of 18. There are, however, other considerations. Eighteen is usually the age at which a boy finishes high school and is ready to enter college or go to work. It is a natural break in his life. If we were to enlist boys at 18 rather than 19 or any other age, it would cause less disruption in our schools and in working careers. Therefore, all things considered, I think 18 should be the age at which our young men should begin their year of UMT.

This year should be considered not only as their contribution to country but as part of their education. The government would, of course, provide sustenance, clothing and other necessaries, but the trainees would be paid only a small stipend—say five or ten dollars a month—in order to have a bit of pocket change for incidentals.

At the beginning of the year, each UMT trainee would be offered the option of enlisting immediately in our regular forces for a two-year term of duty, with all the pay, advances and benefits pertaining thereto, including later education under the G.I. bill of rights. A great many, I believe, would choose this course.

For the large number who *remained* in UMT, the year would be spent primarily in military training. It would include regular daily stints on the training base, athletics, remedial education for those who need it, building vigorous bodies and learning the wisdom of discipline, cleanliness and good personal habits. Youngsters with correctable physical weaknesses—and we have millions of them in this favored land—would benefit from good nutrition, a year of disciplined life, and special medical attention if they needed it.

The boys in UMT could and should be used in times of emergency such as floods, storms and fires. They could be useful in helping to maintain order and in assisting the victims of misfortune. On the other hand, they should not be impressed into any regular work program outside their base. We want no semblance of forced labor in America.

Aftermath? Almost two million boys now reach the age of 18 each year, and in times of peace or small wars we certainly could not use that many in our regular military forces. Consequently, many of our young men would complete their period of service with the 49 weeks of UMT. They would then be free to go on to college or vocational school or to begin their careers without interruption—except in the case of a major war, when all our potential military manpower would be needed.

If the inducements of full pay and later education at government expense did not produce the volunteers that we need for our regular forces, then it would be necessary to draft the added men. To do this in the fairest way, we should employ the lottery. In the beginning, we would have to include in the lottery the large pool of youths who were past UMT age but were still liable to military service. This pool would diminish each year, and after five or six years would cease to exist. From then on, the lottery would apply only to the boys in UMT.

This basic plan is by no means original with me. I have merely selected what I regard as the best parts of many suggested plans and put them together in an integrated whole. It is impossible within the compass of a short article to fill in all the details. For example, how would we fit the R.O.T.C. units, the National Guard and our reserves into the UMT system? I do not believe that these worthwhile services would have to be abandoned. All such complex matters can be worked out through careful study.

The obstacles. A suggested variant is that we adopt a system of universal service but offer each young man the choice of military training or of serving in some civilian group such as the Peace Corps, a hospital cadre or a conservation corps. I strongly doubt the wisdom of this plan, because (1) it would be almost impossible to provide enough useful civilian duties for those who elected this course; (2) the scheme would still be unfair to the boys who have to fight our wars; (3) the important benefits of a year of military education would not reach those who chose civilian service.

I am fully aware that the plan I suggest is not perfect. There are difficulties to be surmounted in putting it into operation.

One is that there would be some disruption of normal procedures on college campuses and in vocational schools. During the first year of UMT, these institutions would have virtually no male freshman classes; the second year, few sophomores; and so on until the end of the fourth year. After that, conditions would return to normal, the only difference being that first-year college students would average a year older—which could be a good thing.

The second obstacle—and this is a tough one—is the cost. Nobody really knows the price tag of UMT, but estimates run from three to six billion dollars a year above present military expenditures. If we wished to cut the training period to six months, costs could be sharply reduced, but I think that this would also seriously dilute the benefits. In the beginning, we would also have to build and equip many new military camps, thus increasing the early costs.

I have no ready-made plan for financing UMT. I wish only to say that a big, powerful country such as ours could surely find a way to pay the bill. Personally, I think the program is far more important than some of the public efforts on which we are now spending so much.

Still another problem is the procurement of training personnel—military instructors, teachers, doctors and so on. I do not regard this problem as insurmountable. We could call in reserve officers for a time if needed, and I am confident that we could find the other necessary people if we had to—just as we did during World War II.

The benefits. Opposed to these obstacles are the enormous benefits that our country would reap from such a system.

First, there are the long-term military advantages. After a few years of UMT, we would have always a huge reserve of young men with sound basic military training. The R.O.T.C. would turn out better officers; the National Guard would be far more efficient. In case of a great emergency, all these men would be ready for combat after a brief refresher course, and in the event of a nuclear attack—the Lord forbid!—a disciplined body of young men in every community would be a priceless asset.

Second, although I certainly do not contend that UMT would be a cure for juvenile delinquency, I do think it could do much to stem the growing tide of irresponsible behavior and outright crime in the United States. To expose all our young men for a year to discipline and the correct attitudes of living inevitably would straighten out a lot of potential troublemakers. In this connection—although I am sure that in saying this I label myself as old-fashioned—I deplore the beatnik dress, the long, unkempt hair, the dirty necks and fingernails now affected by a minority of our boys. If UMT accomplished nothing more than to produce cleanliness and decent grooming, it might be worth the price tag—and I am not altogether jesting when I say this. To me a sloppy appearance has always indicated sloppy habits of mind.

But above and beyond these advantages of UMT is the matter of attitude toward country. If a UMT system were to become a fixture of our national life, I think that resentment against military obligation would die away, that virtually every young man would take pride and satisfaction in giving a year of his life to the United States of America. After all, the good instincts lie near the surface in the young. Patriotism, a sense of duty, a feeling of obligation to country are still there. They are the noblest and the most necessary qualities of any democratic system, and I am convinced that UMT would help call them to the surface once more.

I am aware, of course, that many Congressmen regard Universal Military Training as political poison. I think they are being unduly timid. I am convinced that most Americans believe in the value of such a system, and that many others could be persuaded by an enlightened educational campaign. Most of all, I urge that we act *now*.

ADDRESS AT ATLANTA EXPOSITION [1]

Booker T. Washington

MR. PRESIDENT AND GENTLEMEN OF THE BOARD OF DIRECTORS AND CITIZENS: One-third of the population of the South is of the Negro race. No enterprise seeking the material, civil, or moral welfare of this section can disregard this element of our population and reach the highest success. I but convey to you, Mr. President and Directors, the sentiment of the masses of my race when I say that in no way have the value and manhood of the American Negro been more fittingly and generously recognized than by the managers of this magnificent Exposition at every stage of its progress. It is a recognition that will do more to cement the friendship of the two races than any occurrence since the dawn of our freedom.

Not only this, but the opportunity here afforded will awaken among

[1] A. Craig Baird, *American Public Addresses: 1740–1952,* McGraw-Hill Book Company, New York, 1956, pp. 190–192.

us a new era of industrial progress. Ignorant and inexperienced, it is not strange that in the first years of our new life we began at the top instead of at the bottom; that a seat in Congress or the state legislature was more sought than real estate or industrial skill; that the political convention or stump speaking had more attractions than starting a dairy farm or truck garden.

A ship lost at sea for many days suddenly sighted a friendly vessel. From the mast of the unfortunate vessel was seen a signal, "Water, water; we die of thirst!" The answer from the friendly vessel at once came back, "Cast down your bucket where you are." And a third and fourth signal for water was answered, "Cast down your bucket where you are." The captain of the distressed vessel, at last heeding the injunction, cast down his bucket, and it came up full of fresh, sparkling water from the mouth of the Amazon River. To those of my race who depend on bettering their condition in a foreign land or who underestimate the importance of cultivating friendly relations with the Southern white man, who is their next-door neighbour, I would say: "Cast down your bucket where you are" —cast it down in making friends in every manly way of the people of all races by whom we are surrounded.

Cast it down in agriculture, mechanics, in commerce, in domestic service, and in the professions. And in this connection it is well to bear in mind that whatever other sins the South may be called to bear, when it comes to business, pure and simple, it is in the South that the Negro is given a man's chance in the commercial world, and in nothing is this Exposition more eloquent than in emphasizing this chance. Our greatest danger is that in the great leap from slavery to freedom we may overlook the fact that the masses of us are to live by the productions of our hands, and fail to keep in mind that we shall prosper in proportion as we learn to dignify and glorify common labour and put brains and skill into the common occupations of life; shall prosper in proportion as we learn to draw the line between the superficial and the substantial, the ornamental gew-gaws of life and the useful. No race can prosper till it learns that there is as much dignity in tilling a field as in writing a poem. It is at the bottom of life we must begin, and not at the top. Nor should we permit our grievances to overshadow our opportunities.

To those of the white race who look to the incoming of those of foreign birth and strange tongue and habits for the prosperity of the South, were I permitted I would repeat what I say to my own race, "Cast down your bucket where you are." Cast it down among the eight millions of Negroes whose habits you know, whose fidelity and love you have tested in days when to have proved treacherous meant the ruin of your firesides. Cast down your bucket among these people who have, without strikes and labour wars, tilled your fields, cleared your forests, builded your railroads and cities, and brought forth treasures from the bowels of the earth, and helped make possible this magnificent representation of the progress of the South. Casting down your bucket among my people, helping and encouraging them as you are doing on these grounds, and to education of head, hand, and heart, you will find that they will buy your surplus land, make blossom the waste places in your fields, and run your factories. While doing this, you can be sure in the future, as in the past, that you and your families will be surrounded by the most patient, faithful, law-abiding, and unresentful people that the world has seen. As we have proved our loyalty to you in the past, in nursing your children, watching by the sick-bed of your mothers and fathers, and often following them with tear-dimmed eyes to their graves, so in the future, in our humble way, we shall stand by you with a devotion that no foreigner can approach, ready to lay down our lives, if need be, in defence of yours, interlacing our industrial, commercial, civil, and religious life with yours in a way that shall make the interests of both races one. In all things that are purely social we can be as separate as the fingers, yet one as the hand in all things essential to mutual progress.

There is no defence or security for any of us except in the highest intelligence and development of all. If anywhere there are efforts tending to curtail the fullest growth of the Negro, let these efforts be turned into stimulating, encouraging, and making him the most useful and intelligent citizen. Effort or means so invested will pay a thousand per cent interest. These efforts will be twice blessed—"blessing him that gives and him that takes."

There is no escape through law of man or God from the inevitable:—

> The laws of changeless justice bind
> Oppressor with oppressed;
> And close as sin and suffering joined
> We march to fate abreast.

Nearly sixteen millions of hands will aid you in pulling the load upward; or they will pull against you the load downward. We shall constitute one-third and more of the ignorance and crime of the South, or one-third its intelligence and progress; we shall contribute one-third to the business and industrial prosperity of the South, or we shall prove a veritable body of death, stagnating, depressing, retarding every effort to advance the body politic.

Gentlemen of the Exposition, as we present to you our humble effort at an exhibition of our progress, you must not expect overmuch. Starting thirty years ago with ownership here and there in a few quilts and pumpkins and chickens (gathered from miscellaneous sources), remember the path that has led from these to the inventions and production of agricultural implements, buggies, steam-engines, newspapers, books, statuary, carving, paintings, the management of drug-stores and banks, has not been trodden without contact with thorns and thistles. While we take pride in what we exhibit as a result of our independent efforts, we do not for a moment forget that our part in this exhibition would fall far short of your expectations but for the constant help that has come to our educational life, not only from the Southern states, but especially from Northern philanthropists, who have made their gifts a constant stream of blessing and encouragement.

The wisest among my race understand that the agitation of questions of social equality is the extremest folly, and that progress in the enjoyment of all the privileges that will come to us must be the result of severe and constant struggle rather than of artificial forcing. No race that has anything to contribute to the markets of the world is long in any degree ostracised. It is important and right that all privileges of the law be ours, but it is vastly more important that we be prepared for the exercises of these privileges. The opportunity to earn a dollar in a factory just now is worth infinitely more than the opportunity to spend a dollar in an opera-house.

In conclusion, may I repeat that nothing in thirty years has given us more hope and encouragement, and drawn us so near to you of the white race, as this opportunity offered by the Exposition; and here bending, as it were, over the altar that represents the results of the struggles of your race and mine, both starting practically empty-handed three decades ago, I pledge that in your effort to work out the great and intricate problem which God has laid at the doors of the South, you shall have at all times the patient, sympathetic help of my race; only let this be constantly in mind, that, while from representations in these buildings of the product of field, of forest, of mine, of factory, letters, and art, much good will come, yet far above and beyond material benefits will be that higher good, that, let us pray God, will come, in a blotting out of sectional differences and racial animosities and suspicions, in a determination to administer absolute justice, in a willing obedience among all classes to the mandates of law. This, this, coupled with our material prosperity, will bring into our beloved South a new heaven and a new earth.

APPENDIX C

SOURCES OF INFORMATION AND OPINION

Based on Baird and Knower's *General Speech,* McGraw-Hill Book Company, New York, 1949, Appendix G, "Suggestions for Library Research."

Books

General Encyclopedias

Encyclopedia Americana, 30 vols., Americana Corporation, 1951; Americana Annual, 1923 to date.

Encyclopaedia Britannica, 24 vols., 1960; 11th ed., 1910–1911, 28 vols., generally considered most scholarly of all. Britannica Book of the Year, 1938 to date.

Special Encyclopedias

Encyclopedia of Religion and Ethics, 12 vols., James Hastings (ed.), Charles Scribner's Sons, New York, 1908–1927.

Encyclopedia of the Social Sciences, 15 vols., E. R. A. Seligman (ed.), The Macmillan Company, New York, 1930–1935.

Year Books

American Yearbook, Thomas Nelson & Sons, New York, 1925 to date.

American Annual, Encyclopedia Americana, since 1923.

Britannica Book of the Year, Encyclopaedia Britannica, since 1938.

Collier's Yearbook, P. F. Collier & Sons Corporation, New York, since 1939.

New International Year Book, Funk & Wagnalls Company, New York, since 1907.

Yearbook of the United Nations, United Nations, Department of Public Information, New York, 1947 to date.

Statesman's Yearbook, The Macmillan Company, New York, 1864 to date.

World Almanac, Newspaper Enterprise Association, New York, 1868 to date. Contains a list of organizations in the United States many of which publish material in their special fields.

Directories and Biographical Dictionaries

Who's Who (English), A & C Black, Ltd., and The Macmillan Company, New York, annual, 1849 to date.

Who's Who in America, The A. N. Marquis Co., Chicago, Ill., 1899 to date. Additional volumes of the Who's Who series are available in special fields, e.g., *Who's Who in American Women, Who's Who in Art, Who's Who in Engineering, Who's Who in the Theatre.*

Current Biography, The H. W. Wilson Company, New York, monthly, annual cumulation, 1940 to date.

Dictionary of American Biography, 20 vols., Allen Johnson and Dumas Malone (eds.), Charles Scribner's Sons, New York, 1928–1937; with later supplements.

Dictionary of National Biography, 22 vols., Leslie Stephen and Sidney Lee (eds.), The Macmillan Company, New York, 1908–1909; supplements to 1950.

Directory of American Scholars, 4th ed., R. R. Bowker Company, New York, 1964.

Leaders of Education, 5th ed., Jaques Cattell and E. E. Ross (eds.), Science Press, Lancaster, Pa., 1960.

Magazines

Reader's Guide to Periodical Literature, H. W. Wilson Company, New York, 1900 to date. See also Special Indexes, including *Agricultural Index, Art Index, Biography Index, Education Index, Index to Legal Periodicals, Industrial Arts Index, International Index.*

Psychological Index, Psychological Review Company, annual, 1894–1935.

Psychological Abstracts, American Psychological Association, Inc., Washington, 1927 to date.

Table of Contents of Quarterly Journal of Speech, 1915–1964, *Speech Monographs,* 1934–1964, and *The Speech Teacher,* 1952–1964, Franklin H. Knower (comp.), Speech Association of America, 1965.

Index and Table of Contents of Southern Speech Journal, 1935–1965, *Western Speech Journal,* 1937–1965, *Central States Speech Journal,* 1949–1965, and *Today's Speech,* 1953–1965, Robert Dunham, L. S. Harms, and Richard Gregg (comps.), Speech Association of America, 1966.

Newspapers

New York Times Index, 1913 to date.

Government Documents and Bibliographies

Bureau of the Census, *Statistical Abstract of the United States*, Government Printing Office, annual, 1878 to date.

Bureau of Foreign and Domestic Commerce, *Survey of Current Business*, Government Printing Office, monthly, 1921 to date.

Department of Agriculture, *Agricultural Statistics*, Government Printing Office, annual, 1936 to date.

Department of State, *Bulletin*, Government Printing Office, Official Record of United States foreign policy; issued weekly by the Office of Public Services, Bureau of Public Affairs, since 1939.

United States Superintendent of Documents

Numerical Lists and Schedule of Volumes of the Reports and Documents of the 73rd Congress, Government Printing Office, 1934 to date. Continued for successive sessions of Congress.

United States Congress, *Congressional Record*, Government Printing Office, 1873 to date.

Bureau of Labor Statistics, *Subject Index of Bulletins*, 1915–1959, Bulletin No. 1281, United States Department of Labor.

United States Bureau of the Census, *Census Publications;* catalog and subject guide, Government Printing Office, quarterly, annual cumulation, 1945 to date.

United States Superintendent of Documents, *United States Government Publications: Monthly Catalog*, Government Printing Office, 1895 to date, supplements, 1941–1942, 1943–1944, 1945–1946.

United States Superintendent of Documents, *Price Lists*, Nos. 1–85, Government Printing Office.

Nongovernmental Documents and Pamphlets

Brookings Institution, *Brookings Publications*, Washington, D.C. A checklist issued annually. Material especially useful in the fields of economics, politics, and foreign affairs.

National Association of Manufacturers, Research Department, *National Fact Book*, Washington, D.C. Current statistical service.

Foreign Policy Association, *Headline Series*, Washington, D.C. Summaries and analyses of all aspects of United States foreign policy (74 pamphlets to 1966).

See also publications of other professional organizations (addresses in *World Almanac* and other sources).

Bibliographies, Book Indexes

Bibliographic Index: A Cumulative Bibliography of Bibliographies, H. W. Wilson Company, New York, 1938 to date.

Book Review Digest, H. W. Wilson Company, New York, 1905 to date.

Cumulative Book Index, H. W. Wilson Company, New York, 1898 to date. A world list of books in the English language; supplements the United States Catalogue.

Essay and General Literature Index, H. W. Wilson Company, New York, 1900 to date.

Public Affairs Information Service Bulletin, Public Affairs Information Service, 1915 to date, weekly, annual cumulation. Indexes books, pamphlets, documents, and periodicals in political and social sciences.

Publishers' Weekly, 1872 to date. American trade book journal, lists currently published books.

United States Catalogue, 4 eds., H. W. Wilson Company, New York, 1899–1928, supplements, 1906, 1912–1917, 1918–1921, 1921–1924. A list of all books in print in the English language.

Vertical File Service Catalogue, H. W. Wilson Company, New York, 1932–1934. Monthly, annual cumulation. Annotated subject catalog of pamphlets, booklets, leaflets, circulars, folders, maps, charts, and mimeographed bulletins.

Winchell, Constance (ed.): *Guide to Reference Books,* 7th ed., American Library Association, 1951, and frequent supplements since.

INDEX